SEX OVER 50

Joel D. Block, Ph.D.
with Susan Crain Bakos

PARKER PUBLISHING COMPANY

Library of Congress Cataloging-in-Publication Data

Block, Joel D.
    Sex over 50 / Joel D. Block, [Susan Bakos].
        p.   cm.
    Includes index.
    ISBN 0-13-080968-3 (case). — ISBN 0-7352-0058-0 (pbk.)
    1. Sex instruction.   2. Middle aged persons—Sexual behavior.   I. Bakos, Susan Crain.
II. Title.
HQ31.B569   1999
613.9'6'0844—dc21   98-42503
                                                                                    CIP

Acquisitions Editor: *Doug Corcoran*
Production Editor: *Eve Mossman*
Formatting/Interior Design: *Robyn Beckerman*

© *1999 by Parker Publishing*

Printed in the United States of America

10 9 8 7 6 5 4 3 2 1   *10 9 8 7 6 5 4 3 2 1*

ISBN 0-13-080968-3   ISBN 0-7352-0058-0 (pbk.)

ATTENTION: CORPORATIONS AND SCHOOLS

Prentice Hall books are available at quantity discounts with bulk purchase for educational, business, or sales promotional use. For information, please write to:
Prentice Hall Special Sales, 240 Frisch Court, Paramus, New Jersey 07652. Please
supply: title of book, ISBN, quantity, how the book will be used, date needed.

PARKER PUBLISHING COMPANY
West Nyack, NY 10994

A Simon & Schuster Company

On the World Wide Web at http://www.phdirect.com

Prentice Hall International (UK) Limited, *London*
Prentice Hall of Australia Pty. Limited, *Sydney*
Prentice Hall Canada, Inc., *Toronto*
Prentice Hall Hispanoamericana, S.A., *Mexico*
Prentice Hall of India Private Limited, *New Delhi*
Prentice Hall of Japan, Inc., *Tokyo*
Simon & Schuster Asia Pte. Ltd., *Singapore*
Editora Prentice Hall do Brasil, Ltda., *Rio de Janeiro*

INTRODUCTION: THE BEST YEARS OF YOUR SEX LIFE

Sex does change as we age; and that is the good news. Performance anxieties and many common sex problems occur far more frequently in the young than in those who are old enough to know better. Men and women are still vital, alive, and sexy at 40, 50, 60, and beyond, and they're sexually confident and experienced too. As long as we don't lose our zest for life, we don't lose our lust for lovemaking either.

Couples at 50 are on the threshold of a richer, fuller, and more mature sex life than they have enjoyed in the past. Adults Only Sex not only can but *will* be emotionally satisfying and thrilling physically. While physiological changes dictate that we make certain adaptations to our lovemaking styles, *we are also the beneficiaries of some potent sexual benefits at midlife*. They include:

- Greater sophistication about our own and our partner's sexuality.

- Increased capability of communicating our sexual and emotional needs without fear of "looking silly" or being rejected or misunderstood by the one we love.

- Improved sexual responsiveness in women and a corresponding improved ability to control ejaculation in men.

- Greater willingness to experiment with sexual variations.

- Lessened inhibitions and increased ability to "have fun" with lovemaking.

- And far greater technical proficiency as lovers.

Many of the sexual problems couples experienced in their youth are naturally resolved at midlife. Premature ejaculation, for example, is a young man's problem with some ejaculating in as little as 30 seconds after insertion. By the age of 50, most men's ejaculatory responses have slowed down considerably, to at least the average time of two to five minutes of thrusting and sometimes much longer. Simple remedies can resolve minor problems naturally occurring at midlife such as vaginal dryness in women.

As we age, we evolve sexually; and the sexual maturation process makes lovemaking a far more enjoyable overall experience at 50 than it was at 20. Typically, men and women cross sexual and psychological paths at midlife in a process psychoanalyst Carl Jung described as the "contrasexual transition." Women become more independent and assertive, less in need of reassurance or approval from their partners. Men become more nurturing, more comfortable with intimacy and able to share themselves in ways they never could before. Older men seek the warmth and closeness in sex that some women have waited decades for them to discover. Each partner becomes more like the other in patterns of sexual response.

We know more about ourselves and our intimate partners at this point in our lives than we did when we were young. At 50, we can be bold and tender lovers, unafraid of our passion and our lover's desires. We are more likely to be empathetic, able to feel and understand our partner's feelings, sexual and otherwise. Couples who relegate sex to the storage closet of their life together because they are no longer young are giving up just when the real prize is within their grasp.

Why do some couples make the transition to a higher sexual level while others use aging as an excuse for shutting down?

- Some people subscribe to a series of myths about sex over 40 that lead them to believe passion is the exclusive province of the young.

- Others fail to recognize that physiological changes present opportunities for better sex, not obstacles to it.

- Some fail to adapt their lovemaking styles to accommodate their changing needs and particularly their improved abilities as lovers.

- Many allow boredom, stress, or dissatisfaction with other areas of life—jobs, finances, child rearing, extended families, physical signs of aging—to stifle their sexuality.

In 1996 the first of the 78-million-member, trend-inspiring Baby Boom generation turned fifty. The Boomers, more than the generation preceding them, will not go quietly into the sexual darkness. They don't and won't consider themselves finished with sex because media images of sexuality are predominantly youthful ones.

In fact, some of the advertisers are beginning to get the message that older isn't neutered. Vanity Fair, the lingerie company, reassessed their ad campaigns when market researchers discovered many of the women who purchased their products were 40, 50, and older, considerably older than the teen models hired to display the wares. Now Vanity Fair models are in their thirties, forties, and fifties and, though still abnormally beautiful, display fine lines and graying hair.

Advertisers will increasingly devote more energy to romancing the older consumer as more Boomers cross the fifty mark. That flattering attention will, in small increments, increase the collective sexual self-esteem of those of us who are no longer young. Whether you are pushing 50 or on the far side of it, you'll benefit from Boomer power in the marketplace. New trends in health care promise to keep lovers feeling and looking as fit as possible, too. There has never been a better historical time period for the mature lover.

Sex over 50 helps you make the transition to a deeper, richer, more sophisticated sexual relationship by giving practical advice for overcoming negative attitudes and providing specific erotic directions for upgrading your lovemaking skills. You really are getting better as you get older. What you have to offer your partner now is much greater than it was earlier.

While treasuring the special joy that was youth, you can still embrace the beauty of the present and look forward to discovering the hidden erotic treasures in your future.

CONTENTS

CHAPTER 2

THE BUILDING BLOCKS OF PASSION 17

CHAPTER 3

TAKE CHARGE OF YOUR SEXUALITY 33

CHAPTER 4

GAMES FOR MATURE LOVERS 47

CHAPTER 5

IMPROVING INTERCOURSE   65

CHAPTER 6

DON'T HAVE SEX, MAKE LOVE   83

CHAPTER 7

THE POWER OF MIDLIFE SEXUAL FANTASIES   99

CHAPTER 8

GETTING IN SYNC WITH YOUR
PARTNER AGAIN   117

CHAPTER 9

STRETCHING YOUR SEXUAL BOUNDARIES 137

CHAPTER 10

THE UNLIMITED POTENTIAL OF MIDLIFE ORGASM 157

CHAPTER 11

SEX AND HORMONES   179

CHAPTER 12

OVERCOMING IMPOTENCE   197

CHAPTER 13

SEX AND HEALTH   223

CHAPTER 14

LOVE WITH ANOTHER PARTNER   245

CHAPTER 15
KEEPING THE ROMANCE ALIVE FOREVER   271

CONCLUSION: YOU'RE STILL SEXY   287

INDEX   293

1

CREATE A SEXY FRAME OF MIND

Sex begins in the brain, the most important sexual organ of all. Before you can have great sex, you have to believe you can have it—and change any thinking that stands in the way.

"I thought I was too old for sex," says Jane, a 50-year-old woman, who'd gone through menopause, one daughter's wedding, and the other's leaving home for college when she arrived at this conclusion. The combination of an empty nest and menopause convinced her she was "too old for sex," though her husband certainly thought otherwise. "No periods, no contraception necessary, no girls coming home at all hours of the day or night," she says, laughing. "He thought we were in prime time for sex. 'Are you crazy?' he asked me. 'Don't you recognize liberation when it tickles you in the genitals? We can act like kids again.'"

She resisted his playful mood at first. When he walked around the house naked and encouraged her to shed her own clothes, she was embarrassed, not aroused. Fortunately, he was able to convince her she wasn't "too old" during a romantic second honeymoon cruise

1

around the Greek islands. Over dinner, he lavished attention and compliments on her. Alone in their flower-filled cabin, he massaged her body with scented cream before making love to her, very slowly. After a few days of sexual pampering, she felt young again, desirable, and filled with desire.

What if he'd shared her mind-set or hadn't been so persuasive in changing it? "I was ready to close up shop," Jane admits. "Maybe I would have been ready to open it again in six months or a year, but think of the time we would have lost. Now I would say to other women: Ask yourself why 40 (or 50 or 60) should be the cut-off age? Don't you still have feelings of physical love and desire for your husband? Aren't you still capable of experiencing pleasure?"

THE 12 MYTHS ABOUT SEX OVER 50— AND THE CORRESPONDING TRUTHS

Some of our most cherished sex beliefs are myths. Though we have access to more accurate information about sexuality than any society in history, we still subscribe to many sex myths, especially about aging. A previous generation believed that love alone—or the penis alone— would transport a woman to sexual ecstasy. Now the majority of couples probably know clitoral stimulation is necessary for most women to achieve orgasm, a key ingredient in the definition of "sexual ecstasy." But, like Jane, they may still believe one can be "too old for sex."

Our relentlessly youth-oriented culture entered an attitude-adjustment phase a decade ago when the first Baby Boomers turned 40. The generation who refuses to grow old the way their parents did, they are redefining middle age; and the new definition includes sex. Now the vanguard of the Boomers have hit 50, and the process of rethinking continues. Actresses and models in their forties, fifties, and sixties, women such as Cybil Shepard, Joan Collins, Goldie Hawn, Farrah Fawcett, and others are still considered sex symbols. (Aging men such as Clint Eastwood, Harrison Ford, and Michael Douglas always have been.) *Playboy* magazine has done tasteful nude photo spreads of women over 40, often considerably over. But our private attitudes about sexuality and aging developed through a complex process combining elements of socialization, learning, and personal experience, with current media images representing only a part of the equation. Many men and women can admire Goldie or Farrah and still believe that 50 is "too old for sex" where they *personally* are concerned.

The myths are:

1. *The quality of sex declines for both men and women as they age.* Sexual responses are different, not worse, after 50. A man may not have the hard erections he had at 21, but he is capable of sustaining erection longer and knows how to use a semi-erection to tease and stimulate his partner. More important, he can enjoy the slower buildup of sexual tension and also use the added time to bring her to orgasm before intercourse. At midlife, men can finally be sensual beings, capable of enjoying a wider range of touch and sensation beyond friction applied to the head of the penis. Sex is not driven by the immediate needs of the penis and becomes a whole body experience; and giving satisfaction is as thrilling as experiencing it.

Often women are not comfortable taking the sexual initiative until they are in their thirties. As they age, their sexual assertiveness increases as does their enjoyment of intercourse. A shift in a woman's hormonal balance beginning in her late thirties or early forties increases her libido and her ability to have orgasms.

Men and women achieve in their fifties a level of emotional maturity combined with sexual self-confidence that makes it possible for them to enjoy a superior intimate relationship. The quality of sex definitely improves and continues to remain high for decades.

2. *If a woman does not lubricate sufficiently or a man does not become erect immediately, he or she are not aroused.* That is completely false. Insufficient lubrication is probably a result of hormonal changes, not lack of desire. The situation can be corrected through the use of lubricants such as K-Y jelly or hormone creams or hormone-replacement therapy. In older men, desire does not always immediately translate into an erection. Some men report feeling desire throughout their bodies rather than localized in their penises.

3. *Erection problems are inevitable and incurable without medical intervention.* Often men confuse natural physiological change with a "problem." They think they are not "hard enough" because they aren't as hard as they were at 19. Or, they overreact to an occasional failure

to get or maintain an erection. By the time he is 40, nearly every man has experienced a bout of impotence, and many unnecessarily fear these erotic disappointments will inevitably become regular occurrences. Healthy, physically and sexually active men can continue to achieve erections into old age without medical intervention. According to the National Institute of Health, only between 15 percent and 25 percent of men over 65 have erectile dysfunction severe enough to preclude intercourse; and the majority of their problems are caused by over-the-counter or prescription medications, illnesses such as diabetes or hypertension, or alcohol abuse.

4. *Female desire declines dramatically following menopause.* Many women report *increased* desire following menopause. In a 1990 survey of women over 50 conducted by the Robert Wood Johnson Medical School in New Brunswick, New Jersey, a whopping 72 percent reported no complaints—including declining desire—about their sex lives. When women do have less interest in lovemaking following menopause, the causes are typically hormonal imbalance or negative thinking. Each can be easily resolved. In addition, desire at any age is affected by many other factors including health and fitness, relationship issues, and stress factors outside the relationship.

5. *Once a man is no longer aroused by the mere sight of his wife, he will have great difficulty making love to her.* The older a man gets, the less likely he is to have a psychogenic erection, in other words to become erect merely by looking at his partner or another arousing female. That doesn't mean he isn't aroused or isn't interested in making love to her. After 35 or 40, a man needs direct penile stimulation to get an erection. When midlife men have difficulty making love, the cause is more often rooted in relationship conflict than in the physical appearance of aging bodies. As men become more psychologically in tune with women, they also find their feelings can get in the way of sexual expression, something that may have happened to them rarely if at all when they were young. When they express those feelings rather than keeping them inside, they become more passionate.

6. *Men peak in their teens.* Men achieve erection more quickly in their late teens than they ever will again in their lives. Those erections are also harder than they will be once a man is old enough to know what to do with them. If male sexual performance is judged purely in

fast and hard erectile terms, the peak is indeed young. But isn't it more realistic to view sexuality in broader terms? A man can't be truly said to "peak" until he has become a good, even great, lover, with ejaculatory control and the ability to please his partner in many different ways; and that's unlikely to happen at 19.

7. *Women peak in their thirties.* For most women, sex does gets better in their thirties, but their level of responsiveness doesn't plateau and then level off in later years as many people mistakenly believe. Women's increased ease with their bodies and confidence in lovemaking continues to grow after the thirties. And a woman's orgasmic capacity, including the ability to have multiple orgasms, is undiminished by age.

8. *Youthful orgasms are more intense.* Too many of us believe that sex is only for the young and beautiful. A corollary of this belief is the assumption that sexual ecstasy is more intensely experienced by the young. Not true. Women often report that orgasms are more intense after the age of 40. While men may notice that the force of their ejaculation isn't as strong in midlife as in youth, they will also feel a more diffuse orgasm in other parts of the body including the entire genital area, not merely the head of the penis.

9. *Men and women with heart or other problems should avoid sexual activity.* A study of 1,600 people conducted at Boston's New England Deaconess Hospital found that the risk of a heart attack during sex was roughly equivalent to the risk of a heart attack from getting out of bed in the morning. According to Dr. Robert Butler, former director of the National Institute on Aging, heart attacks during intercourse account for less than 1 percent of all coronary deaths—and 70 percent of those occur during extramarital liaisons where the stress level can be assumed to be higher. Sexual activity is actually good for all of us. Lovemaking has many physical and psychological benefits, from reducing stress to preventing depression.

10. *Sex has to end in orgasm.* Both men and women can find satisfaction in lovemaking that doesn't end in orgasm. Sometimes couples are tired or rushed, yet want to kiss, caress, and fondle each other. Orgasm isn't a goal that must be reached each time. In fact, some mature lovers deliberately make love without orgasm to intensify the experience when they do have one.

11. *Oral sex is for the very young.* According to studies cited by *The Janus Report on Sexual Behavior* and *The Kinsey Institute New Report on Sex,* couples are more likely to have oral sex at 40 than at 20. Younger people have more inhibitions without performing sex acts including fellatio and cunnilingus. They are also more likely to be unsure of their erotic skills and hold back because of performance anxiety, something modern women suffer too.

12. *Intercourse is the only kind of sex that counts. Anything else isn't "sex."* That intercourse equals sex is a modern Western concept. In the ancient Indian text, the *Kama Sutra,* many forms of lovemaking were celebrated. Is it coincidence that the Eastern erotic acts became popular again when the Boomers entered their forties? Most of us learned as teens that "foreplay" was the kissing, caressing, and touching a man had to do to get a woman "ready" for intercourse. "Loveplay" is a better word, encompassing all the ways men and women have of giving each other sexual pleasure. By midlife, a man craves this touching, kissing, and caressing as much as a woman does, requires it for erection, and may sometimes be satisfied with oral or manual lovemaking, even intercourse that does not end in ejaculation. There is so much more to "sex" than intercourse.

OVERCOMING THE MENTAL OBSTACLES TO GREAT SEX

The obstacles to great sex are not age-related factors. Anyone at any age can suffer from boredom, be "too busy" for sex, or let duties get in the way of pleasures. But some people use age as an excuse for failing to surmount these obstacles to sexual pleasure. They are:

- *Simple boredom.* If we don't seek out new challenges and experiences at midlife, we can fall into a state of ennui, an emotional comma induced by familiar, safe, and repetitive patterns. Boredom is a condition not conducive to passion.

- *Assigning low priority to romance and lovemaking.* Members of the "sandwich generation," caught between the needs of growing children and aging parents, not to mention jobs, can feel guilty about planning a romantic evening together when they "should" be taking care of others.

- *Allowing daily life stresses and time demands to stifle desire.* Too tired, too tense, too busy, wound up too tight for sex?

Men are as apt to find their libido trapped under one of the big three rocks as women are; and they may have more trouble acknowledging the real problems. (Another myth: Women lose interest in sex before men do.) For her fiftieth birthday Anne, a vibrant 52 year old, gave herself a career change from a corporate job to running her own decorative-arts business. Rather than being inspired by her energy and enthusiasm for life, her husband was alternately baffled and annoyed by those qualities in her. He was comfortable in blaming external circumstances for his own lack of energy, enthusiasm, and sexual desire.

"John turned 50 six months after I did; and he gave himself a case of the blues instead of a celebratory gift," she says. "He felt trapped in a job that hadn't challenged him in years, yet he was certain he was too old to do anything else. Whenever I suggested any kind of change, from professional to personal, he had excuses for not trying anything new. Our sex life suffered too. He teased me about being a 'horny old broad' when I tried to initiate lovemaking, but he was insistent about pushing me away."

Another woman might have allowed rejection and criticism to dampen her own ardor. When one spouse loses interest in sex, he or she typically brings—or attempts to bring—the other down to the same level. Apathy loves company. A change in attitude is the first step toward surmounting the mental obstacles to great sex. If changing your own negative attitudes can be difficult, how is it possible to help change your partner's thinking?

FIVE STEPS FOR OVERCOMING THE OBSTACLES

1. *Open a discussion.* Get your partner to talk about why he or she believes there is no time for romance, no room for change, no reason to feel like a sexual being at this point in life. Saying the reasons out loud forces us to examine them for validity.

Anne insisted that John both talk and listen to her. At first she didn't challenge his opinions and attitudes. "I knew he would mull over what each of us had said in his own time," she says. "If I'd forced him to respond to my thinking, he would have rejected it."

2. *Agree to remove critical language from the discussion.* Neither can accuse the other of being "horny" or "sex obsessed," hinting that such a state is inappropriate to one of a certain age, or of being "frigid" or "impotent" or "over the hill." Each partner should be able to express a desire for sex, or a lack of desire, without fear of being judged or ridiculed.

3. *Be clear about your motives.* Do you want more sex? A better, closer relationship? Are you concerned about helping your partner pull out of a funk?

"I wanted more for both of us," Anne says. "At first he thought I was being selfish, wanting more sex at a time when he didn't think he could meet my needs. I was able to convince him I wanted more than sex for us. I wanted him to be alive again and for the two of us to enjoy these golden opportunity years together in every way."

4. *Test the validity of your attitudes.* Is it a fact or an opinion that one can be too old for sex? A fact or an opinion that duties and obligations must always come before pleasures? Present your partner with some facts about midlife sexuality and ask him or her to consider them. Examine your own attitudes and prejudices too.

5. *Be open to change, not merely sexual change.* Trying a new intercourse position; renting an erotic video; making love in the morning, not evening; or introducing some other change into your lovemaking routine may not be the place to start. You wouldn't begin an exercise program with a half hour of aerobic activity if you hadn't been physically active in months or years. Start with easy changes, such as trying a new restaurant, having mango and kiwi fruit instead of orange juice in the morning, buying a brightly colored shirt or blouse, not another white, black, or beige.

"I got John to agree to sign up for some continuing education classes with me," Anne says. "Our first course was on wine. John became something of a wine aficionado in no time at all. Just having a new interest made him more lively in bed. The night he suggested we take our wine into the bedroom, I was hoping we wouldn't drain our glasses before making love; and we didn't."

REMOVING BOREDOM FROM YOUR LIFE

Boredom, more than anything else, dulls desire. Maybe a 25 year old can be awash in ennui yet still function sexually. As we get older, our sex lives increasingly reflect what is happening in the rest of our lives. You can't live a routine no-habits-changed-in-years life and have passionate sex. Lasting passion is not an end in itself, something to be achieved by following the sex-guidebook numbers, but a consequence of living an adventurous life, in bed and out.

To remove boredom from your daily existence, you have to live a counterphobic life, which means working against your fears rather than giving in to them. Here are the five steps for doing that:

1. *Acknowledge your fears.* List your fears in escalating order of importance, from fear of spiders to fear of sharing embarrassing intimate information with your lover. What do all fears have in common? They represent loss, such as loss of control, power, esteem, and love. Some fears are healthy, such as the fear of walking alone in a dangerous neighborhood after midnight. Most fears hold us back. Don't be discouraged and give up. Tell your partner you need support, not ridicule. Insist. It's that important.

Beside each fear on your list, note what you are afraid of losing. Then ask yourself: What is the worst thing that can happen to me if my fear is realized? Face that scenario. Imagine yourself dealing with it. If you are afraid of driving alone at night, picture yourself stranded in a car with a sudden mechanical problem. You have a cell phone in the car; calmly you're dialing for help with the doors locked and the flashers on. You will survive. How reasonable is it to assume that the worst will happen anyway?

Share your fears with your partner, who undoubtedly knows what some of them are but may be surprised at others. A man might be avoiding sex because he fears performance failure, something his wife doesn't suspect because she thinks she no longer excites him. When he shares his vulnerability with her, he gives her more than the gift of trust. He tells her she's desirable.

What if your partner doesn't understand your fears? Or even laughs at them? That's possible, of course, but is it likely? If it does happen, remember that one who ridicules another's fears probably has more fears of his or her own.

2. *Eliminate guilt.* How does guilt interfere with the ability to lead a counterphobic life? Guilt can stop you from taking a risk. The guilt-ridden have a multitude of reasons for not taking the chance they suspect will improve their lives. A man stays in the family business rather than pursuing a career of his own because his parents need him. A woman sacrifices her educational plans to support a husband's goals and later to carpool the children to every activity that interests them. The couple put sex and romance at the bottom of their priority list because they feel guilty about doing anything selfish, indulgent, not for the benefit of others. For the guilty, self-denial has become a habit, one they've elevated to a virtue in their minds. It isn't.

Denying self in the name of duty only makes one less a person, less a full and loving partner, parent, adult child, sibling, friend. Don't confuse *selfish*—"I want what I want at any cost"—with *I am worthy, I count.* You give less to the people you are sacrificing to serve because you have less to give; you are less. Make a list of everything you've given up—including lovemaking—because you would have felt guilty if you hadn't. Do these sacrifices make sense? Examine your life. What do you want that you haven't let yourself try to have? Guilt is a comfortable excuse; and it's time you threw away this particular security blanket.

3. *Stop being so cautious.* There are two kinds of caution, physical and psychological. They can overlap, for example, when a couple won't try anal sex or light bondage or spanking—practices that excite them both in fantasies—because they might experience initial discomfort or "look silly." For some people, physical risks such as bungee jumping, are exhilarating, whereas psychological risks, such as sharing hidden fears, are very frightening.

If you were raised by cautious, fearful parents who warned you against every possible accident or injury, you probably grew into a cautious, fearful adult unlikely to leave home without an umbrella on a mildly overcast day. At middle age, you may be leading an unnecessarily restricted life, protecting yourself from every imagined hurt. Is it possible to experience thrilling sexual passion inside that cocoon? Not likely.

Start throwing caution to the proverbial wind. Take a walk in the rain. Share a secret about yourself. Head out for a weekend trip without planning every aspect of it. If a little voice inside your head says, "I can't/shouldn't do that," tell it to shut up.

4. *Push back your personal boundaries.* We all have limits and rules that constitute our personal boundaries. In addition, we draw a set of imaginary lines around our possibilities and don't let ourselves dream or plan, reach or hope beyond them. Some people have too many rules, and their limits are narrow, confining, the lines they've drawn too far within the limits of what they might achieve. By midlife, they have become rigid people who can be approached only in certain ways, like the potentates of small countries. Pushing back the boundaries may be difficult for them, almost physically painful, but ultimately liberating.

You can push back your physical boundaries in small ways. A man who isn't comfortable with public displays of affection might hold hands with his wife while walking down the street. A woman who hasn't put on a sexy dress in years can buy one, wear it to a party, and flirt with her mate. Hug a friend, express a painful feeling, admit a mistake to your son or daughter. Ignore the initial discomfort and push the boundaries back so the people you care about can come a little closer. Extending yourself outside the imaginary lines takes a little more effort, like asking for the raise, applying for the promotion, or changing jobs.

5. *Take risks.* Risk taking is the backbone of an exciting, passionate life. Without risk, a life doesn't stand tall and move forward with vigor. Ironically, at midlife when many have a secure financial and emotional base from which to take more risks, they shut down and take fewer. This is why some men and women who have achieved financial success seem so curiously dull and flat when cornered in conversation outside the office. Risk is essential to continued personal growth. People who remain interesting and sexy are risk takers in all areas of their lives.

That doesn't mean you have to register for a skydiving class, take up mountain climbing, or quit your job without having another one lined up. The high-stakes risks are often emotional ones. Admitting fear, expressing anger, daring to be vulnerable can be huge leaps of faith across a scary chasm. Taking these risks leads to change; and the move is fearful because there's no guarantee that the ensuing change will be for the better. In risking, we let go of something: a sense of security, a false belief, a protective habit, a tenuous investment or relationship. What will we get in exchange? Maybe something wonderful; and maybe nothing at all.

A risk that will improve your sex life is not having unprotected sex with a stranger on a business trip, but it might be telling your long-term partner about a previously undisclosed erotic fantasy or wish. On the other hand, going back to school, joining a gym, or confronting a buried issue in your family of origin could also have unforeseen erotic benefits. If you felt sexier when you were young, you also took more risks then. Do you see the connection? Life was more exciting; and so were you.

TYING IT TOGETHER

"My libido began limping like a guy with an old football injury in my late forties," says Ron, a chemical engineer. "I attributed the situation to aging, though my wife, only a few years younger, was more interested in lovemaking.

"For years I'd been employed by the same small firm. One day I was told by someone in the field whose judgment I valued that I was considerably underpaid for my job given my years of experience and level of performance. When I told my wife, who is an investigative reporter, she researched the subject and told me how poorly compensated I really was. She and my best friend began hassling me to ask for a raise or look for another job. I countered that there were advantages to working for this small firm, but I was rationalizing. I was really afraid of asking for a raise, afraid of having my boss tell me that I was worth only what he was paying me.

"But my wife and my friend kept up the pressure, so I finally had the talk with the boss. He said he'd get back to me. For two weeks, he said nothing. I felt better about myself for asking, but when he didn't respond in a timely fashion, I realized I'd have to ask again. By this time, I wasn't getting any outside pressure. Asking was something I wanted to do for myself.

"He offered me a good raise. If he hadn't, I was prepared to begin looking for another job, something I'd been afraid to do before. The real surprise to me was the lasting effect this incident had on my libido. I felt more sexual after asking for that raise than I had in years; and the feeling persisted."

As soon as Ron began working against his fears, he changed his life. His lack of libido was an indicator that he hadn't been happy for a long time. He'd kept himself strictly within a tight set of boundaries, living at a level of discomfort he associated with safety, which perversely felt like comfort to him. In pushing those boundaries, he freed his libido.

FIVE TIPS FOR CREATING A SEXY MINDSET

1. *Pretend that you're dating again and sex is a delicious possibility, not a certainty.* After a couple have been together for years, they each know when the other is "in the mood" for sex. One partner makes a move, gauges the other's response, and knows if the answer is affirmative or negative. Not knowing creates erotic tension.

2. *Rather than squashing erotic thoughts unless they can be carried to completion, indulge in fantasies of lovemaking when you know you won't have the opportunity to do it.* In youth, people encourage and enjoy their fantasies, which is one reason they always seem to have sex on the brain. Later, they sternly shut down sexual thoughts until it's "time" for sex. The result? The erotic hour arrives; and the sexual thoughts remain suppressed.

3. *Laugh together.* Laughter unlocks the emotions. It is an erotic elixir more potent than good wine.

4. *Learn how to tease your partner, visually and verbally, to create desire.* Mother said, "Don't be a tease," but Mother was wrong. In the early stages of sexual attraction, men and women tease each other with suggestive comments, seductive gestures. Later, they become overly direct, eliminating the playful aspects of their sexual relationship.

5. *Take care of your body through exercise, a healthy diet, and vitamins.* You'll get this message more than once here, because it's that important.

Sizzler # **1**

WE'RE STILL SEXY

"Grandparents!" Jill said. "She's six months along now; and I still can't believe it. I'm happy, of course, but . . ." Her voice trailed off. Steve reached across the bed for her hand. It was limp and cold in his. "Grandparents," she repeated. "We're old, Steve. Old."

"I don't feel old," he said, a suggestive note in his voice. "I couldn't wait for the kids—his term for their son and daughter-in-law—" to leave so we could be alone. We didn't make love once the entire ten days they were here." Or how long before that? He couldn't remember, but he did know that Jill's disinterest in sex dated back to the day they'd been told they were going to be grandparents.

She caught the suggestion, took her hand from his, and rolled over so that her back was to him. He moved to her side of the bed, fitted himself against her back, and put one arm around her, his hand resting against her stomach, gently rounded and softly warm to his touch. She flinched lightly. How long had it been since she'd teased him that she didn't dare turn her back on him if they hadn't made love in a few days. He liked to enter from behind. Her ass had always been beautiful to him. Sometimes when she bent over, he had to resist the impulse to fall to his knees and bury his face in her cheeks. He wanted to worship his wife's body; she was a goddess to him.

"I'm tired," she said. "Sleep well."

Sleep well! His wife was consigning them to a sexless old age in their early fifties. And he was supposed to sleep?

Steve tossed and turned that night and, in his frustration, developed a plan. He called it Operation We're Still Sexy. The next morning he got up before she did, hurriedly showered, and then took the kitchen calendar off the wall and slipped it into his briefcase. When he got to the office, he asked some colleagues to help him come up with the names of sexy celebrity grandmothers and grandfathers. They included Lonnie Anderson, Raquel Welch, Sean Connery, Clint

Eastwood, and others. He skipped lunch and went to a newsstand where he bought magazines featuring the stars. Back at the office, he made a new calendar: The Sexy Grandparents Calendar.

Jill laughed when he hung it up, but it was a good laugh. She liked the calendar. Over the next several days, he bombarded her with small romantic gifts and cards. His behavior toward her was tender and affectionate, but he didn't push for "sex," even when she pressed her body against his in the night. One day he brought home an expensive midnight-blue silk kimono. And finally, he gave her the pièce de résistance: A day spa for two. When he'd called to arrange their day of total pampering at a local spa that advertised "couple days," he'd asked the receptionist to book them with other "mature" couples. Steve wanted Jill to see other older women reveling in their sensuality, to notice the quiet passion he was sure she would see simmering in couples who had taken the time to be together in a different way.

As they lingered over their spa luncheon, sipping champagne in thick white terry robes, she reached across the table and stroked his hand. "I haven't felt this good in years," she said. "I can't thank you enough for planning this day."

"You'll think of something," he said lightly. Beneath the robe, his penis grew hopefully stiff.

That night she put on the midnight-blue kimono and curled up beside him on the sofa. Stretching her torso languorously like a cat, she whispered, "I'm not wearing any underwear." He put his hand between her legs. The silk of the cloth gave way to the softness of her inner thighs. He caressed her skin and slowly moved his hand up her leg. She sighed happily, leaned forward into his arms, and kissed him passionately. His thumb parted her labia. She was moist, hot, anticipating him. "I want you," she said.

The words thundered in his ears. He lowered his face and slowly licked her clitoris until her breath came in that short, jagged pattern he knew so well. *We've still got it,* he thought, as she began to come for the first time that night.

THE BUILDING BLOCKS OF PASSION

In Chapter One I encourage you to throw out those tired old negative sex attitudes with the nonrecyclable trash. You're *not* too old for sex. Both you and your partner are capable of experiencing a rich and rewarding erotic life together. It is possible to become joyously sexual again even for partners in a sexless marriage. You have a new attitude. How do you move up and out of the sexual doldrums now that you believe it's possible to do so?

Begin by replacing the old attitudes with new ones. Attitudes are like emotional building blocks. Your old foundation was made of negative building blocks. The new positive building blocks will build a new sex-positive foundation for your life. Those building blocks, the emotional qualities that lead to great sex, include:

- *Sexual self-esteem.* People who have enjoyed good sexual relationships before forty usually have sexual self-esteem, but it may be at low ebb now. They are relatively free of sex guilt, confident about their desirability and erotic skills, yet at midlife they may suffer a setback rooted in body-image anxiety or misinformation about the effects of aging on sexuality.

- *Enthusiasm.* Enthusiasm for life and for lovemaking is contagious, and so is the lack of it. One partner's loss of the zest for life typically has an impact on the other.

- *Optimism.* Optimistic people tend to see the challenge in change while pessimists look for the downside. To a pessimist every setback, from failing to get a promotion to failing to get an erection, is a catastrophe. Optimism is an energizing sexual force.

- *Playfulness.* Sex is one way that adults play. When couples complain "sex isn't fun anymore," they have stopped being playful with each other. Put the play back in your sex life and the orgasms will follow.

The negative feelings, the building blocks of the old foundation that sap sexual energy are:

- *Anger.* People who can't acknowledge or express their anger typically try to suppress it. What else can they do with it? Eventually stored anger dulls sexuality. People who are chronically angry stifle their sexual feelings and alienate their lovers.

- *Guilt.* As noted in the previous chapter, guilt is not a sensuous emotion. Whether you feel guilty about having sexual desires, participating in certain activities, or taking time away from duty for lovemaking, it will cost you. The guilt price is diminished sexual satisfaction and decreasing opportunities for sex.

- *Depression.* Nothing dulls desire as effectively as depression. A man or a woman who is deeply or persistently unhappy about other areas of life isn't likely to have good sex until the underlying causes of the depression are resolved.

- *Fear.* Fear leads to protective behavior that makes it difficult to be intimate, vulnerable, and playful with a partner. When we're fearful, we create avoidance patterns rather than reach out to connect.

TEAR DOWN THE OLD FOUNDATION AND CREATE A POSITIVE SEX FOUNDATION

"I prided myself on never refusing my husband sex even when I was angry at him," says Fran, 49 and married to Morris for 24 years. "Shortly after our twentieth anniversary, I started to lose interest in sex, but I never said "no." I faked orgasms. I thought I was doing my share.

"Two years ago he came home from a real-estate brokers convention in Boston and confessed that he'd had a fling with a woman he'd met there. I was devastated, then furious. How could he do that when I'd always been so accommodating to his needs?"

Morris told her he'd been "insulted" by her sexual accommodations. He wanted to be wanted, not tolerated. She was, he said, "emotionally flat," in bed and out. When she told him he hadn't given her an orgasm in years, he responded that he'd suspected she was faking for years. "You never broke a sweat," he accused, "and your orgasms were too perfectly timed to coincide with mine. How real is that?"

For six weeks, they alternated between not speaking to each other and sharing heated, angry exchanges where each told the other how unsatisfactory they were as sex partners. Repressed anger, mild depression, and fear of aging and an accompanying loss of sexuality were building blocks in both their foundations, but they didn't recognize that at the time. Some couples in a similar situation would either get divorced or stay together in a sexless marriage. Fran and Morris were lucky.

"Looking back, we see the explosion of anger on both sides as a positive thing," she says. "We got rid of a lot of feeling that we'd been keeping inside. Our big advantage, however, was in having the right confidants. He talked to his brother, and I talked to my best friend. Some brothers and friends might say, 'You're right and your spouse is wrong.' They helped us see the other person's side.

"My friend Lorraine told me that Morris was right when he said I'd become 'emotionally flat.' Hearing it from her was like a splash of cold water in the face. She also said it took a lot of courage for him to confess his infidelity to me, and she was right. That fling was his act of desperation."

When they were a little calmer, Fran and Morris were able to examine some of their emotional issues, such as anger and depression, and their underlying sexual attitudes. They had both assumed a female orgasm was a gift a man gave a woman, like handing her a single red rose. That put all the responsibility for her sexual pleasure on him and encouraged her to fake as a way of rewarding him for his effort. (A nice girl says "thank you" even if the rose is a little wilted and hasn't much fragrance.) Not surprisingly, he had concerns about his sexuality he'd never shared with her. Would he have trouble with erections soon? And how would he handle that when and if it happened? They both had misconceptions about sexuality and aging and harbored secret fears about performance and desirability.

"When I noticed his erection wasn't as hard as it used to be," she says, "I thought he was a little turned off by my body because my breasts aren't as perky as they used to be either."

Voicing these concerns brought them closer together. When they made love for the first time after his infidelity, they were more vulnerable to each other than they could ever remember being. They both regard that lovemaking session as a new beginning.

"I'm learning to speak up," she says, "to tell him when I do or don't want to make love, to be more comfortable about asking him to touch me the way I want to be touched. I read an article advising women to touch themselves during lovemaking; and I tried that. Before everything happened between us, I would have felt silly masturbating myself with my husband next to me in bed. I would have been embarrassed. But it was exciting for both of us and liberating for me."

A crisis of fidelity led Morris and Fran to tear down their old foundations and begin to build new ones, something you and your partner can do without a motivating trauma.

HOW TO BUILD SEXUAL SELF-ESTEEM

Studies have shown that people who have high self-esteem live longer, healthier lives, continue to enjoy sex throughout their lives, and are more optimistic about the future. At midlife, most of us suffer an occasional blow to our esteem. We look in the mirror and recoil at the image of our mother (or father) looking back at us. Wrinkles, sagging skin, receding hairlines—this is not the stuff of romantic legend as we learned it when we were sure our parents never had sex except for the purpose of pro-creation. A man may have trouble getting erect or ejaculating, a woman in lubricating sufficiently for intercourse. How we feel about our bodies affects our sexuality; and rare is the person of any age who hasn't experienced feelings of angst rooted in body image or performance issues.

"I stopped feeling sexy after I caught a glimpse of myself in the bedroom mirror while making love," says Kim, 49. "I looked at my image and thought, 'Who is this old fat broad on top of that man and why is she letting everything hang out?' Not a flattering self-analysis, but it seemed true to me."

Kim's partner, with whom she lives, did not share her negative evaluation of her body. Men typically are more forgiving of women's figure flaws than women are. They are capable of lavishing admiring attention on her good parts and putting the less attractive ones in soft focus, like selective photographers. A man often looks at a longtime partner, especially while lovemaking, and sees not the woman she has become but the woman she was when they first met. But her physical appearance was a problem to Kim, one that interfered with her sexual enjoyment. For her, a diet-and-exercise program were the first steps toward restoring sexual self-esteem; and they may work the same magic for many midlife people. Toning the body and improving appearance can have an aphrodisiac effect on most people at any age.

You can also restore your confidence by:

1. *Challenging your inferiority feelings.* Midlife inferiority feelings come from four major areas: physical appearance, sexual performance, financial status, and worldly accomplishments.

The great majority of people never have model bodies, perfect hair, ideal faces. Why compare yourself to Cindy Crawford or George Clooney when you're looking in the mirror? At forty we castigate ourselves for having fallen from a state of physical grace few of us ever attained in the first place. Set reasonable, attainable physical standards for yourself. Improve what you can and be accepting of your physical imperfections. Even models know they aren't perfect and are often unhappy with certain body parts.

While men are susceptible to insecurity about their physical appearance, women have more concerns in this area. When it comes to sexual performance, however, men take the number-one position. Though most middle-aged people are more enlightened about gender and sexuality issues than they were 30 years ago when they were on the brink of adulthood, they nonetheless were indoctrinated in the belief that women's sexual role is to attract while men's is to perform. That message is imbedded deep within the psyche. Her biggest fear is losing the ability to attract while his is losing the ability to perform. Both have to let go of impossible, often imaginary, standards and replace them with reachable goals.

"I finally stopped competing with my adolescent self," one man said in explaining how he overcame the feelings of sexual inferiority that had begun to paralyze him after 40. "My ejaculate doesn't shoot powerfully. You can't hang a cowboy hat on my erection anymore. But I'm a better lover than I was then. I was more impressed with myself at 19 than my partners were with me. A woman would rather have a tender lover than watch a young stud in action."

Some men who never considered themselves "young studs in action" may develop sexual anxiety more rooted in their fiscal performances than erectile abilities. In our time, corporate downsizing has created a sizable pool of unemployed or underemployed middle-aged men and women. Job loss or even the perceived failure of achievement can affect a woman's sexuality, too. Increasingly, women measure themselves in terms of money and position earned. Rare is the older adult who can weather downsizing or being passed over repeatedly for promotion without experiencing at least a temporary loss of sexual desire.

How can you challenge those inferiority feelings and begin to restore desire?

- Stop idealizing your youthful self. When you look backward in time, try to retrieve the memories of the insecurity and callowness of youth. Haven't you evolved into a better, more loving person? Most of us do.

- Make a list of your attributes and strengths, sexual and otherwise. It's a much longer list than you thought it was, isn't it?

- Whether or not your job provides self-esteem benefits (such as good pay or other less tangible compensations), look outside the workplace for them. Volunteer. Go back to school. Take up an artistic pursuit. Develop a hobby into a paying enterprise. Consider supplementing your income with consulting work. A woman forced into early retirement at fifty used her severance package to start her own mail-order bonsai business and has "never been happier."

- Help your partner build his or her self-esteem. As each grows stronger, so can the other.

2. *Accepting yourself.* Surprisingly, studies show that middle-aged and older people are actually more comfortable with their bodies than younger people, particularly women, are. We may not love what we see at 40, but we don't loathe it the way many do at 20. After a certain point, most of us learn how to practice personal forgiveness when we look into the mirror. If you have achieved this level of body comfort, work at extending the concept to the rest of you. Accept your personality quirks, small character flaws, and less-than-sterling résumé with as much equanimity as you accept a slightly crooked nose, a receding hairline, a few extra pounds.

Look over the list of attributes again. Juxtapose it to the little debit column you carry in your head. Doesn't the balance tip over to the positive side? At midlife especially, self-acceptance is necessary to continued growth, change, improvement—and to a good sex life.

3. *Paying attention to your partner's sexual self-esteem needs.* What's the best sex advice for a woman whose partner has lost his erection during lovemaking? Encourage him to please her. Nothing takes a man's mind off his own perceived shortcomings like his partner's pleasure.

The same advice applies to either a man or a woman with low sexual self-esteem: Take your mind off your own perceived shortcomings by lavishing erotic attention on your partner. Put your own feelings aside and do something to boost his or her sexual self-esteem. Compliment appearance. Give an unrequested back rub. Nuzzle a neck and murmur kind words about the scent and feel of your lover's skin. Say, "Lie back and let me make love to you; I want to do all the work this time." When you make your partner feel more desirable, you feed the cycle of desire shared by both.

THE FOUR SEXUAL SELF-ESTEEM EXERCISES

There are other, more physical ways, of building sexual self esteem. They are:

1. *Masturbation.* Many people include masturbation after marriage on their internal list of sexual "shoulds" and "shouldn'ts." Reasoning that sex is something you do with a partner unless you don't have one, they believe only the single "should" masturbate. Women

are more prone to make this assumption than men and may even regard masturbation as a form of "cheating."

Masturbation is a normal, healthy form of sexual expression for everyone, male or female, married or single. Through masturbation, we learn about our sexual responses, too. A man can teach himself better ejaculatory control by practicing techniques while masturbating. A woman can learn how to reach orgasm via masturbation if she's had orgasmic difficulties. Women who are comfortable with masturbation are more likely to help their partners please them because they know when, where, and how touch is needed.

As the ultimate form of sexual self-love, masturbation also serves a higher purpose. Lovingly stroke yourself. People who feel worthy of self-love are more apt to consider themselves desirable to their partners.

2. *The indirect request.* Help your partner please you by providing more nonverbal guidance. Some couples lose interest in sex because lovemaking becomes "mechanical"; in other words, they have been making love in the same way for years. The patterns of arousal and response that once worked for them may have become dulled over time.

Maybe he would like to take her head gently in his hands and guide it to his penis at just the point where she typically stops manual stimulation in preparation for intercourse. Maybe she would like to put his hand on her vulva and show him how to massage her in a new way. Habit, fear of change, and uncertainty prevent them from translating wishes to realities.

Be bold. Lead your partner in a different direction. Then be enthusiastic in your response to change.

3. *The direct request.* Ask your partner for what you want. Just as your self-esteem rises when you ask for a raise, request redress for a wrong or state an opinion in conflict with another's, so does your sexual self-esteem increase with the direct request. What do you want? More oral sex, more stroking and caressing, more variety in practices and positions top most people's sex wish list. Share yours with your partner.

What stops couples in long-term relationships from making the direct request? Fear of looking silly, being refused, being "judged," or having the other suspect infidelity. "Where will she/he think I'm getting these ideas?" silences some of us, but in our society, inundated with sexual information and imagery, that's not a good excuse. You got the idea from a book, a magazine article, a movie, a glossy advertisement for expensive perfume. Now express it.

4. *Practice enlightened sexual self-interest.* Be sexually self-interested. Nothing is more exciting than an excited partner. Here are some suggestions for raising your own temperature:

- Don't have sex to please your partner if you're not in the mood. Ask to be seduced.

- If your partner is not in the mood for sex, masturbate where your partner can watch, if this is acceptable. Ask first.

- Ask him or her to devote a lovemaking session to pleasing you alone.

- Splurge on sensuous accessories for your own pleasure, such as bath oils, scented creams, lingerie meant to arouse you, not necessarily him. Maybe all your silk undies are black, for example, because he likes black. Buy something in your favorite color.

WHY ENTHUSIASM ENCOURAGES PASSION

Enthusiasm for life in general, and work, hobbies, family, spiritual, and other pursuits in particular, makes one more passionate. Lust for life leads to lust in the bedroom. If there is a great fallacy in our approach to sexual problems it is the isolating of "sex" from the relationship, from the rest of life. Only in the young and intensely hormonally driven does "sex" happen regardless of what else is going on. They can mope their way to orgasm; you can't anymore. The disaffected midlife man or woman, disillusioned and discouraged, is not going to be an exciting lover, no matter what his or her partner pulls from the little bag of sex tricks.

People who have lost their enthusiasm for life have also set up negative patterns in living and loving. They have less and less interest in their jobs, families, and relationships, which causes employers, coworkers, families, friends, and partners to interact less and less with them. They have less and less sex, which causes them to desire less and less sex. The patterns of giving less, receiving less, and wanting less become habitual.

If you're caught in the habits of less, you have to do something to put the vitality back into your life.

THE HIDDEN SEXUAL POTENTIAL OF OPTIMISM

Some people lost their enthusiasm for life as a natural result of losing their sense of optimism. They have allowed negative life experiences, difficult challenges, rejections, or setbacks to quell their sense of hope in the future. By middle age, the habit of pessimism has begun to take a toll on sexuality.

Optimism goes much deeper than believing the glass is half full. Optimism is characterized by:

- Assigning *temporary* causes to bad events. A pessimist says, "I can't get an erection; I must be impotent," while an optimist says, "I can't get an erection because I'm tired and ate and drank too much tonight; I'll try in the morning."

- Being *specific rather than global.* A pessimist says, "Jim didn't call after our first date; I'm a loser," while an optimist says, "Jim may not be interested in a relationship with me, but there are plenty of other men."

- Assigning *external* rather than *personal* explanations for things. A pessimist says, "Jim didn't like me," while an optimist says, "Jim may not be ready for a relationship."

Numerous studies show the connection between optimism and achievement. In one study, students who had hope for academic success overcome a bad test score in an early exam to raise their grade levels by end of term while those who expressed little or no hope after the initial failing grade didn't recover from it. In the business world, people with high hopes set higher goals and continue working toward them when they suffer setbacks. Optimism gives us more than solace when times aren't good; it plays a role in reducing anxiety, alleviating the emotional distress accompanying many life events, and motivating us toward achieving personal and professional goals.

The habit of optimism has powerful sexual benefits. If you are pessimistic about the effects of aging on sexuality, you'll likely suffer sexual problems at midlife. On the other hand, if you're optimistic about your continued sexual future, you probably won't have difficulties or will certainly be able to work around them. What you believe is possible (or not possible) often is.

"In the past five years I've been treated for diabetes, mild heart disease, and a prostate problem," says Robert, 65. "Every time I had a medical situation, someone told me that meant the end of my sexual potency. I never believed that; and it never happened. I get erections. My wife and I have intercourse and enjoy that as we do other variations of lovemaking.

"I will never be an impotent man."

Robert is a born optimist. A tendency toward optimism (or pessimism) may well be inborn, but you can develop optimism too. If you are practicing the steps for leading a counterphobic life as listed in chapter one, you're already on the way toward adopting a more optimistic view of life and sexuality.

Injecting some elements of play into lovemaking, passion's final building block, will help make the new sex foundation sturdier.

FIVE TIPS FOR MAKING SEX MORE PLAYFUL

1. *Don't take your clothes off.* Remember groping, making out, dry humping? Remember being so desperate for your lover's body that you didn't take the time to remove clothing, only pushed aside the necessary items? Start kissing on the sofa and recapture the feelings.

2. *Combine food and sex.* Even grown-ups like to play with their food occasionally. Take food to bed with you. Feed each other. Get more creative than that.

3. *Paint your bodies.* Use water soluble finger paints or body paints— some come flavored—to decorate one another's nude bodies. Paint yourselves to look like the members of primitive tribes and make love the way you imagine they do.

4. *Wear a mask.* Not a rubberized Nixon mask, but something light and feathery. Use the feathers to tickle your partner during oral sex.

5. *Eroticize your environment.* Create a romantic, erotic bedroom and bathroom. Include poetry and erotic fiction into your nightable reading. Buy leisure clothing and fragrances that arouse you and your partner. Indulge in flowers and other accoutrements of gracious, sensual living.

CONQUERING THE THREE EMOTIONS THAT SAP SEXUAL ENERGY

They are, anger, guilt, despair. You've seen how these emotions dampen ardor and squelch passion. You can conquer them by using simple cognitive behavioral steps.

1. *Acknowledge.* On a conscious level, tell yourself the things your unconscious already knows. Anger, guilt, and despair are often stored below the conscious surface, where they can do the most damage. Don't tell yourself, "I'm not angry at my partner for treating me badly, I'm just annoyed." You're angry.

2. *Address.* What is behind the feelings of anger, guilt, despair? Look at your emotions as objectively as possible. What causes the feelings? How long have you had them? What can you do to change them?

3. *Express.* Talk to your partner about your feelings. Don't blame everything on the other person. That will only create a defensive response.

4. *Resolve.* Some issues can be resolved by negotiation with your partner. And some issues are yours personally, like the sex guilt you brought into the relationship. Work on your own issues. Fix what you can and learn to live with the rest.

5. *Release.* Let go of old feelings, old resentments, old arguments. Release them into the atmosphere as if they were helium balloons going up into the sky.

OVERCOMING FIVE FEARS THAT STEAL PASSION

The five fears are:

1. *Fear of intimacy.* For some people, intimacy is associated with early memories of an overly involved or protective parent. They may subconsciously fear losing their own identity in an intimate relationship as an adult. Rather than risking being overwhelmed by a partner, they protect their vulnerability by shutting down emotionally.

2. *Fear of rejection.* Men may fear sexual ridicule, especially at midlife when performance anxieties increase. Women may fear abandonment, again especially at midlife when younger women are perceived as a real threat to the relationship. Ridicule and abandonment are devastating forms of rejection.

3. *Fear of performance failure.* Stronger in men, the fear of performance failure also strikes women. What if she isn't as "good" in bed as another woman might be? Will she lose him?

4. *Fear of hidden (possibly "kinky") sexual desires.* At midlife, kinky desires come more readily to the surface as people come to terms with who they are and what they want. A repressed desire for sexual variation can become an almost unbearable itch at this point. For some, a search for sexual innovation is part of the quest for eliminating boredom.

5. *Fear of (unseemly) passion.* Men and women who have subscribed to the sexual myths are sometimes afraid of their own passion. Do they look foolish? Is their behavior inappropriate, even perverse?

You can overcome these fears by relinquishing the sex-negative myths, leading a counterphobic life, and following the cognitive behavioral steps listed here.

Sizzler #2

SEX PLAY

Exciting sex was not on Helen's agenda. Nor on her husband Jim's. Married 30 years, they had recently suffered the deaths of both their mothers, stood by one daughter through a difficult divorce, consoled another following a miscarriage, and endured the humiliation of "downsizing" on their jobs. As Helen said often to friends, they were "emotionally tired."

Jim suggested they needed to learn how to laugh again. "If we don't," he said, "we'll turn into miserable old farts nobody wants to invite over for dinner." Helen laughed at that remark, and she had to admit laughing felt good.

It was the week before Halloween so Jim made his usual stop at a discount store to buy candy for the neighborhood children and their grandson. On a whim, he picked up a handful of masks, too, a glittering sequin and feather mask on a stick for Helen, the ubiquitous mustache, nose, and glasses, a rubber monster face, and a Batman mask with accompanying headgear.

"I've always fancied myself the Batman type," he said to Helen when he came in the door wearing that mask.

"I'm more the Marx Brothers type, don't you think?" she teased, pulling the mustache, glasses, and big nose out of the bag and putting it on her face. While preparing dinner together, they played with the masks, inventing dialogue to go with their new identities. Helen vamped when she held the sequin and feathered mask in front of her face. "We should wear these for the trick-or-treaters," she said; and he agreed.

"Why stop at masks?" he said. "Remember how we turned the porch into a Halloween display when the girls were small? Let's do it again. The kids will love it."

They shared a lot of laughter while planning and putting together their Halloween fantasy. Though they had for months and by mutual unspoken consent avoided anything but the kind of brief and occasional sexual contact they'd referred to as "necessary quickies" in happier days, they began touching each other more often, especially when they were laughing together. On a crisp afternoon, Helen watched from inside as Jim created a scarecrow on the porch. Bits of straw clung to his sweater and his hair. She was overwhelmed with the desire to pluck them away and went outside to join him. As she pulled the straw from his hair, he looked deeply and tenderly into her eyes. They kissed with their eyes open.

By Halloween night, the front porch was filled with lighted pumpkins and piles of apples. Ghosts and smiling witches hung from the ceiling. The bemused scarecrow and his pal the tin man, a masterpiece of aluminum foil and cardboard, stood guard on either side of the steps. Jim wore the Batman mask and headgear with his tuxedo, part Bruce Wayne, part Batman, he explained. Helen, an elegant witch, wore a long black dress and held the silvery mask in front of her face. The living room was softly lit with candles of all shapes and sizes, and a fire blazed in the hearth. With the light at her back as she answered the door and distributed candy to the little ones, she had never, he thought, been more beautiful. A small boy shyly told her she looked like the beautiful and good witch in *The Wizard of Oz.* The compliment made her glow.

When the lights were out in the pumpkins, they sat side by side on the sofa, sharing a bottle of red wine and memories of holidays past. They laughed repeatedly at the familiar family stories. Then Helen put down her glass, picked up her mask, and again played the vamp.

"My Wayne," she said in a throaty voice. "I'd love to see your bat cave."

They walked arm in arm to the bedroom. Slowly they undressed each other. They teased one another with their hands and lips and tongues, building up the desire in delicious increments as they hadn't done in a very long time. Erotic requests tumbled from their mouths. "Please kiss my pussy," she begged. "Touch my cock," he whispered. "Put it between your breasts." The words aroused them to greater heights.

Finally, she put her hand on his penis and said, "I want you to fill me up. I want you to take me, own me, possess me now." He felt exactly like Batman when he did.

3

TAKE CHARGE OF YOUR SEXUALITY

Imagine a couple lying side by side together in bed after having told each other they were "too tired and stressed" for sex an hour ago. She's reading a novel; he's watching an old black-and-white movie on television. An erotic passage in the novel arouses her. If he were paying attention, he would see her nipples briefly stiffen beneath the silk of her nightgown. Like the heroine, she wants to be taken "hungrily" by a man whose "desire cannot be refused." Beside her, he watches the screen intently. A woman in a low-cut gown leans across the table so the man seated opposite can light her cigarette. Her breasts sway seductively forward. Under the sheets, he feels a slight stirring in his penis, a movement that quickly subsides. After a while, she puts her novel on the table, turns out her light and tells him goodnight. He falls asleep before the movie is over. Sometime in the middle of the night he will awake, reach for the remote control, hit the "off" switch, go back to sleep.

In a way both husband and wife are like Sleeping Beauty. Each would like the other to wake him or her from this sexually somnolent

33

state. Maybe they harbor unspoken anger and hold private grudges. Maybe they are simply bored, with themselves and with each other. The flames may have died down, but the fire is still alive, buried inside each of them.

Are you waiting for your partner to rescue you sexually?

Stop waiting. With this chapter, you take charge of your own sexuality and stop hiding behind the stress excuse, the intimacy fear, the need to control. Light your own fire, and your partner will get caught up in the flames. You are about to become an irresistible sexual force.

THE SEX AND STRESS CONNECTION

Stress isn't all bad. Can you envision a life without tension? As Americans we overreact to every perceived threat to our physical or psychological health, and we make too much of stress. A bird in a gilded cage has a stress-free life. Too much stress, however, or more likely an inability to handle a reasonable amount of stress can have a negative impact on libido and sexual performance. Couples who avoid lovemaking opportunities, pleading "stress," will find at midlife that they aren't very interested in sex when at last they have the opportunity for the perfect island vacation of their dreams.

The primary sources of stress include money, jobs, the responsibilities of parenthood, household chores, health issues, extended families, and marriages or other intimate relationships. Typically people respond to stress in both active and passive ways. They may cry, snap at others, exercise, eat, drink, or take a time-out from the world through reading, going on a nature walk, playing with a pet. Others seem sanguine in the face of every emergency yet develop health problems such as fatigue, headache, neck or back pain, irritable bowel syndrome, or nausea. Many people let stress get a chokehold on their libido.

Some people function well under stress, and they may consider sex a good outlet for tension. But, while stress can be an energizing factor, motivating one to exercise or tear into that mess in the attic, basement, or garage to relieve tension, *it* is more likely to have a debilitating effect on sexuality for most of us. During periods of unusual stress, even loving couples with a good sex life probably experience a lack of desire.

"My husband completely lost interest in sex while his construction business was going into bankruptcy," says Sharon. "We didn't make love for six months. At first I was understanding, then irritable, then really worried. I wanted him to see a counselor but he wouldn't. Eventually, he found a job and began putting his entrepreneurial failure behind him, and we had sex again. He didn't tell me until long after the fact that he hadn't wanted to make love to me because he was afraid he wouldn't be able to 'perform.' I wish I'd know that at the time."

A man who is already under great stress may avoid sex because the added sexual performance pressure is more than he can handle. His partner feels rejected, and she begins avoiding opportunities for sex, too. They are careful to go to bed at different times, develop headaches or stomachaches late in the evening, or choose the eleventh hour to make long-distance phone calls to chatty relatives or friends on the opposite coast. For other couples under stress, sex seems like another chore, one they can put off until later.

Couples who are too stressed to make love only add to their stress level by the habit of erotic avoidance. They may feel guilty for not making love. Unresolved and perhaps unrecognized sexual tensions begin to mount. Without lovemaking to smooth the rough edges of the relationship, they find each other more irritating and annoying as the days go by. The stress level increases again.

How can you remove the stress from your sex life?

- *Never put sexual pressure on a spouse who is under extraordinary stress.* Death of a parent, loss of a job, and other major life traumas almost inevitably take a sexual toll. Be patient and understanding. Offer affection without strings.

- *If sex has become a chore, suspend performance criteria.* Forget intercourse. Don't count orgasms. Agree to touch, stroke, caress, fondle—with no goal in sight. Touching can be as satisfying as intercourse and will often lead there without the pressure of the goal.

- *Reduce some of the tension in your life.* Do you chronically over-schedule free time? Make too many outside commitments and promises to family and friends? Cut back. Consider relaxing your housekeeping standards or hiring occasional help if you don't already have it. Simplify meal preparation with smarter shopping, easier menus, family participation. Divide household responsibilities equitably among family members.

- *Make it possible for your partner to move toward you, not away from you.* Stressful events can being couples closer together, but stress can also trigger two distancing responses, withdrawal and smothering. The stressed partner may withdraw, leaving the other feeling rejected. Or the partner under stress can feel smothered by the other's solicitousness. Be supportive without being smothered, and don't respond to withdrawal by pulling back yourself.

SEVEN SEXY STRESSBUSTERS

1. *Hit something together.* Buy a punching bag. Or a pair of soft bats. Or designate two pillows as your stress removers of choice. Take turns hitting the punching bag or whacking the bed with the pillows. You'll eliminate some of the tension from your body and probably share a laugh at the same time.

2. *Practice erotic touching.* Touch your partner everywhere and anywhere except the genitals, from shoulder kneading to full-body massage. Too many couples touch only when they are signaling their intent to have sex.

3. *Take regular joy breaks, brief sensual/sexual interludes.* Plan a joy break at least once a week. Don't be inhibited by fear of looking foolish. Joy breaks can include a candlelight bubble bath, dancing together in the living room, breakfast in bed.

4. *Practice deep-breathing exercises together.* Get into a comfortable position, perhaps facing each other. Take a deep breath. Let it out slowly. Relax. Repeat. Look in the library or bookstore for books on meditation for more varied and advanced breathing exercises.

5. *Do something physical together.* Plan a shared physical activity, such as biking, hiking, swimming, at least once a week. Exercise is a natural tension reducer.

6. *Do something spiritual together.* You need not attend organized religious services. For some, a nature walk is a spiritual experience.

7. *Take turns letting each other off the hook.* Everyone needs a day, a night, even two hours free of obligations. Give each other regular minivacations in which one partner handles the chores, calls, family demands.

The Intimacy Fear

You may have noticed them sitting at a nearby table in a restaurant. Well-dressed, middle-aged, attractive, the man and woman exchange few words. When they speak, they look past each other as often as they look at each other. They are together, but they don't connect. Most observers would rightly guess they're married and have been for many years. You've seen them. In fact, you and your partner may be them.

Some couples don't make the transition to a deeper level of lovemaking at midlife because one or both of them are afraid of becoming truly intimate with each other. They are together, but they know how to connect only through the genitals. Without recognizing it, they got stuck at the level of hormonally driven sex and are ready to give up on each other now that the wake of the roiling hormones has subsided. Sexual passion isn't dead between them, but it has to be reached through a different path. If they don't find that path, they have few alternatives: boring sex, no sex, changing partners.

"When Matt and I got married 25 years ago, we lived in the hot zone," says Beth, 49. "Passion was everything to us. We sustained a high level of pure physical passion longer than our other married friends did, but gradually things began to change for us too around our tenth anniversary. He had the first affair; and then I had one. The excitement generated by the affairs, the tearful confessions and angry recriminations, the dramatic reunions made our relationship hot again, but we couldn't sustain the heat.

"Eventually he did the predictable thing. He left me when I was 40 for a woman half his age. Exhausted from being the drama queen, I went into therapy where I learned we could probably have saved our marriage and our sex life if we'd been vulnerable and open to each other. But we didn't; and I've moved on. My second marriage is different, better. We are more connected to each other on all levels than Matt and I ever were. At almost 50 I'm having the best sex I've ever had—and, in my case, that's saying a lot. This time the sex is deeply emotional."

Passion doesn't always predict pleasure. While Beth shared explosive, orgasmic lovemaking in the early years with Matt, some women, with matching passion and equally avid partners, don't have the orgasms. When we envy the very young, we often forget that women in their twenties are less likely to be orgasmic than older women, that men in their twenties are more likely to have problems with premature ejaculation, that both genders have less erotic sophistication than their elders. Beth, easily orgasmic, was lucky; and even Beth says the sex is better now, the second time around in a marriage with a man who shares more than his genitals. What does that tell you about the erotic power of intimacy?

Being open with a longtime partner should be easy, but it isn't for many people. Years of squelching their anger, denying their guilt, and suppressing their emotions have left them afraid of being honest. To be honest is to be vulnerable. What if your feelings are rejected? What if your partner harshly judges and withdraws? Emotionally disrobing in front of another person is more frightening than physically disrobing, yet more necessary for great sex at midlife. That kind of intimacy will seem less fearful to you if you learn the following.

FOUR WAYS TO MASTER MIDLIFE INTIMACY FEARS

1. *Comfort yourself.* Don't make your life harder than it needs to be. Rather than waiting for your partner or someone else to notice you need a break, take it. "Comfort" doesn't mean bingeing on food, drink, or another substance, but finding ways of helping yourself feel calmer, quieter, soothed.

2. *Stop taking your partner's behavior personally.* A partner's tension, anger, or sadness may have nothing to do with you, and you aren't responsible for solving all the problems. And don't assume his or her unhappiness or frustration signal, "No lovemaking tonight, dear." Admittedly it's difficult *not* to take a partner's angry, defensive, or sullen behavior as a form of rejection. Keep telling yourself: This isn't about me. I didn't cause it; and I can't fix it.

3. *Turn off your own negative thoughts that inhibit sexuality.* You may be angry about something that happened at work or unhappy with your body following a weight gain. Those negative thoughts make you too angry or uptight to be loving. Your partner may be more accustomed to making assumptions—"reading" you, often incorrectly—then asking questions and may thus assume the negativity is a "keep-away" sign rather than asking, "What's really bothering you?"

4. *Use your vulnerability to be a better lover.* At midlife, we may be more comfortable with our own vulnerability and can therefore be more understanding of, and comfortable with, a partner's insecurity and doubt. *Expose* rather than *protect* yourself emotionally. This openness will allow you to touch your partner in a more intimate way.

Let Go of the Need to Control

Before you can take charge of your own sexuality, you have to stop trying to control your partner. Few of us ever do really control our partners' behavior sexually or otherwise, though we expend a lot of energy in trying. Maybe you think your sex life would improve if your partner took the initiative more often or were more willing to try different positions or make love at the times you would prefer or would wear high heels to bed or brought home flowers more often.

Let it go. Work on yourself. In growing and changing, you will excite your partner. The more you become a complete person—as opposed to half a couple—the less you need to control the other.

The five steps to letting go are:

1. *Own your own issues.* Stop blaming your partner for your mistakes, bad behavior, problems with your family of origin. These are your problems, your issues, your solutions to find.

2. *Don't personalize your partner's anger, need for privacy, or mood swings.* Grant him or her the space to resolve personal issues too.

3. *Stop judging your partner.* And don't accept judgments from your partner either.

4. *Don't lecture.* Too many married couples behave like each other's parent, nagging about the chores, the checkbook, work, and personal goals. Is there anything sexy about a nagging parent?

5. *Don't insist that your partner change so you can.* Change yourself. Let your partner be.

TEN TIPS FOR CREATING AN ELECTRIC SEXUAL ATMOSPHERE

You can improve the quality of your sexual relationship. Rather than saying, "If only he/she would fill-in-the-blank, then I would be a better lover," take positive steps to becoming one.

1. *Make time.* Don't wait for your partner to set aside the time. Plan a romantic evening. Ask him or her out on a date.

2. *Stay as fit and healthy as possible.* Aren't you more attractive when you do? Don't wait for your partner to join the health club with you. Get started on your own.

3. *Be fully present in every erotic encounter.* Banish thoughts of chores, duties, responsibilities, and don't watch the clock. Focus on your sensations and your partner's responses.

4. *Communicate your feelings as well as your needs.* Make the difference clear. "I feel . . ." doesn't mean "I expect you to give or do."

5. *Give positive feedback, both verbally and in nonverbal ways.* Compliment appearances. Say "thank you" for kindnesses and favors. Caress your partner's neck when he/she is tired.

6. *Take responsibility for your own pleasure, sexual and otherwise.* A man does not give a woman an orgasm. A woman can't intuit when a man wants the sensations changed. Communicate.

7. *Don't make sex "work."* You don't have to live up to the average numbers you read in a magazine reader survey. Sex is not another chore. Nor is it an athletic event with points for orgasms.

8. *Keep a sense of humor, in bed and out.* Laughter has been shown in various studies to promote physical and psychological healing. If you can laugh and can make your partner laugh, nothing seems terrible.

9. *Have courage to explore new areas of being together, to say the things you've been holding back.* Express your fears. Show your vulnerability.

10. *Expand your definition of sex beyond intercourse if you haven't already.* The following chapters will help you do that.

How to Become an Erotic Consumer

"Every now and then a relationship needs a jolt of the new," says Todd, 52, and married to Janey for 30 years. "My wife is game to try a lot of things other women aren't, including white-water rafting, fly fishing, and going up in a hot-air balloon, but she is more reluctant when the adventure is an erotic one.

"I really wanted her to wear lingerie for me. She kept saying she wasn't that kind of woman. I know she thinks the twenty pounds she's gained over the years make her less appealing to me, but she couldn't be more wrong. I like her body better now. It's softer, rounder, more womanly. I love her dimpled knees, which she can't fathom.

"Then my daughter-in-law gave her a beautiful silk robe for Christmas. She loved the feel of it, and she let me make love to her while she was wearing it. I bought her a set of silk tap pants and camisole to match the robe; and she surprised us both by loving those too."

If you've never or rarely purchased erotica or sex toys, rented videos, or bought lingerie or other items of sexy clothing for you or your partner, now is the time to become a sophisticated shopper. These items can inject a note of play into lovemaking, introduce new ideas, open the lines of communication, spark desire. Never mind the budget. Sometimes you can't afford not indulging yourself. In the past, some couples may have refrained from visiting the X-rated section of the video store or the sex-toy shop because it was nearly impossible to find quality among the schlock. Many of the toys, like foot-long dildoes and edible panties, were of the gag-gift variety; and most of the video material was designed for male arousal, not female, much of it crudely designed.

Bookstores and video stores now have an unprecedented selection of erotica written by and for women, including the most highbrow and hard-core material available. Videos in both the entertainment and sex-instruction categories are increasingly produced by women and marketed to both women and couples. Sex-toy shops have gone upscale, selling everything from expensive body oils and creams and pasta in the shape of penises to elegant corsets, then leather whips, and gold and silver jewelry meant to be worn in pierced nipples, belly buttons, and genitals.

What if your partner balks at the introduction of videos or sex toys into the bedroom?

- Start with erotic reading material. Erotic thrillers available in paperback include *In the Cut* by Susannah Moore and *Topping from Below* by Laura Reese. The Literary Guild always has a selection of erotic books if you don't feel comfortable buying them at the mall book store. Take turns reading a chapter a night to each other in bed.

- Rent arthouse films (that probably didn't play in your city if you don't live in New York, Chicago, or L. A.) with erotic themes, such as *Damage, Female Perversions,* and *Bliss.* Check one of the video guides for other ideas.

- Don't pressure him or her into watching the video or trying the vibrator. Ask. Suggest. If the answer is "no," say, "Okay, but I'm going to enjoy this myself." Don't accuse your partner of being a sexual prude.

- But don't be deterred from pursuing your own independent pleasures.

- If a reluctant woman consents to watch a video, choose one aimed at couples, with a more romantic storyline such as those produced by Candida Royalle's Femme Productions. Don't rave about the actresses' bodies. Many women compare their own bodies to those on screen and feel inferior.

- If a reluctant man agrees to vibrator play, treat the toy as an adjunct to, not a replacement for, his penis. See 62 for suggestions on how you can give each other pleasure with a vibrator.

- Buy lingerie cut to fit and flatter her figure. And don't forget him. Buy some silk boxer shorts or, if he is trim and fit, perhaps a silk bikini or g-string.

- Leave catalogues from two good sex-toy stores on the night-stand. Order them from: Good Vibrations, 1210 Valencia Street, San Francisco, CA 94110 and Eve's Garden, 119 W. 57th St., New York, NY 10019. The ubiquitous Victoria's Secret lingerie catalogues are also a good source for gifts and inspiration.

DEVELOP YOUR OWN EROTIC LESSON PLAN

"My husband is always working on perfecting his golf swing," a woman complained, "but he hasn't changed his lovemaking style in 28 years."

Her husband needs to apply the principles of the counterphobic life to his sexual technique. Yes, technique does matter. Anyone who says it doesn't probably needs a few erotic lessons. No amount of loving, caring, and sharing will bring a woman to orgasm unless either she or her partner make sure she gets adequate clitorial stimulation.

Sex education is not just for the young. Lack of knowledge is a contributing factor to sexual boredom in midlife couples. Many are unaware of how the physiological changes associated with aging can be used to their advantage in lovemaking. They continue to have sex in the same old way they've been having it for years and wonder why they're bored.

Why shouldn't we apply creativity to our sex life as we do to other pursuits? Think about the way you make love now and then imagine how you would like to make love. What did you see in the fantasy? Is there any reason it can't be made real?

In coming chapters, you'll learn some new techniques for cunnilingus and fellatio, ways to adapt the standard intercourse positions to changing bodies, and many other things. For now, develop your own lovemaking goals. Know what you want: This book can take you there. Here are the steps for developing your lesson plan:

- *Make it personal.* This is not a list of suggested changes for your lover to make to please you. What can you do to increase your pleasure and your mate's?

- *Be aware of the physiological realities associated with aging, but don't be unnecessarily limited by them.* You can't learn to have the erections you had at 19, but you can learn to make better use of the erections you do have.

- *Be specific.* Rather than "I want to perform cunnilingus better," say, "I want to learn new ways of using my tongues, lips, teeth, and the tip of my nose to increase her arousal, prolong her excitation phase, and induce a stronger orgasm."

- *Look beyond the genitals.* Remember there is more to lovemaking than intercourse, genital play, or even orgasm.

- *Build on your strengths.* If you're a great kisser, you can be equally adept at oral sex. And if you give a wonderful back rub, you can learn to bring your partner greater pleasure through manual stimulation.

- *Take your partner's needs and desires into consideration.* What would constitute his or her idea of better lovemaking? If your partner has desires you've never explored, can you learn how to do that comfortably and safely now?

- *Expand your erotic horizons.* What have you been afraid or ashamed to try—and why? In later chapters, you will learn the facts about anal sex, bondage, spanking, and light S/M; and you may decide they are worth trying as an occasional alternative.

Try making a to-learn list of at least two or three and maybe as many as ten points. A point can be as simple as learning how to give an erotic backrub or perfecting the art of the whispered endearment. Either will likely create sexual excitement in a long-term relationship, if for no other reason than that it introduces the element of surprise.

Sizzler #3

THE TAKE-CHARGE LOVER

Jessica prided herself on being a "sensitive" woman. At 55, ten years into her second marriage to a slightly younger man after being widowed, she had grown accustomed to responding to the emotional needs of Brian, her husband, her grown son and daughter, granddaughters, stepchildren, even other relatives and close friends, before they had to articulate those needs. Especially now that she was retired from her university teaching position—an early retirement ostensibly taken for the purpose of writing the book she was letting languish largely in her mind—Jessica "felt," then endlessly analyzed her feelings and those she projected on others before acting. She was, in fact, becoming sexually paralyzed by her own sensitivity.

"We don't make love very often," she told her best friend. "When we do, it's routine, tepid. Brian is so tense around me. I know he's unhappy about some aspect of our relationship, but I don't know what it is. When I ask him to talk, he says there's nothing to talk about. Everything is fine."

"Maybe it is," her friend responded. "There's more to his life than your relationship. Maybe he is worried about his job or turning fifty or any number of things."

"Then why won't he share his concerns with me? And why doesn't he want to make love very often anymore?"

"Because you put everything in the context of 'you'?" her friend posited, stunning Jessica with what she perceived was criticism.

That blow was followed by her daughter's advice: Stop overanalyzing everyone, stop living through others, and harshest of all, "stop believing 'sensitivity' makes you better than the rest of us." Hurt, Jessica retreated into her own work. She didn't initiate sex, but waited for Brian to take charge. He didn't. Feeling better about herself now that she was working again, she began to feel dissatisfied with her sex life, not because unsatisfying marital sex might reflect upon her inability to meet his emotional needs but because her sexual needs weren't being met.

She wanted more sex. How was she going to get it? Obviously demanding an explanation for his lack of interest wasn't the answer.

First, she became more affectionate with Brian. She took his hand when they walked, rubbed his shoulders or neck when they watched television together, occasionally leaned her head against his shoulder at a movie, while seated side by side on a restaurant banquette, or riding together in a cab. Her easy affection seemed to relax him.

One night she shyly asked him if he would masturbate her to orgasm. At first he seemed uncomfortable with the request, but he did comply. After bringing her to several shuddering orgasms, he was clearly aroused. She kissed him and, offering her profuse gratitude, fell asleep in his arms. The next morning she woke early to the delicious feeling of Brian's erection moving rhythmically against her buttocks.

"Are you awake?" he whispered.

"Uhmm," she replied, moving her body against his, in tune with his urgency.

His hands massaged her breasts, her clitoris. She angled her hips, to make his entry easier. Shortly after he penetrated her, she began coming. After his own orgasm, he clung to her, their sweaty bodies bonded together.

"You're so hot these days," he whispered appreciatively in her ear.

Later that morning she left a message on his voice mail telling him how much she'd enjoyed their time together. The afternoon brought flowers, a dozen yellow roses, her favorite. He followed that by calling to make a dinner date with her.

They made love again that night. For several days afterward, Jessica felt like a woman embarking on a second—no, third—honeymoon. After their passion was reestablished, Brian confided in her about some problems he'd been having with one of his major clients. Her best friend and her daughter had been right: Her "sensitivity" had been perceived by her husband as a suffocating demand for attention on her part. When she got involved in her own life again and went after her own sexual satisfaction without trying to understand his reasons for withdrawal, she turned him on.

"I can't believe how much you turn me on these days," he told her. "You've changed."

She smiled enigmatically and put his hand on her crotch.

4

GAMES FOR MATURE LOVERS

"Several years ago, I realized my lovemaking wasn't having the same effect on David anymore," says Elizabeth. A professional couple in their midfifties, they have been married for 20 years, the second marriage for both. "I thought he was tired of me, maybe there was another woman. After 50, a woman thinks everything that goes wrong can be blamed on her sagging breasts. I stopped initiating sex. When he suggested making love, I agreed, but I was holding back. I felt tentative, insecure. I couldn't let go."

"I knew she was holding back, but I didn't understand why," David says, taking up their story. "Finally I just asked her. I'd learned from going through one divorce that it's better to ask what's wrong before you inadvertently make it worse by stumbling around in the dark, pretending there are no obstructions in the path."

Elizabeth told him she knew she wasn't "turning him on" anymore. He vehemently denied that was true. "If I excite you, why does it take you so long to get an erection?" she demanded. It didn't before." David gave her a lesson in the facts of midlife.

"My rhythm has changed," he says, "and I like the change. Now that she understands and has adapted to the slower pace of my arousal, she likes it better. I respond more slowly but more fully than I did."

READING YOUR PARTNER'S SEXUAL RHYTHMS

As previously noted, some normal changes in arousal and sexual performance patterns are associated with aging in both men and women. Things are different now; they aren't worse. *Different.* These changes don't lead to a loss of pleasure unless a couple misreads and misunderstands them. In some ways, a man and a woman who have been together for many years need to get sexually reacquainted at midlife. If she continues to treat his penis like a gun that might go off at any minute while he hands on to the innocent belief that she always prefers cuddling to intercourse, they aren't reading each other's rhythms.

After 40, a man probably does not get an immediate, strong erection, and the intensity of his need to ejaculate may diminish. Some men may no longer need to ejaculate every time they have sex. (In a later chapter, men will describe how they can have orgasms without ejaculating.) Most men report their need for both affection and more prolonged caressing during lovemaking increases. A woman's sexual-response cycle speeds up as a man's slows down. One of the hurdles standing between this couple and great sex is simple misinformation. Once a woman understands that her partner's slower arousal patterns are not a negative reflection on her lovemaking skills or desirability, she can relax. And once a man understands that his partner can be more easily aroused and satisfied than she was in the past, he can relax too.

"This is really the best time in our sex lives," Elizabeth says, "because I don't have to worry that he will ejaculate while I'm performing fellatio or come too soon after we begin having intercourse. Sex has a more luxurious feel now. I can give him blow jobs like I never could before. I never feel rushed to have my own orgasm. There is time for everything."

HOW TO FLIRT SHAMELESSLY WITH YOUR MATE

At midlife the tempo of the seduction dance changes too. Take advantage of the new beat by putting more energy into the prearousal phase of lovemaking. Too many married couples in every age group skip this part altogether. They think it's enough to kiss or cuddle briefly before sliding a hand suggestively down the other's body or even to ask with no erotic preliminaries, "Do you want to?"

Consciously flirt with your mate whether you have the opportunity for sexual activity or not. Flirting is really nothing more than letting the other know she or he is attractive and appreciated, with no demands or expectations implied. It keeps the spark alive. If you've forgotten how, here are the four elements of flirting for lovers:

- *Eye contact.* How often do you look into each other's eyes while talking? Hold a gaze longer than a nanosecond? Seek your lover's eyes; and lower your voice a bit as you hold them. The gaze need not be soulful or studiedly romantic. Let your eyes convey warmth, amusement, a hint of erotic availability.

- *Body language.* Don't sit across from each other at a table or beside each other on the sofa with arms and legs protectively crossed. Use open inviting body language.

- *Light verbal bantering, with sexual innuendo.* In a gently suggestive tone, praise your mate's physical appearance. Be witty if you can. Tease, but don't criticize in the guise of teasing.

- *Touch.* Use sparingly, like spice in food. Touch your lover's hand or arm to emphasize a point while speaking. Run a finger down his or her cheek, stroke your thumb across a hand, brush a leg under the table with your foot.

HOW TO BEHAVE LIKE A TEENAGER IN LUST

Young lovers and for that matter lovers of any age who face repeated and/or prolonged separations know the joys of delaying intercourse, even orgasm. When preserving virginity or "waiting" until a suitable length of courtship time had passed were conditions under which most of us chafed, we played arousing, teasing love games. Such play can work for you and your partner now. Agree to a moratorium on penetration for a while. Ratchet up the sexual tension over a period of days or weeks. Intercourse will seem like a holiday.

Games teenagers play—or did play when we were teenagers—include outercourse, petting, and dry humping, all stopping short of "the act." Why not return briefly to the glory days of youth? Tell your mate you've been revirginized and won't "go all the way."

- *Petting.* The object of the game for the boy was to get his hands inside her bra and panties. For the girl, it was holding the elastic line. Tongues in mouths are more than acceptable. They're mandatory. He touches her a lot more than she touches him. Get in an upright seated position. Start with a clench.

- *Dry humping.* He's lying flat out on top of her on the back seat of the car, the parents' sofa, the floor, carpeted preferably—or she's lying on top of him. They move together simulating intercourse. If she has an orgasm from the friction, he's a stud. But if he comes inside his jeans, they're both a little embarrassed. He should stop the rocking motion when he feels ejaculation is imminent and substitute the flat of his hand pressing against her vulva.

- *Outercourse.* Clothes may be loosened and pants pulled down in the heat of the moment, but the underwear stays on. He rubs her clitoris through her panties. She may take his penis in her hand if it spontaneously falls out the slit in his shorts or briefs. He may continue rubbing her until she has an orgasm. If she masturbates him to orgasm or allows him to come on her stomach, she loves him.

BE A TEASE

There is simply not enough "play" in sexplay. By midlife, the average couple has become far too serious about sex. Teasing is something they, particularly she, might have done to one another a very long time ago. Now teasing is what they tell each other not to do to the dog or the grandchildren.

Stop being so forthright about sex. Tease your partner. Torment eventually gives way to delight. You do remember delight, don't you?

Some teasing games include:

• *The feather tease.* Chinese courtesans once used peacock feathers to tease their titled lovers. You can use any feather—peacock, ostrich, the feathers attached to gift-shop pens. Tickle and caress your partner's genitals with the feather. A silk scarf can be used in the same way. Experiment with other fabrics or soft household items, such as those dishwashing implements made of soft fingers of sponge on a handle.

• *The visual tease.* You're dressed, running ten minutes late, hurrying out the door. Your partner is still getting dressed or lingering over breakfast. On your way out, flash him or her. Yes, flash. Quickly expose a breast, hike a shirt to show an inner thigh, unzip and let the penis show.

When you want to make love, use visual-seduction techniques. Put a little jiggle in your walk. Stretch out your legs encased in silk stockings. Let her watch as you slowly unbutton your shirt. Show what you like about your body and *then* dim the lights.

• *The verbal tease.* Make promises you aren't going to keep—yet. Tell him what you're going to do with his penis. Then make him wait until next time. Tell her exactly how you're going to make her come, and then make her ask for it in very specific terms.

• *The breast tease.* Men love women's breasts. For many men, making love to a woman's breasts is a fantasy they'd like to make come true. If you're unhappy with your breasts, buy a sexy push-up bra and leave it on. Take his penis between your breasts and let him have intercourse with your cleavage.

• *The penis tease.* Use the end of your penis to tease her nipples, inner thighs, clitoris, labia. The silky texture of the head makes the penis more effective than a rose petal at stroking and stimulating sensitive places. A bonus: Stimulation works both ways. Your penis may get harder than it normally does when you use it as a teasing device.

IMPROVING HER ORAL LOVEMAKING SKILLS

"Like a lot of Baby Boom women, I learned how to perform fellatio by practicing on a green banana with a copy of *The Sensuous Woman* by 'J' in one hand," says Delia, 48. That book, first published in 1969 and reissued many times in the ensuing years, was outrageously bold in its day. "The author made fellatio sound like fun, not an onerous marital duty or a sin, and I took enthusiastically to instruction."

When Delia got married a few years later, her husband Andy was delighted with her oral skills. Now, she says, he gently pushes her head away when she tries to perform oral sex on him. She doesn't understand what's wrong. How could a technique he considered "perfect" suddenly not work? Andy's response pattern has changed. Though he enjoys receiving oral sex as much as he ever did, he doesn't get an erection as soon as she takes him into her mouth when he's flaccid. He probably doesn't want to disappoint her if it takes him too long to achieve an erection.

By adapting your fellatio technique, you may be able to bring your partner to erection more quickly or help him get a harder erection than he has been getting lately. But it isn't necessary to perform fellatio endlessly. If your jaw gets tired, alternate oral with manual stimulation.

THE NEW BASIC FELLATIO TECHNIQUE

1. Spend more time kissing, licking, sucking, caressing his inner thighs than you did in the past.

2. Put his balls carefully in your mouth. Pull down gently with your mouth. With your thumb, massage his perineum (the area between the anus and the base of the scrotum) lightly.

3. Either with his balls still in your mouth or not, depending on what is comfortable for you, lovingly stroke his penis from the head down to the base of the shaft. The downward stroke is more arousing to most men than stroking up the shaft. Spend more time stroking than you did in the past. While stroking, again lick, kiss, suck his inner thighs.

4. Get into the most comfortable position, which might be the basic P-M (penis/mouth) position, the man lying on his back, the woman kneeling at his side at a right angle to his body. Take his penis gently in the palm of your hand and run your tongue around the head to moisten it.

5. Circle the head of the penis with your tongue, then work your tongue down the shaft, licking lightly with the tip. Repeat the stroke while massaging his testicles, gently pulling them downward. Alternate the testicle massage with the perineum massage. (See following.) Do not be concerned if he doesn't become erect.

6. Follow the ridge of the corona with your tongue while massaging the shaft with both hands, the penis sandwiched between them. Keep the fingers together. Use the palm of one hand and the backs of the opposite fingers to create a rolling pressure, a slightly firmer pressure than you used on him in the past.

7. Wet your lips and stretch your mouth to cover your teeth, forming a ridge on top and bottom. Grasping the penis firmly in both hands, repeatedly move your mouth down toward your hand at the base of the penis and back up to the head, varying the speed.

8. When your mouth is tired, vary the routine by repeating steps five and six. Keep a firm grip on the penis at all times.

FELLATIO VARIATIONS

• *The Deep Suck.* Some men say their erections grow stronger with this kind of sucking: Gradually suck into your mouth the full length of his penis—the slower the better. Move your tongue around the shaft as you're sucking in. Once he is all the way in, pull in the sides of your cheeks to create suction. Relax the back of your throat. Give the penis several hard sucks. Open your mouth to release the suction. When you close it, pull in the sides of your cheeks again before sucking.

If you can, tease the corona with your tongue while you're sucking. With practice, you may be able to lick the corona down the shaft. To stop the gag reflex, swallow frequently. Also, it may help to keep your tongue flat against his penis.

The "Deep Throat" is nothing more than the deepest suck. Linda Lovelace's trick in the X-rated film of the same name was positioning her head so that her mouth and throat formed one long continuous passage, easiest done by fellating him while flat on your back with your shoulders at the edge of the bed and head thrown back. Experiment to find the right angle for you. Another position that works: Straddle him and kneel over his penis, facing his feet. Your throat and mouth will be at the right angle to accommodate his entire penis.

- *The Butterfly Flick.* Flick your tongue back and forth lightly and rapidly across the delicate corona. After several flicks, run your tongue from the base to head, then flick it up and down the same path, before resuming your ministrations to the corona.

- *The Silken Swirl.* Continually circle the penis with your tongue while sliding it in and out of your mouth. Combine with the Butterfly Flick.

- *The Jade Flute.* Hold his penis firmly at the base in one hand. Hold the head in your mouth. Purse your mouth into a slight O and suck the head while playing up and down the shaft with your finger pads.

Some general hints: Don't use your teeth. Remember that you can and should devote more time to fellatio than you did in the past. Concentrate most of your attention on the top one third, the most sensitive part of the penis. The head and coronal ridge are the most sensitive parts of the penis. On the shaft, the raphe, that seam running down the underside of the penis, is the only very sensitive part.

IMPROVING HIS ORAL LOVEMAKING SKILLS

"When we got married 27 years ago, we were very much in love, but our sex life was disappointing to both of us," says Roger, 51. "I had a problem with premature ejaculation. Foreplay was quick and not inventive. Anita rarely had an orgasm. We had a family before we knew how to give each other pleasure, which is a little sad.

"We didn't discover oral sex until we'd been married for ten years. Her sister gave us a copy of *The Joy of Sex* as an anniversary gift. It was a revelation. I immediately loved performing cunnilingus. Anita was reluctant at first, but after her first orgasm this way she was a convert. When she started going through the perimenopausal phase, she would sometimes pull away when I started to go down on her or take my head away before I'd hardly begun. I read some of her menopause books and guessed she had concerns about losing her sex appeal after menopause.

"I was wrong. She was more sensitive than she'd ever been and was embarrassed by that. I find it an amazing, delightful turn of events. I can give her multiple orgasms via cunnilingus now. She goes higher than she ever has. It's incredible."

Sex surveys done in the past 25 years show increasing numbers of couples engaging in oral sex, with the rise in cunnilingus particularly marked. Like Roger, men learned that they could be more sure of giving a woman an orgasm via cunnilingus than by any other route. By the 1980s sexual etiquette almost dictated he give her an oral orgasm first before taking his pleasure.

At midlife, being a gentleman is easier than it was. If a woman felt some embarrassment about receiving cunnilingus, she, having been liberated from youthful hang-ups, may be embarrassed no longer. With erotic senses heightened, she may have an orgasm after minimal oral contact, allowing her partner to practice more sophisticated patterns of stimulation to tease her to the brink and bring her back repeatedly. For the first time, she may be multiply orgasmic.

THE NEW CUNNILINGUS TECHNIQUE

1. Stroke, massage, nibble, suck, kiss, lick, and otherwise tease her body, avoiding the genital area until she is fully aroused. Pay special attention to her breasts and inner thighs. Massage her aureole with flat open palms, then play with the nipples as you kiss slowly down to her navel. Lick the inner thighs. As you are licking one side, use the finger pads of one hand to spider walk, up and down the opposite inner thigh.

2. Caress her perineum as you use your fingers to part her outer vaginal lips, making her clitoris accessible. Lick and suck the area

surrounding the clitoris. Some women at midlife reach orgasm after initial licking and sucking of this area.

3. Cover her venus mons, the point where the clitoris begins, with your mouth. Suck, using *gentle* pressure. Some women enjoy having this area nibbled lightly, which is nothing more than letting your teeth touch the flesh, then pulling back, touching again and pulling back. No biting. Other women find this too much pressure. Remember that she may like more pressure, or less, than she did in the past. Vary your technique and gauge her response.

4. If her clitoris is well back inside the clitoral hood, exert minimal pressure with your fingers along the side of the hood to lift and expose the clitoris.

5. Indirectly stimulate her clitoris by putting your lips around the sides. Hold them in a pursed position as you suck. Alternate the sucking with licking of the sides of the clitoris and surrounding tissues. Her clitoris may be so exquisitely sensitive now that she won't be able to tolerate direct stimulation—or, on the other hand, will be highly orgasmic this way. Pay attention to her as if she were a new partner whose responses can surprise you.

6. When she is nearing orgasm, you can vary the sensation by covering the clitoral area with your mouth. Suck around the sides of the clitoris. Stimulate her labia with your hands or stroke her inner thighs or tease her nipples or alternate those stimuli.

7. Try gently inserting a finger into her anus during cunnilingus. (Be careful not to put that finger into her vagina later.) Or stimulate her perineum.

How to Give Your Partner Manual Pleasure

Don't focus exclusively on the genitals. Touching that isn't programmed to lead directly to intercourse is often neglected in relationships. Couples use touch sparingly when they aren't stroking to arousal. Yet the need to touch and be touched varies in intensity from person to person and within the same person at different ages and stages of life. For many people at midlife, touch becomes increasingly important.

"The skin is one continuous erogenous zone," says John, 61, a retired movie-set designer living in California with his third wife, Juanita. "I didn't appreciate that until I took a workshop in erotic massage to surprise her on our twentieth anniversary last year. She was really surprised. First we got into the hot tub together. Then after serving her champagne and strawberries, I oiled my hands and began massaging her from head to toe. I started by gently kneading the base of her neck, then making long gliding strokes down her body to her buttocks, which I caressed.

"Combining the basic strokes the instructor taught us and adding a few fancy erotic techniques I picked up from one of the books on the recommended reading list, I gave her an experience she was begging me to repeat in a few days. Sometimes we make love afterward and sometimes I masturbate her to an orgasm. I enjoy giving her pleasure this way at least as much as she does receiving it."

In our haste to reach the genitals, we forget that our entire bodies have erotic potential. Before moving on to erotic massage, you and your partner might benefit from going back to square one. In the initial stages of sex therapy, couples are instructed not to have intercourse. Instead they are given homework assignments, series of pleasurable sensuous interactions called "sensate focus" or "nondemand exercises." They are not demanding because they are not expected to lead to intercourse. Derived from the more varied and subtle arousal techniques taught by Oriental sexologists hundreds of years ago, sensate focus is a good first-touch step.

Here is a variation of the basic technique:

One partner lies on his/her belly. The other uses hands and lips to kiss, caress, and stroke the skin. Each concentrates on the feeling of touch and nothing else. The partner being stroked can ask for a change in pressure or speed.

The Erotic Massage

Unlike the typical invigorating massage that can include sometimes painful kneading of knotted muscles, an erotic massage, focused on skin, not muscle, is softer, the pace more languid. Use small amounts of lightly scented oil, warming the oil in the hands before rubbing into skin. Combine the following strokes in a pattern pleasing to your partner:

- *The Glide.* Run your hands smoothly in long strokes that blend seamlessly together. Best for large areas of the body, such as back, thighs, legs.

- *Kneading.* Be careful not to be too vigorous. Use sparingly. You are trying to arouse, not loosen tight muscles. Most effective on the buttocks.

- *Spider Legs.* A highly arousing touch. Use the pads of your fingers as if they were spider legs wandering up and down your lover's body. Keep it very light and teasing.

- *The Single-Finger Stroke.* Most effective on delicate areas such as eyelids and ears. Also thrilling on the throat. Simply run one finger very lightly along the skin.

- *The Walk of Love.* Walk your fingers around your lover's body. This touch is most exciting when you move from one erogenous zone to the other. Move more slowly and apply more pressure than in Spider Legs.

- *Love Bites, Pinches, and Slaps.* An occasional bite, pinch, slap, squeeze—always done lightly in the spirit of play—intensifies the arousal for some people. Slaps are particularly effective on the buttocks because they bring the blood closer to the surface, making the flesh more sensitive to the touch. Some men and women enjoy having their nipples teased by love bites or pinches—and some *hate* it.

- *The Nipple Stroke.* Use the palm of your hand to brush lightly over nipples, his as well as hers. Gently rub the nipples between your fingers. Blowing over nipples wetted with saliva creates a pleasant tingling sensation.

- *The Breast Stroke.* Women can use their breasts on any part of the male anatomy. Press your breasts against him. Use the nipples to tease with light touches. Hold your nipples against his. Or take your nipples in hand and rub the tips against the tips of his.

Here are some specifically sexual massage techniques:

Manually Stimulating the Male Genitals

1. Lightly stroke the perineum with fingertips.

2. Move your fingers to the back, bottom, and front of the scrotum in a quick, almost tickling fashion. Then cover the same ground in soft caressing touches. Alternate tickles and caresses.

3. Fondle his testicles tenderly.

4. Grip his penis with palms and fingers firmly near the tip and move your grasp smoothly down the shaft toward the base. Use the fingertips of the other hand to stimulate the head. Firmness of touch is the critical factor. Don't be too gentle.

5. Run a fingertip along the underside of the erect penis, outlining the head and the corona, the ridge surrounding the base of the head and the most sensitive area of a man's penis.

6. Lightly pump the shaft up and down while caressing the head.

• *The Perineum Massage.* Some older men, or men who have become adept at holding back their ejaculation, may have prolonged intercourse to the point where ejaculation is difficult. For many of them, the perineum massage induces orgasm. Try it, and don't be dismayed if it doesn't have the desired effect. Male response varies widely.

With the flat of your hand or your thumb, massage the perineum while continuing intercourse, manual stimulation, or fellatio. The key lies solely in the force of your pressure. Exert firm, not harsh, pressure as you massage.

Manually Stimulating the Female Genitals

1. After using the glide on her thighs, stroke her labia using the Single-Finger Stroke.

2. Lightly stroke above, below, and at the sides of the clitoris.

3. As she becomes aroused, use a soft vibrating side-to-side motion, which is achieved by placing finger pads on either side of the clitoris, touching gently, and vibrating the finger pads.

4. Alternate the sensation by moving finger pads further apart and/or vibrating more quickly or more slowly.

5. Place one thumb lightly at the root of her clitoris and stroke her labia or inner thighs with the other hand.

• *The G-Spot Massage.* Some sexologists says it doesn't exist, while others vociferously argue that it does. Some women claim they don't have one, can't find it, or have found the supposedly miracle place to be just another cluster of cells, not an erotic hot spot. Others swear they have wonderful orgasms if it's manipulated properly. The G spot, named for German gynecologist Ernst Grafenbert, who rediscovered it in the 1940s, was known to the authors of the *Kama Sutra.* They reported that stimulating the area produced a pleasurable response.

Locate the spot by inserting your index finger into her vagina, the back of the finger against the anterior wall. Move your finger in a tickling or "come-here" gesture. The rough patch of skin—which may be somewhat spongier than surrounding tissue—is the G spot. The size and shape of a small bean, it is located about two inches inside the vaginal opening on the front wall of the vagina, the side toward the belly button. Massage the G spot in a smooth, rhythmic motion.

THE JOY OF MUTUAL MASTURBATION

"Ryan wasn't in the mood for sex one night, so I asked him if he would mind if I masturbated in bed," Jessica says. She and Ryan, both in their forties, have been lovers for seven years. "He feigned nonchalance, but I could tell he was titillated. I'd wanted to do this for years, but I was afraid I'd look funny or be too self-conscious to have an orgasm while he was watching me. Suddenly my inhibitions were gone. I wanted to show off. I was confident of my ability to have an orgasm any time I wanted one.

"I sat up with my back against the headboard, my legs open, bent up at the knees. First I massaged my nipples, slowly, slowly, with the flats of my hands. I took each nipple between my fingers and twisted gently, then massaged with the fingers. Moving my hands down toward my genitals at a leisurely pace, I caressed my body. By the time I parted my lips and placed two fingers in V position alongside my clitoris, Ryan was watching me with glazed eyes.

"'Touch your penis,' I told him; and he obeyed me in an erotic trance. We masturbated to climax, watching each other, watching ourselves, catching glimpses in the dresser mirror. It was an intensely erotic experience that energized us for days afterward."

Many women, particularly when young, find the idea of masturbating in front of their partner unappealing or intimidating. They think masturbation "should" be private or that couples "shouldn't" masturbate at all. Many men, no matter their age, rate watching a woman masturbate at the top of their sex-wish list. Fortunately, at midlife more women are willing to experiment with this very private form of exhibitionism. In this as in so many other ways, the genders come together.

Why mutual masturbation?

- Watching one another fondle genitals from a slight distance is a unique, intensely arousing experience.

- Each partner's excitement feeds the other's, creating a higher level of arousal than either would experience masturbating alone.

- The gift of masturbation increases intimacy between partners.

- It allows both partners to explore their own bodies at their own pace while being stimulated by their lover's presence.

- There's no clearer way to show a partner how you would like to be touched. If your needs have changed and your partner's love-making hasn't, play a little show rather than tell.

- And, it's the safest sex if you're having an affair, becoming intimate with a new partner, or if one or both is recuperating from an illness or surgery that makes other forms of lovemaking more problematic.

For more variety, introduce the vibrator, first through using it on yourself during mutual masturbation and gradually adding it to the occasional lovemaking session.

FIVE TOP VIBRATOR TIPS

1. Most women reach orgasm with the vibrator by pressing it against the clitoris, not through vaginal insertion. Experiment by varying the pressure and speed. If the vibration is too intense for direct contact even at low speed, move it to the side of the clitoris or wear silky panties.

2. Men can enjoy vibrator play too. Start on low speed. Run the vibrator along the shaft, then press it against the base, the scrotum, and the perineum. Experiment with higher speeds and firmer pressures.

3. First use the vibrator to massage your partner's body. Use it on the back, arms, legs, neck. Move slowly to the genitals, just as you would if you were using your hands in a full-body massage. Take turns massaging each other.

4. A man can combine penetration and vibrator use during intercourse. Hold the vibrator on her clitoris while slowly thrusting into her vagina with your penis. He can also use the vibrator while manually stimulating her. Hold it against the back of his hand as he strokes her labia and the sides of her clitoris.

5. A woman can use the vibrator to vary stimulation while caressing her partner's genitals in manual loveplay. Hold a vibrator against the back of her hand that is cupping his scrotum or holding his penis.

Sizzler # 4

THE LOVE GAME

When they were young newlyweds almost forty years ago, Cal and Maggie made up for what they lacked in sophistication, experience, and erotic expertise with boundless enthusiasm and passion. Now they overcome the erotic lethargy that can accompany long-term relationships by utilizing the sexual skills they've developed together. Sometimes they make love, Maggie says, and other times they play sex games.

"The intensity and purity of sexual passion in youth is a beautiful thing," Maggie says. "But we have idealized that phase of lovemaking in this culture. There are other beautiful things. Cal and I have become consummate sexual-game players. Sometimes lovemaking is about a tender union of souls. Sometimes it's not. We use props and costumes, play roles, and experiment with the occasional sexual variation, such as spanking and bondage."

A favorite game is the pick-up. They arrange to meet at a bar and agree that they will pretend not to know each other. The partner who arrives second has to play the "pick-up artist." The last time they played, Cal was waiting in a lobby lounge in an expensive Chicago hotel. The ambiance was elegant. A long, highly polished mahogany bar was flanked by a mirrored and richly carved back bar. The drinks were expensive. The clientele looked well off. When Maggie took the bar stool one over from Cal's, he pretended to ignore her, affecting the expression of world-weary ennui worn so well by the rich and celebrated.

Though she doesn't smoke, Maggie pulled a cigarette from her tiny handbag. She pretended to search for a light before turning to Cal and murmuring, "I can't find a match. Do you have one?"

"No one smokes anymore," he replied, half turning away from her.

In response, Maggie made a half turn toward him. She uncrossed and recrossed her still fabulous legs. And she simply looked at him with a bemused expression on her face until he couldn't resist looking back at her.

"I was quite sure you were aware of me," she said, pitching her voice seductively low.

"It would be hard to miss those legs," he said.

"Are you a leg man?" Maggie asked. She put a manicured hand on one knee and slowly moved it up her thigh, exposing a little more leg encased in sheer black stocking as she did. Lowering her head and raising her eyes, she looked at him from beneath the broad brim of a stylish black hat.

"I can be," Cal said, deliberately not meeting her eyes, but keeping his gaze on her leg.

"I'll bet you can," she said. "Are you staying in Chicago long?"

"I live here," he said, turning to face her now, his leg brushing hers. "And you?"

"I'm here only to collect an inheritance," she said. "My lover died."

He raised his eyebrow and grinned. That was a new one. He put his hand on top of hers, the hand that was still resting on her thigh.

"Let me buy you a drink," he said; and she knew she had him.

An hour later, they were groping each other passionately in his car parked in the hotel garage. They were going to "his" place. She was, she said, a little drunk and ready to toss her "virtue" aside.

"I like it hard and hot," he whispered in her ear. "How about you?"

For an answer, she took his hand that was covering her breast and squeezed his fingers until they compressed her nipple tightly. A shiver ran up her spine. He roughly pushed aside the fabric of her V-necked dress, reached inside her black-lace bra, and found her nipple. As he thrust his tongue deeply into her mouth, he twisted her nipple. She moaned appreciatively.

Before he started the car and began the drive home, he shoved her skirt up, exposing her genitals. She was wearing a garter belt and stockings, no panties. At every stoplight, he insinuated a finger into her vagina. By the time he pulled into the garage at "his" apartment building, she was wet.

Inside the apartment, with a panoramic view of the city before him, he took her the way he said "a man takes an expensive slut": From behind, as she was bent over the sofa. Her orgasm was both profound and prolonged. He deliberately stopped himself from ejaculating because, he knew, after they had changed clothes and driven back to the hotel to get her car, they would make love again, playfully yet more tenderly this time.

IMPROVING INTERCOURSE

"I have always loved the feel of my man inside me during intercourse," says Monica. "When I was in my twenties and early thirties I almost never had an orgasm during intercourse, but I still enjoyed it because of the feeling of closeness you can't get from anything else. Now, at fifty, I am often orgasmic during intercourse, partly because I have orgasms easier, but mostly because I am more comfortable with stroking my clitoris.

"Intercourse is also better because foreplay lasts much longer now. My husband isn't in the rush he once was. He needs the time to get a good erection and be ready for intercourse. He needs the foreplay even more than I do."

Traditionally, the period of lovemaking known as "foreplay" has been considered something a man has to do for the woman to get her ready for intercourse. Presumably he is always ready. That was never quite true, and by midlife it is quite untrue. Studies and surveys show that women enjoy intercourse now more than they did when they were younger, while men enjoy other forms of loveplay more than they did.

Men want and *need* more touching, kissing, caressing, and stroking before they are ready for intercourse.

SEVEN TIPS FOR HOTTER LOVEPLAY

1. *Start on warm.* Sex begins in the brain for everyone. The mental fires need tending, particularly for the couple who've been together a long time. Get in the habit of indulging your fleeting sexual thoughts and fantasies, rather than banishing them until "a suitable hour." Start thinking about lovemaking hours in advance. Share your erotic thoughts briefly and graphically with your lover during the day if you can. The busiest, executive has a few minutes to make or receive a husky-voiced call.

2. *Get romantic.* The details are more important now, and typically the couple are paying less attention to them. Set the stage for lovemaking in little ways. Is your bedroom a haven for romance? Consider fresh decor, softer lighting. Add fat candles in glass or pottery containers, plants, fresh flowers, photos of the two of you when you were younger. Bring each other small gifts. Perform unexpected favors.

3. *Go slower.* Begin making love in the living room, at the dining table, in the restaurant. Start by paying close attention to each other. Remember how flattered you were when your lover listened carefully to everything you said? Flirt. Later, when you begin making love in earnest, kiss and caress each other's entire bodies, but not the sex organs yet. Sucking a finger or toe is sexy.

4. *Lavish attention on his other erotic zones.* Don't go straight for the penis. Many men have sensitive nipples, scrotums, and perineums. Stimulating these areas orally or manually may make it easier for him to get an erection when you do take his penis in hand.

5. *Give her an orgasm, manually or orally.* She has an orgasm more easily and is more likely to have multiple orgasms. Giving her the first orgasm takes the performance pressure off, and watching her come is very arousing, possibly arousing enough to make his erection harder.

6. *Spend more time stimulating his penis.* Some men have trouble getting and sustaining a good erection because their partners continue to treat their penises gingerly. He is unlikely to reach the ejaculation point too quickly. Grasp him firmly. Don't let go too soon.

7. *Experiment with varying touch and rhythms.* Use a little more or less pressure than your lover expects. Arouse your partner, then back off at the point where you typically build up the stimuli. By teasing, you increase the level of arousal. Your lover never knows if you will continue stroking or stop and change the pattern. His or her excitement is increased by anticipation. It's also a lovemaking style that invites the other to make verbal and nonverbal requests.

THE INTERCOURSE POSITIONS

There are really only six basic positions for intercourse, but a lot of possible variations within them. No one position is inherently better than the other, and complicated certainly doesn't mean better. If you have looked through the *Kama Sutra*, you may have wondered, "Is this really possible?" Some of the more elaborate and distorted positions may be possible for gymnasts but they couldn't be maintained comfortably by anyone for long. More important, they probably wouldn't lead to a scintillating genital connection.

One need not be an athlete to have erotic command of several positions. The overweight, the aged, those with bad backs, trick knees, tennis elbows—all can find pleasure in intercourse. Put each suggested position to this simple feel-good test:

- Can you comfortably get into the position and hold it easily enough so that you won't be distracted by trembling muscles or minor pain? If not, how could you adapt it with the help of pillows or bolsters?

- Is this position conducive to female orgasm? The majority of women don't reach orgasm via intercourse alone. Does the position allow her or her partner room to stroke and caress her genitals?

- Is it visually stimulating to your partner without being embarrassing to you?

Most people are restricted in their choice of positions more by habit than necessity. They have intercourse in the same way they have always done and wonder why it has become routine and boring. The positions are:

1. Female Superior Position, or Women on Top

- *The basic step and some variations.* The man lies on his back as the woman straddles him and lowers herself onto his penis. Some men put a pillow under their buttocks to raise their hips for a more efficacious angle or easier entry. To change the angle of penetration and give her greater control of thrusting, she can lean back or forward, resting her hands on the bed behind or in front of her. In the final moments of intercourse prior to orgasm, she may flatten herself out on top of him, clench her thighs together, and roll her clitoris into him.

- *The pros and cons.* Many women find they are more apt to reach orgasm in this position than in others. The woman has greater control over the angle and degree of thrusting and can get more clitoral stimulation. She or her partner can easily provide manual stimulation of her breasts and clitoris. Many men say it is the most visually stimulating position because they can admire her breasts and see her face when she reaches orgasm. Sexually passive women find it difficult to assume this level of control.

- *The midlife secret.* Body-image anxiety stops some women from getting on top. If his reassurances aren't enough to allay her concerns, she can wear a bustier, camisole, a short silk robe or nightie, or any sexy piece of lingerie that makes her feel more appealing. A man and woman don't have to be completely nude to make love. Clothes can give a woman confidence, even in bed.

- *Comment.* "This is a great position for a woman who knows how to excite a man," says Shelley, "a fiftysomething" bride who says her sex life is better now than when she was younger. "Make eye contact with your man, especially when you come. My husband told me that his first wife always closed her eyes when she came. He felt cheated because she hid her vulnerability from him. Use your hands. A man gets very aroused watching a woman touch herself during intercourse. And, be a little dominant when you're on top. Lean over and tweak his nipples occasionally. Or take his wrists and push them over his head."

2. The Missionary Position or Man on Top

- *The basic step and some variations.* Legend has it that Pacific Island natives named this position after the missionaries who used it exclusively. Unfairly maligned, the man-on-top position may be the most common one for intercourse in the Western world. The woman lies on her back with her knees bent and legs opened outward. Some women place a pillow under their buttocks or the small of the back to make penetration easier or the angle of penetration less deep or more arousing. The man largely controls the speed of thrusting.

  For very shallow penetration, the woman can lie on her back with her hips at the edge of the bed so that her legs hang over the sides, feet touching the floor, with the man standing and leaning into her between parted legs. And for deeper penetration, she can, in the classic position, open her legs more widely and bend her knees, either keeping her feet on the bed or placing them on his shoulders.

- *The pros and cons.* One of two face-to-face positions, the missionary promotes intimacy, encouraging deep thrusting and full penetration. A couple can also kiss during intercourse. This is generally considered the best position for male orgasm. A man may choose to switch to it when he is ready to ejaculate if he doesn't get sufficient friction from thrusting in another position. If she is the partner more interested in lovemaking or he is suffering from fatigue or back problems, another position, requiring less masculine authority, would be a better choice.

- *The midlife secret.* By keeping her feet on the bed, knees bent, or placing her feet on his shoulders, she can create the effect of a tightened vagina. That may enable him to remain inside her with a less-than-firm erection. It may also cause him to become more erect.

- *Comments.* "The missionary is a good position for older couples," says Marilyn, fifty-four. "It's bad only if you use it exclusively. My husband and I like to finish in the missionary position after having intercourse in at least one other position. We put a pillow under my buttocks. I put my feet on his shoulders. The pillow and the right positioning of my legs enable us to get good penetration for him to reach a climax. With my feet on his shoulders, I have room to stroke my clitoris. Often now we can have an almost simultaneous orgasm this way. When he has a semi-erection, we use the position differently. I keep my feet on the bed, knees bent, and hold the base of his penis as he thrusts."

3. Rear Entry

- *The basic step and variations.* The woman is on knees and elbows, her hips elevated. The man kneels and enters her vagina from behind. She can kneel at the edge of the bed with the man standing behind her. To elevate her hips at a steeper angle, she can rest her chest on the bed. In America, the position is often referred to as "doggy style," which connotes negative images for some people.

- *The pros and cons.* Men tend to like rear entry better than women do, though both can move freely and vigorously. Women complain about lack of intimacy—no eye contact—and worry about how their buttocks look from the rear. Actually, they look better in this position than when a woman is standing nude with her back to her partner. The arched position smoothes out the sags and bags. It is an excellent position for manual clitoral stimulation by either partner. Some women claim the G spot is more easily stimulated during rear entry, too.

- *The midlife secret.* With her chest lowered to the bed, the position has an elongating effect on her vaginal barrel, creating a tighter fit. His erection will feel more powerful to both of them.

- *Comments.* "My wife didn't like the rear-entry position very much until recently," says Paul. "She is more assertive and enthusiastic in her sexual participation than she was. Now she says the rear-entry position makes her feel powerful. She pushes back against me, matches me thrust for thrust. We really go at it in this position, especially if I stand behind her and she lowers the front half of her body to the bed. I love looking at her ass. Intercourse is hard and hot, like it was when we were young, only better because it lasts longer."

4. Side by Side

- *The basic step and variations.* The couple lie side by side facing each other. One puts a leg over the other. In a variation, often called "spoons," the man faces the woman's back, her buttocks angled against him. Each are bent slightly at the knees and waist. He may put one of his legs between hers and enters her vagina from behind. In another adaptation, the "scissors," the man lies on his right side, with the woman lying next to him on her back, her right leg between his thighs and her left leg on top.

- *The pros and cons.* This is a warm and intimate position for a couple who are too tired for vigorous sex. It's also a good starting position for intercourse. They can caress and fondle each other's genitals easily. On the other hand, deep penetration isn't really possible.

- *The midlife secret.* She lies half on her side, half on her back, drawing up the leg on which she is lying. The man faces her. In this position, penetration is limited, but the couple can make very good use of a semi-erection. She can stroke her clitoris with the head of his penis and vary that with partial insertion.

- *Comments.* "We call the side-by-side position our 'maybe we will and maybe we won't' position," says Iris, 40 and married for fifteen years to a 61-year-old man. "It feels good to us to get into this position and stroke each other as we talk. We've found we're able to say things to each other in this position that we haven't said before. The unpressured physical intimacy encourages sharing of thoughts and feelings as well as bodies. Sometimes we get excited and move on to more active lovemaking, and sometimes we fall asleep this way."

5. Sitting

- *The basic step and variations.* The man may sit in a chair with his feet on the floor or on the bed, his ankles tucked under his legs toward his groin. The woman sits astride him. He holds onto her buttocks. She has her hands on his shoulders and her legs around his waist or she may squat over him, keeping her folded legs to the sides of his body. Or they may sit facing each other in the middle of the bed, legs wrapped around the other's bodies. She will probably need to sit on a pillow to elevate herself for easier entry and a better angle of penetration.

- *The pros and cons.* This can be a very intimate position because of the close eye contact the partners share. (In a later chapter, you'll learn the tantric version of the sitting position.) Her clitoris is easily accessible to him for stroking. But it may be difficult for partners with chronic knee problems to hold the position comfortably.

- *The midlife secret.* The sitting position is probably not a part of the average couple's repertoire, which makes it an excellent choice for introducing change into a lovemaking routine. The eye contact makes a deeper intimacy almost unavoidable. This may be the erotic jolt your relationship needs. Place stacks of pillows behind your backs.

- *Comments.* "My husband has a very large penis," Ginny says, "and we have always found the sitting position a good one. We can see his penis going in and out of me, and the position limits the depth of penetration. It still works for us. He gets more aroused when he can watch himself having intercourse. I find that more arousing now, too, than I did. I have become more of an erotic visualist, which surprised us both."

6. Standing

- *The basic step and variations.* He enters her from the rear while she is standing, slightly bent forward. To achieve insertion, the man will probably have to squat while the woman lowers herself on to him. She can wrap one leg around him, keeping the other on the floor. Or in another version, if he can hold her, she can put both legs around his waist, her back against the wall, as he cups her buttocks while energetically thrusting.

- *The pros and cons.* This is a great position for spontaneous love-making after a physically fit couple have fondled and caressed each other to the point of near orgasm. Who hasn't had, or imagined having, a quickie in an airplane restroom or the bathroom of someone else's house, her back pressed against the wall, his pants around his ankles? It's not, even for the young, a position meant to be held for long.

- *The midlife secret.* In the movies a strong young actor lifts up the actress, holds a hand under her buttocks, and supports her while he thrusts. In real life she can sit on a bar stool, kitchen counter, or other surface of the right height while he stands, her legs wrapped around his waist. The exciting elements are still there for dramatic, urgent lovemaking.

- *Comments.* "A couple times a year I have to make love standing up, if for no other reason than to prove I can still do it," says Denny. "My wife is accommodating. The position dictates a quickie. The last time we did it, she really got into it. I don't think some kinds of sex work for young women. I tease her about being a horny old broad at forty. A woman has to be forty before she thinks sexually like a man."

THE DYNAMICS OF THRUSTING

There's more to intercourse than position. Coital dynamics—the style, angle, and depth of penetration and the speed and force of thrusting—define the experience as much or more than the position does. The hard, deep, and regular thrusting pattern considered the ideal in Western society leads to ejaculation in minutes, if not seconds. A man can prolong intercourse by varying the thrusting pattern. There are also ways in which women can change the coital dynamics.

Taoist sex manuals devote a lot of space to techniques for prolonging intercourse and withholding ejaculation. At midlife a man can readily adapt some of them to his own lovemaking style. He may also find that changing the coital dynamics helps him to maintain an erection during intercourse.

The names of these thrusting patterns may sound a little off-putting. Try them anyway. They've been working for thousands of years. Each method can be used in any position. Concentrating on the count will distract a man from performance concerns if he has them.

- *The Eight-Slow, Two-Fast Thrusting Method.* The depth of penetration varies in the slow strokes from shallow to deep. The two fast strokes are deep. Exhale on the outward strokes. Inhale on the inward strokes.

- *The Nine-Shallow, One-Deep Thrusting Method.* The Taoists believe the number nine holds powerful "yang," or male, energy. In the nine shallow thrusts, the penis enters only two or three inches into the vagina, which is supposed to create a vaginal vacuum. The deep thrust forces the air out of the vagina, making the penis feel more tightly held. Some women may feel G-spot stimulation from the shallow thrusts.

- *The Japanese Set of Nines.* He performs nine shallow thrusts, withdraws, pauses, enters again. Then he performs eight shallow thrusts, followed by one deep thrust, withdraws and pauses. Now seven shallow and two deep. The set continues in this manner until he takes nine deep strokes, which is supposed to bring her to orgasm.

"I was skeptical," says Michael, who was "dragged" to an Eastern erotic-arts weekend workshop by his wife in search of a cure for the sexual blahs. "I thought I would feel silly counting strokes. It sounded like a game. Well, I was wrong.

"Changing the thrusting pattern was very arousing for her. She had an orgasm during intercourse for the first time in months. I also found increased pleasure. When I use these methods, I don't lose my erection. I feel more powerful too. We both think my erection is harder."

HER COITAL DYNAMIC POWER

He isn't the only one who influences coital dynamics. Varied genital movements during intercourse create different kinds and degrees of stimulation for both the woman and her partner. She can change the dynamics most easily in the female superior position where she controls the angle and degree of penetration and the speed of thrusting. But she can get different sensations in every position simply by shifting her body so that his penis enters her vagina at a slightly different angle. Women who achieve orgasm during intercourse may consciously or unconsciously do this.

The following techniques are taught in Tantric workshops:

- *The Oval Track.* Typically, a woman moves up and down in the female-superior position. She can vary that dynamic with the oval track. In the movement down onto his penis, she leans forward slightly and pushes her pubis a little to the back, stimulating her clitoral area with his shaft. On the upward movement, she leans slightly backward and pushes her pubis a little forward, stimulating her G spot by the head of the penis.

- *The Pause.* In any position, at the moment of his deepest penetration, she grasps his buttocks, holding him tightly and prolonging the moment of contact. This is even more effective if she has strong pubococcygeal (PC) muscles. (See page 78 for PC-strengthening exercises.)

- *The PC Flex.* She times the flexing of her PC muscles with her partner's thrusting. She keeps the muscles relaxed until his penis is inside her vagina. Then she contracts them. Vary the flexing in intensity and duration.

"I always wanted to be more active during intercourse," says Kathryn, Michael's wife, "but I didn't know how to do it until we took this workshop together. Simple changes in your movements, like the oval track, produce big results. By using the pause or the flex, I can help Michael maintain his erection.

"We have extended the concept of subtle change to other areas of lovemaking. We've been experimenting with different ways of kissing and caressing, for example. Like many couples who've been together for a few decades, we thought we knew everything about each other's bodies, but we didn't. I would recommend learning a new sex trick to any couple. The technique is not an end in itself. It's more like the key to a door opening into a bigger room of pleasure. The willingness of both partners to learn something new has an energizing effect on the relationship as a whole."

THE SIX SECRET HOT SPOTS—AND HOW TO IGNITE THEM

Most people know that a woman's clitoris (and the surrounding tissue) and the head of a man's penis are the most sexually sensitive places on their bodies. Her clitoris is a small pink organ, often compared to a tiny penis because of its shaftlike shape, located at the point where the inner labia join at the top of the vaginal opening. The head is the part of the penis set off from the shaft by a thick ridge or crown, the coronal edge, also sensitive to touch.

Many men and women have a number of other "hot spots" that, when stimulated, produce pleasurable sensations and often orgasm. Though referred to as "spots," the term isn't precisely accurate. They are more like areas than spots, not magic buttons, but places particularly susceptible to erotic touch. Some sexual positions hit more of them than others do.

As men's erections lose some of their firmness and women lose some of their vaginal tone—a situation that can be largely remedied by exercises described on page 78—the same old positions may not work in the same way because the spots aren't being hit. Intercourse isn't thrilling anymore? That could be why. The good news: Hot-spot combustion can almost always be rearranged.

His hot spots are:

- *The F Spot.* The frenulum is that loose section of skin on the underside of the penis, where the head meets the shaft. This area is highly sensitive to touch in most men. Some men can be brought to orgasm if the F spot receives intense stimulation during intercourse.

- *The R Area.* The R area is the raphe, the visible line along the center of the scrotum, an area of the male anatomy typically neglected during lovemaking. The skin on the raphe is similar to the skin of a woman's labia, very sensitive.

- *The P Zone.* The perineum, that area an inch or so in size between the anus and the base of the scrotum, neglected by Western lovers. Rich in nerve endings, the perineum can generate a tremendous erotic response in many men.

Her hot spots are:

- *The G Spot.* See page 60 for directions on locating and massaging the G spot. Consider the quest for the G spot a treasure hunt, not a sexual-performance test. Some women report no unusual sensitivity here.

- *The U Spot.* Unlike the G spot, the U spot, for urethra, has received minimal press since its discovery as a possible trigger for orgasm was reported in 1988 by Kevin McKenna, Ph. D., an associate professor of physiology and urology at Northwestern University Medical School. Because urine is expelled through the urethra, we typically don't think of this tiny area of tissue above the opening as a sexual pleasure point, but it is. The U spot is just above the clitoris.

- *The AFE Zone.* The anterior-fornix erotic zone is across from the G spot on the opposite vaginal wall. Think of a sofa facing a chair, with the sofa being the larger AFE zone and the G spot the chair. Not marked by the rough-texture characteristic of the G spot, the AFE zone is indistinguishable at first touch from the rest of the vaginal wall. You'll know you've found it when her vagina begins lubricating from stroking the spot alone. Stimulate it first by sliding a finger up and down the area. Then move from the AFE zone to the G spot and back again. Stroke the AFE area in clockwise, then counterclockwise motions.

Don't forget the private hot spots, the places unique to each of us. They include but are not limited to the backs of knees, ears, throat, inner thighs, and instep.

Midlife Hot-Spot Adjustments

- In the female-superior position, improve the hot-spots connection by changing the angle, either leaning slightly forward or slightly backward.

- In the rear-entry position, elevate your hips at a steeper angle. He should get more friction on his F Spot and R area.

- In the missionary position, keeping your feet on the bed with knees bent or wrapping your legs around his neck may intensify connection with his hot spots and yours. Placement and size of pillow or pillows under her back or buttocks can also influence the hot-spots' connecting patterns.

- Modify the side-by-side or "spoon" position to the "X" or "scissors." He lies on his back facing her, while she lies next to him on her back, her outer leg between his legs and inner leg on top of them.

- In any position, experiment with pillows and bolsters to change the angle and depth of penetration, the key to improving the hot-spot connection.

FOUR ADDITIONAL WAYS OF ENHANCING INTERCOURSE AT MIDLIFE

1. *Strengthen the PC muscles, his and hers.* Strong PC muscles help both men and women achieve stronger orgasms. Her vagina will feel tighter to him because she will be able to use those muscles to grip his penis during intercourse. He will have better ejaculatory control. In addition, they correct mild urinary incontinence in women.

Kegels, named for Dr. Arnold Kegel who developed them in the 1950s, are exercises for strengthening those muscles. Here's how to do them:

- Locate the pubococcygeus muscle, part of the pelvic floor in both genders, by stopping and starting the flow or urine. Practice this stopping and starting several times to become familiar with the PC.

- Start with a short Kegel squeeze. Contract the muscle 15 or 20 times at approximately one squeeze per second. Exhale gently as you tighten only the muscles around your genitals (which include the anus), not the muscles in your buttocks. Don't bear down when you release. Simply let go. Do two sessions twice a day. Gradually build up to two sets of 75 per day.

- Add a long Kegel squeeze. Hold the muscle contraction for a count of three. Relax between contractions. Work up to holding for ten seconds, relaxing for ten seconds. Again start with two sets of 20 each and build up to 75. You will be doing 300 repetitions a day of the combined short and long and be ready to add the "push out." After releasing the contraction, push down and out gently as if you were having a bowel movement with your PC muscles. Repeat *gently*. No bearing down.

- Now create Kegel sequences that combine long and short repetitions with push outs. After two months of daily repetitions of 300, you should have a well-developed PC muscle. You can keep it that way by doing 150 repetitions several times a week.

2. *Alternate intercourse with others forms of lovemaking.* Too many men think that they have to continue thrusting to climax once intercourse has begun, a belief that creates undue performance pressure at midlife. Alternate intercourse with oral and manual stimulation. The lovemaking experience will last longer. She will likely be more orgasmic. And a waxing and waning erection won't seem like a problem.

3. *Change positions.* Changing positions changes the coital dynamics and alleviates muscle strain. The sensations are different. Lovemaking lasts longer without putting stress on muscles and joints.

4. *Use your hands.* By midlife, women are less self-conscious about asking for additional clitoral stimulation from their partners or touching themselves as needed. He shouldn't be afraid to ask her for more manual support either. If she grasps the base of his penis during intercourse, she may be able to help him maintain an erection. Also some men find perineum massage during intercourse very stimulating.

Sizzler # **5**

TAKE ME, I'M YOURS

Damp tendrils of hair clung to her face and neck. The red flush of orgasm covered her chest. As her breathing subsided, she reached across the space between them and put her hand on his penis. He took it away from his semi-erect organ and muttered, "I'm too tired to come tonight, Baby."

A sophisticated lover, Tracey knew that "sex" was more than intercourse. When she and her husband, Ned, were young, they had rarely made love without having intercourse. Now in their early fifties, they often did. Too often, Tracey thought.

Mutual masturbation and oral sex were Ned's preferred ways of making love. Often, after a prolonged session of what she considered "foreplay," he brought her to orgasm with his hand or mouth, and then rolled over on his back as he had tonight. The "rollover" was his signal that he didn't want to, or couldn't, enter her.

"I miss feeling you inside me," she murmured.

"Tracey," he said; and she caught the warning note in his voice.

He didn't want to talk about whatever was wrong. Holding his hand, she pretended to fall asleep. Soon his light snoring told her he really had fallen asleep. She slipped out of bed and grabbed her robe that had fallen to the floor. Pulling it around her, she walked softly down the long hallway into the living room. She curled up on the sofa where she eventually fell asleep. He woke her the next morning.

"Have trouble sleeping again?" he asked, tenderly stroking her cheek.

She wanted to tell him why, but she kissed his hand instead. Dismissing her sleep problem as caused by job anxiety, she hurried to take a shower while he made the coffee. Another day of avoidance had begun.

A few days later, Ned, lying beside her, asked, "Are you feeling amorous tonight?"

"Maybe," she said.

He held his penis in one hand and put the other against her crotch.

"Here," she said, taking his penis into her own hand, "let me do that."

Expertly, she stroked his member until it was standing at half-staff. His ministrations to her labia had sufficiently lubricated her for entry, especially a "soft" entry. Tonight, she was determined, they wouldn't masturbate each other to orgasm side by side. She wanted him inside her, and she was going to take control and put him there.

She turned on her side. Still holding his penis, she kissed him deeply. Then teasing his lips and tongue with hers, she gently straddled him without letting go of his member.

"Uhm," he murmured.

She sensed a note of concern beneath the pleasure, but she persisted. Holding her hand firmly around the base and lower part of his penis, she used the head to tease her clitoris. His excitement grew with hers. When she was very hot and moist, she carefully inserted his penis holding on with her hand. As long as she held him, he wouldn't fall out. She could feel him simultaneously relax in his body and stiffen in his penis.

Flexing her PC muscles, she gripped the head of his penis. He grinned at her. She was showing off her muscular expertise, and he liked it. Then she pulled a little more of his penis inside her. As he grew harder, she moved her hand down, until only her first finger and thumb formed a ring around the base.

Maintaining an even pressure with her finger ring, she rode him. He was fully aroused and gloriously erect inside her. Gazing into her eyes, he threw himself into the act of intercourse more enthusiastically than he had in months. In a few strokes with his erection, she came. And she came again when he did, minutes later.

She collapsed in his arms. He held her, stroking her face and hair, whispering endearments until she fell asleep. In the morning, she woke happily in her own bed.

6

DON'T HAVE SEX, MAKE LOVE

"When Don wants to make love, he asks me, 'Do you want to have sex?'" Julie says. "I have told him I would prefer he called it 'lovemaking,' not 'having sex,' but he says he doesn't see the difference. I do. If he did, maybe we'd make love instead of have sex. I'm tired of having sex. I'm turned off to having sex. He blames it on my age, 48, and wants me to take hormones or something so I can 'keep up' with him.

"We have had an active sex life for the twenty years we've been married, which is saying more than most couples probably can. I want more now; and I'm not getting it. So he's getting less. He just doesn't understand what I'm talking about; and he seems to have no interest in figuring it out yet."

Don and Julia have reached an erotic stalemate. He wants more sexual activity than he thinks she wants. In truth, she probably does want as much activity as he does, but she wants a different kind, lovemaking, at least sometimes. Pressuring her for "more sex" isn't the way for him to get his needs met. He needs to learn how to make love to his wife.

There is nothing wrong with "having sex," sharing a purely physical erotic event with your partner. Quickies, for example, are "having sex." Indulging in the occasional quickie can make a man and woman feel very young again. "Having sex" can also last a lot longer than a quickie. Sometimes a couple want nothing more emotional than sex play, simple release, or vigorous erotic exercise. But "sex" alone won't carry them into a glorious golden age together, even if their techniques and style could be used in teaching videos. People get bored, frustrated, and turned off to lovemaking when they are "having sex" all the time and not making love. There is a full range of erotic expression, including intensely emotional lovemaking, in a lasting, exciting relationship.

FIRST, CLEAR THE EMOTIONAL AIR

Remember the *Seinfeld* episode about George and Susan's "make-up" sex? George was desperate to replenish her contraceptive supply after a fight because they were going to have "make-up" sex, the "best" sex, and he wasn't going to miss the opportunity for lack of contraceptive sponges. Early in relationships couples tend to have more make-up sex than they do later after they've developed entrenched patterns of mutual resentment.

"We never fought," says Veronica, "but we were always to some degree miffed at each other. The resentment was there, like an underground stream. We rarely made love. Rick said he just wasn't interested in sex. One day, after I had made some caustic remarks about his lack of sexual interest, he dropped the bombshell.

"He told me he found other women sexually attractive, but he wasn't attracted to me anymore. I was hurt and angry. The anger came out first. I let fly with everything I'd been holding back for years, and he did the same. We screamed at each other for what seemed like hours, but couldn't have been in reality. Part of the time I was crying.

"Then a funny thing happened. We were standing toe to toe glaring at each other, both of us breathing hard. By mutual unspoken consent, we fell into each other's arms and began kissing hungrily. We had the most passionate sex we'd had in years."

While telling your partner you find others, not her or him, sexually attractive isn't the best way to start a "fight," the sex benefits of a good emotional fight were definitely there for Veronica and Rick.

How Fighting Can Turn You On

An emotional argument involves both mind and body. When you're engaged in a spirited verbal battle with someone you love, your heart beats faster, your skin tingles, the blood seems to race through your body. That's not unlike the experience of sexual arousal, is it?

People who are afraid of their emotions try to shut them down at the first heated flush. They withdraw, which creates a sexual shutdown too. Emotional withdrawal becomes a protective habit, one that's hard to break after years of behaving this way. Every emotion seems frightening, a threat to the hard-won personal sense of peace. A couple in emotional withdrawal may rarely or never "fight," but they probably rarely or never make love either. Resist the urge to pull back from confrontation.

Remember that a "fight" is verbal and emotional, not physical. And follow:

Six Rules for the Good Emotional Fight

1. *Stay on focus.* No fair her dredging up the mistakes he made twenty years ago or him saying again how much he hates her interfering mother. A fight is not an opportunity to rehash old grievances.

2. *Define issues.* Be clear and specific about the problems. Don't get off track.

3. *Listen.* Really, listen. Don't just pause until it's your turn to speak again, with your mind formulating the next sentences while your partner talks.

4. *Don't interrupt.* You can be angry without being rude or bullying.

5. *Don't personalize.* Stay with the issue—he doesn't pick up his clothes, she doesn't take her fast-food trash out of the car—without calling the other names like "lazy slob."

6. *Recognize "his" and "her" conflict styles.* Men and women have different conflict styles as well as intimacy styles. Respect the differences. Also understand that aging softens some of those differences. A woman may not cry so easily, may be more direct and confrontational now than she was, while a man may be more protective of vulnerable feelings she didn't know he had.

Three Ways to Make Up with Great Sex

1. Make a concession or an apology followed by a prolonged kiss.

2. Continue the verbal sparring, on a less contentious level, as you begin to undress.

3. Acknowledge that you are aroused and get your partner to admit she/he is too.

AWAKEN EACH OTHER'S SENSES

Ben and Christine had reached a sensual dead end together by their twenty-fifth anniversary, but they didn't realize they had. Like other world-weary and jaded people, they were so accustomed to having the classic song "Is That All There Is?" whispering in their brains, they scarcely noticed the tune anymore. Discriminating consumers, skilled lovers, and intelligent, witty companions—they were everything the other could want in a partner. Weren't they?

"We didn't know we had a problem so we didn't look for help," she says. "Looking back, we know we were on autopilot for years." What kicked them into a higher gear? "We borrowed a friend's cabin in Vermont for a ski trip and got snowed in. The propane tank was running low. Ben and I spent three days conserving fuel and relying on roaring fires to keep the main room warm. We made love on chilly sheets in the bedroom one night and found the experience enormously arousing because it was such a different physical sensation.

"The next morning we made love on the floor in front of the fire, another new sensation. We went outside and played in the snow, something we hadn't done since the kids were small. There we were stuffing snow inside each other's pants and running back in the cabin to pull off our clothes and turn our naked backsides to the fire. When the snowplows finally came through and we were driving home, we agreed that we'd discovered magic.

"We'd always thought that traveling, dining out, or buying each other expensive gifts was the way to put excitement back in our marriage, and we'd been quietly disappointed when those things didn't work the way we'd hoped they would. Now we look for ways of being more sensual together, from making love on the beach at night in the Caribbean to licking honey off each other at home."

Lovemaking is much more than the sum of the technical parts. It's a sensual as well as sexual experience, involving the whole body, not only the genitals. Sensual people make better lovers for their partners and for themselves. If you and your lover have lost touch with your sensuality, reawaken the five senses one at a time. Through this reawakening the emotional connection between the two of you will deepen—and "the sex" will be better too.

The five senses and their midlife status are:

1. *Taste.* The sense of taste serves a dual function in lovemaking, helping the lover define what part of the body is being touched as well as tasting it. You feel a partner's genitals with your tongue when you're licking them, and, if you are a sensual person, you feel the difference in the skin texture from one part of the labia to another, from the head of the penis to the underside of the shaft. Some couples become turned off to kissing, particularly French kissing, in midlife because their partners have become less conscientious about brushing teeth and freshening breath before lovemaking. Sometimes the medications taken for minor health problems change taste or the ability to taste. Overindulgence in food, alcohol, or chronic smoking may also have changed the way one partner tastes or the other's ability to taste.

Be alert to your partner's responses to the way you taste.

2. *Smell.* The sense of smell is obviously an integral part of sexuality. Semen and vaginal secretions have a scent. The scent of semen in particular can be affected by chronic heavy alcohol consumption, smoking, poor eating habits. Many men and women also use personal fragrance as a seductive tool. Hormonal changes in women can produce chemical changes in the body that impact the interaction of skin and perfume. The scent worn for a lifetime may no longer carry the same fragrance to a lover's nostrils. In some men and women, the ability to detect scent isn't as sharp as it once was, leading one or the other to wear too much perfume, light one too many scented candles.

3. *Sight.* When lovers are young and/or new to each other, the sense of sight may be working overtime, compensating for the other neglected senses. The curve of her buttocks, the line of his shoulders,

a profile, a glimpse of thigh, genital, or pubic hair can arouse a lover so thoroughly that the delights of the senses seem like the cherry on the erotic dessert. Visually delighting your partner is still possible now, but requires a little thought. At just the point in life where many women eschew the sexy lingerie, they should be continually adding to their supply. Erotic wardrobe, lighting, unexpected touches such as a flower behind the ear, and other simple changes create visual excitement.

4. *Touch*. The feel of a lover's skin may seem too familiar to be arousing, but that's only because the couple have allowed their sense to become dulled with familiarity. A woman's skin may actually be more sensitive to touch during perimenopause and after. And a man, as noted earlier, becomes more capable of sensual, rather than purely sexual, expression with age.

5. *Sound*. The sound of a lover's voice may also seem too familiar to be arousing. Again, that need not be true. Some midlife couples have fallen into rigid communication patterns. They say the same things to each other in the same tones of voice. Their voices no longer show great animation or register seductive depths.

Five Exercises for Reawakening the Senses at Midlife

1. *The sensory surprise*. Incorporate some unexpected sensory delights into your lovemaking. If she loves roses, spray the room lightly with rosewater and put fresh roses beside the bed in bud vases. Sprinkle some loose petals on the bed and use one later to massage her nipples or clitoris. Try to add a detail that will ignite each one of the five senses. That's not as hard as it seems. Soft music, candlelight, and flowers are such effective romance aides because they appeal directly to the senses.

2. *Practice the technique of "touch focusing."* Close out everything else and concentrate solely on what you are touching. First, try sitting with bare backs, back to back, eyes closed. How does your lover's skin feel against yours? How does the feeling change when one moves? Then feel the skin under your hands as you stroke his or her body during lovemaking. Note how the texture of the skin

changes from one area to another, how varying the pressure makes touch a different experience.

3. *Add the technique of "touch expansion."* Introduce some unusual materials into lovemaking. Fur, silk, feathers, velvet, leather, ice, flower petals—all can be used to erotic effect on genitals and other sensitive places.

4. *Play with sound.* Yes, bring music into the bedroom, but don't forget that your voice is also an instrument of sound. Move it up and down, out of the octaves so familiar to your mate. Be creative in your pillow talk. Have phone sex occasionally. Sing to each other. Even if you can't carry a tune, you can elicit a giggle.

5. *Expand your awareness.* Every day for at least ten minutes pay attention to your surroundings in a new way. On a familiar street, for example, note architectural details you've missed, examine new growth on shrubs and trees. Take this heightened awareness home.

CREATE EROTIC TRUST

"I love Sharon, but she's not an easy woman," says Joe. "She's hard driving and has high standards for herself, both personally and professionally, standards she expects me to meet, too. Our sex life has been pretty good until recently. I had some erection problems, which led to a confidence problem. She was understanding to a point.

"Our grown son teases her that her life motto should be: Deal with it. That's certainly her attitude regarding my crisis of sexual confidence. She says, 'You had a few failures. So what? Let's make love.' I've been avoiding lovemaking for the past several weeks, and she's furious with me.

"I will give Sharon credit for not being intimidated or taking my lack of erection personally. She doesn't blame herself as some women would, just me, for being a 'nervous Nellie.'"

Ask Joe if he "trusts" Sharon, and he'll probably say he does. With the car, the credit cards, his life maybe—but does he trust her with his sexual vulnerability? Not likely. If he did, he would be willing to risk another erectile "failure" because he'd have confidence that she wouldn't make him feel worse. Some risks can be taken only with people who are accepting.

Doesn't erotic trust naturally exist between longtime partners? Not necessarily. Frustration, discouragement, misunderstanding, and rejection, perceived or real, create distrust. Sometimes nonsexual issues erode trust. For example, a couple who have developed a pattern of saying hurtful things to each other in anger have also learned to protect their vulnerable spots, such as sexuality, from one another. They never remove all the armor. In that kind of atmosphere, neither will admit to hidden desires, secret fears. Another couple might have lost trust for a reason similar to Joe's, a partner's impatient response to a sex problem. Unable to help their partners feel truly accepted, some couples may have never built erotic trust and by midlife the lack of passion in their lovemaking reflects that.

Acceptance doesn't mean going along with everything the other wants. You don't have to make love whenever your partner does or agree to participate in sexual activities you find unappealing. Say "no" without stating or implying your lover is unattractive or not desirable—or worse, "perverted" or "sex-obsessed." (And accept "no" without being angry, resentful, judgmental.) How partners confront their sexual differences helps determine the strength of the erotic trust bond and nourishes the emotional commitment they share.

The Four Steps to Building Erotic Trust

1. *Make a trust zone.* In addition to being a sensually inviting room, the bedroom a couple share should be a safe emotional place, a sanctuary from the storms outside. Many midlife couples have spoiled the sanctuary by using the bedroom to settle their differences away from the hearing of children. Agree not to balance the checkbook, argue about the bills, criticize each other, air grievances, fight about the children, or ambush one another with bad news in the bedroom anymore. Couples can put their defenses down and share confidences, as well as lovemaking, in the trust zone.

Less than a month after establishing their trust zone, Van and Melissa, who hadn't made love in several months, began reaching out to each other in bed again. "When our daughter moved back in with us after college and his mother came to stay with us to recuperate from heart surgery, we began treating our bedroom like the command post," Melissa says. "We lay side by side every night agonizing over what we were going to do. Everything we didn't want either of them to hear was discussed in our bed. It was deadly."

2. *Have the sex talk.* How long has it been since you talked to each other about sex? Some couples have never had a frank discussion about sexuality, while others haven't shared information about their erotic likes and dislikes in many years. Each assumes the other "knows." As their sexuality evolves, a couple need to communicate comfortably and clearly about their needs, desires, fears, fantasies, and secret sexual wish lists. It's also helpful if they tell each other what they really like about their lovemaking in specific terms, like "I love the way you suck my nipples."

"We can't talk about sex in bed," says Grace. "It's too threatening. We need to be fully dressed. We take walks together at least once a week; and for us, that is the right time to talk about sex. Last week my husband told me he wanted me to take his whole penis in my mouth sometime when I performed fellatio. I'm willing to try this. I might have felt intimidated if he'd sprung it on me while we were making love because I need to think a little about things before I do them."

3. *Establish a trust position.* Experiment with ways of holding each other to find the position where both feel closely and warmly connected, yet not pressured to perform or respond sexually. In the trust position, a man and woman become each other's calm harbor from anxiety, depression, sadness, or the frustration that follows a sexual disappointment. Some couples lie side by side, facing each other with their bodies touching from foreheads to toes. Other possibilities: "spoon" fashion, where one partner lies with chest against the other's back; the man lying on his back with the woman's head on his shoulder; one partner lying down, perhaps on a sofa or leaning against the pillows in bed, with the other's head in his or her lap. While the trust position will make verbal sharing easier, talking isn't always necessary.

"When my husband and I were having some sexual difficulties last year," says Gail, "we got into the habit of holding each other in our favorite afterplay position, with his chest against my back, and his arms around me, even when we had no 'after.' We didn't talk about the sex and why it wasn't working. Sometimes we didn't talk at all; and other times we talked about our feelings and our memories. We got a lot closer to each other than we had been in a long time."

4. *Schedule an emotional conference.* Make a 15-minute date for an emotional conference at the same time each week. The agenda is feelings. Each partner spends five minutes talking about how the other's actions have affected him/her emotionally. The actions may have occurred at any time during the relationship, all the way back to the first date. The speaker should begin by briefly describing the incident. After one speaks, the other summarizes what was said and tries to empathize. The few simple rules are:

- Use "I" statements. You are talking about your feelings, not casting blame on the other person.

- Absolutely no interruptions.

- The listener summarizes the major points, without editing, analyzing, interpreting, or judging.

- Each should have a separate agenda. The second speaker doesn't get to rebut what the first person said. Otherwise the conference degenerates into one asking, "How could you see it that way?" and the other countering, "Why don't you see it the way I do?"

What is the point of the emotional conference? It's hoped that both partners will consider how their actions affect each other and learn to listen attentively. This exercise is also a weekly reminder that no two people, even the long and happily married, view incidents and actions in exactly the same way.

Andy, 53, and Ruth, 50, patients of mine in couple counseling, had been in a relationship for five years when they began having weekly emotional conferences. In the early weeks, they continually interrupted each other, challenged each other's "inaccuracies," and began "innocent" discussions afterward that erupted into arguments. After five months, Andy was able to tell Ruth that he was avoiding intercourse, which she strongly favored over other forms of lovemaking, because he was afraid of not getting or maintaining a hard erection. That led him to admit he feared erectile failure would diminish him in her eyes because he'd secretly struggled with inferiority feelings all his life. In summarizing his statements, Ruth neither offered comfort nor defended her enjoyment of intercourse. She would say, for example, "I hear you say that you are avoiding intercourse because you fear failure." No editorializing.

"That conference didn't have an immediate dramatic effect on our sex life," Andy says, "but it did bring us closer. She'd never seen me as someone who felt inferior or insecure."

MASTER THE ART OF SURRENDER

Surrender is the opposite of control. In the context of erotic a "surrender" is often the word used when the heroine allows herself to be swept away by the hero's passion. That's a very narrow view of erotic surrender. It limits the woman and leaves out the man entirely. Think of erotic surrender as the act of letting go while aroused, not ceding control to one's partner.

Most people enjoy the feeling of being in control of their lives, even though much of what happens to them is clearly beyond their control. Successful people are admired not only for the money they earn and their accomplishments but also for the amount of control they exert over their environment and the others inside it. People who practice self-discipline are also admired. In lovemaking, the man who can "control" his erection and ejaculation and the woman who can "control" her partner's arousal and her own responses are idealized. Where does surrender fit into this picture?

Surrender is an integral part of true intimacy. Letting go into full arousal is intrinsic to the higher level of sexual pleasure possible for couples after age 50. It is an art, but one you can learn through practicing the following exercises, which I prescribe for my own patients:

1. *Turn yourself over to your partner.* Offer to be your partner's sexual slave for a night. She/he can create a sexual script within reason. You may discover a new dimension to your sexuality this way.

2. *Write a short essay on "Why I don't let go sexually."* State all your reasons. Then describe how your life might change if you surrendered to your sexuality. Elaborate. Don't merely say, for example, "I would be embarrassed." How would the embarrassment feel? How would you and your partner handle it?

   Put your essay aside for a few days. Read it again and write a rebuttal.

3. *Play a role opposite to the one you typically play in bed for one week.* If you are the passive partner, become the active one. Initiate lovemaking. Be bold and assertive in getting your needs met. If you are the active partner, be passive in all aspects of lovemaking. Don't be afraid of the new feelings these changes will generate. Give in to them.

TURN UP THE EMOTIONAL HEAT

"Jerry and I read some books on Tantric sex to liven things up," says Lisa. She and Jerry, both divorced and in their early fifties, have been in a monogamous relationship for ten years, though they don't live together. "The best ideas were the simple ones, especially keeping your eyes open during lovemaking. I'd gotten in the habit of using favorite fantasies during lovemaking, and I thought I couldn't come without them. So I closed my eyes, and had my own fantasies; I was having sex almost alone. Once I began keeping my eyes open, I didn't need the fantasies as often. I began really paying attention to Jerry, feeling and experiencing him in a new way, as well as experiencing my own arousal on a deeper level.

"The eye lock, looking deeply into one another's eyes and holding the gaze, is the most intensely intimate experience either one of us has ever had. The first time I looked into his eyes at the point of orgasm, I was blown away by the emotions I felt. The orgasm was so much more complex. He has had the same experience. Opening your eyes is the best way to connect more strongly with your partner."

Studies have shown that 90 percent of women close their eyes while kissing. Only a third of men do. During orgasm, men are still more likely to keep their eyes open than women, but the majority of both genders either close their eyes or look away from their partner at the moment of climax. Men often bury their faces in a woman's neck or a pillow. There are several reasons for this behavior. Some people may fear that open eyes will disconnect them from their own sensations. They may feel emotionally distant from their partners. Body-image issues may force them into hiding behind their own eyelids. Or they may feel awkward about exposing themselves this way. We are never so vulnerable as when we allow our sexual arousal to be seen.

Rather than diminishing erotic pleasure, keeping your eyes open during lovemaking turns up the emotional heat. Some Tantric sex positions utilize this concept to help lovers transcend routine lovemaking and achieve a deeper, more spiritual union—as does the Kaballah, a book of Jewish mysticism—but don't skip this section if you balk at the word "spiritual." Meaningful eye contact during sex intensifies the physical sensations by deepening the emotional connection between lovers. That is not an esoteric concept. It's a hot sex tip.

Try the following ways of making sex more eye-opening:

1. *Open your eyes occasionally while kissing.* The visual stimulation will probably increase your arousal, as well as provide your partner useful feedback on how well his or her kissing techniques are working. Some studies have shown that men bond more intensely with women when they make eye contact during kissing.

2. *Practice the eye lock.* Look deeply into each other's eyes as you are caressing each other. Hold the look. Do this more than once. You probably won't realize how little you do look into each other's eyes during lovemaking until you practice the eye lock.

3. *Make frequent eye contact during oral sex.* Glance up from your partner's genitals while performing oral sex. Make eye contact. The impact may be electrifying.

4. *Look into each other's eyes during intercourse.* The face-to-face intercourse positions encourage eye contact. Utilize the opportunities inherent in those positions. Don't look away when you feel arousal increase, exactly the point when connecting will intensify the feelings.

5. *Open your eyes during orgasm.* Eyes open orgasms may feel more explosive and emotional than other orgasms; the afterglow may be more tender and prolonged. Looking into your lover's eyes at the point of orgasm is like giving an erotic gift. Even if the concentration isn't always intense, the practice is likely to generate greater feelings of closeness between a couple.

Sizzler #

6

THE LOVE ENCOUNTER

Ben and Christy were a greatly admired couple. Successful business partners, loving parents of two fine college-age sons who'd given them little trouble as teens, physically attractive and fit individuals, they were liked, loved, and trusted by family, friends, and colleagues. After Christy discovered Ben's brief affair with a younger woman, he begged her forgiveness and ended the liaison. No harsh words were exchanged between husband and wife in public or private, and their handling of the event seemed only to enhance their standing as an *über*-couple.

"We have always had great sex and still do," Christy confided to a friend over lunch one day. Then she had a thought she didn't articulate: They had sex, but did they make love? She brushed the question aside, but later that night it came back to her as her erotically talented husband was running his tongue exquisitely in circles around her left nipple. Again, she closed out the intruding question and willed her body to respond.

"That was great," Ben said later, after they had satisfied each other.

"Great," Christy echoed.

Within minutes, he was asleep. She lay listening to the soft sounds of his snoring and realized she was angry at him. Not merely angry, she was furious inside. When he woke in the morning, Christy was gone. She'd packed an overnight bag, checked into a hotel, and left him a note asking for a divorce.

Ben was stunned. He and soon their family and friends were all sure she must be having an affair of her own, obviously a more serious affair than the one he'd had. What else could explain her inexplicable behavior? (They surely would have blamed it on menopause, if she hadn't already negotiated that passage.) For weeks, she refused to see him outside their business. Finally she consented to have dinner with him to discuss issues surrounding the divorce he didn't want. He prevailed upon her to come to the house for that meal so they would have the kind of privacy a restaurant doesn't afford.

"I'm angry at you, Ben," she said in an even voice.

"You don't sound angry," he replied, in an equally rational tone.

"I am furious." She selected a dinner roll from the basket, examined it briefly, then suddenly pitched it across the table at him. The roll bounced off his forehead.

"What!" he yelled. "What was that for?"

"For your little bimbo!" Christy shouted. She threw another roll, and then another, until the basket was empty. He let them strike his face without putting up his hands to deflect them. "How could you do it?" she asked, her voice breaking. "How could you have a fling with someone young enough to be your daughter? Didn't you imagine how I would feel when I pictured your hands all over her firm unblemished flesh?"

She began crying. He got up and walked around the table, arms open to comfort her. She pushed him away with sufficient force to cause him to lose his balance. He fell backward on his ass.

"Bastard!" she shrieked.

"You fucking bitch!" he yelled back. "You fucking perfect bitch! I have sex with someone else, and all you care about is how your skin tone compares to hers."

He got up. She stood to leave, but he grabbed her arms and held her in place. For several minutes, they screamed into each other's faces. Then he took her blouse in both hands and ripped it open. Her heaving breasts seemed to be overflowing her bra. He tore off the bra and hungrily took one breast in his mouth. She gasped and tried to pull away, but he held her firmly. He forced one thigh between her legs and rubbed rapidly back and forth. She yanked angrily at his hair, but he wouldn't take his mouth off her breast. He felt her yield.

Finally he lifted his mouth to hers. They kissed passionately and sunk to the floor together. Crying and kissing, they caressed and fondled each other. With shaking fingers, she unbuckled his pants, pulled them down, and took his penis in her mouth. He hadn't felt so hard, so powerful and strong in years.

After they made love on the floor, they moved to the bedroom where they talked and cried for hours, then made love slowly and tenderly again.

7

THE POWER OF MIDLIFE SEXUAL FANTASIES

"I've always had a fairly active sexual fantasy life," says Wanda, 50, who's been in a relationship for five years with a slightly younger man she met at the baby-viewing window in a hospital maternity unit. Both their daughters had given birth to sons. "I revisit old favorite fantasies sometimes, particularly when masturbating. Two that never fail me are having sex on the beach with Frankie Avalon—he's left Annette Funicello for me—and some version of my assertive sex-goddess fantasy. I am wearing the highest heels and very hot clothes, maybe leather or a skintight short red strapless dress, and I am dominating my partner, who has to service me.

"My lover and I talk about our fantasies sometimes. He gets very aroused when I tell mine, which are usually erotic stories I've made up for him, not fantasies I've actually used during masturbation or intercourse. If I get him excited by the stories, I may use them as fantasies later, incorporating his responses into the scenario. My fantasy life is as rich now as it's ever been, maybe richer, because we do talk about them. I'd never been with a man who liked to hear my fantasies before.

He's encouraged me to be more creative with him, which is paying off for me alone too.

"One big change in my imaginary sex life since I was a young woman: I no longer have those fluffy romantic fantasies where most of the story is about pursuit and the sex at the end is NG, No Genitals, in view. Now I picture the genitals, mine and his, and I watch them connect in full juicy color. I see a big penis, always a big penis, and every detail, including the little drops of pre-ejaculate like dew on the head."

WHY FANTASIES HAVE SUCH EROTIC POWER

Fantasies have often been compared to private movies running in the theater of our mind. Researchers believe that sexual fantasy is a nearly universal experience among women as well as men, with some of these erotic daydreams being nothing more than fleeting thoughts, like the clips of coming attractions, while others are full-blown features. A man may glimpse a flash of thigh in a restaurant when a woman crosses her legs and may briefly imagine touching her. A woman may light candles in her bedroom, put on soft music, and leisurely masturbate while fantasizing to multiple orgasms. Each is having a sexual fantasy.

The tangled roots of fantasy probably lie in childhood. Dr. John Money, one of the world's leading researchers in human sexuality and the pioneer in studying the origins of sexual fantasies, says they *originate* before puberty, between the ages of five and eight, and then *emerge* in adolescence. The child who played at his mother's feet may become the teenager fantasizing about a cheerleader's legs and eventually the adult who proudly refers to himself as a "leg" man. Beautiful female legs will likely play a featured role in his fantasies throughout his life. Some fantasies, like those involving less mainstream practices, such as spanking, foot or other fetishes, and bondage, may have less obvious origins, but Money believes that their roots can be traced to childhood events. A little boy who gets an erection when spanked or a little girl who becomes aroused during a spanking, for example, may as adults have spanking fantasies that they don't necessarily want to act out. The awesome power of erotic fantasies comes from these deep, twisted roots embedded in the adult psyche.

People use fantasy to aide arousal during masturbation and love-making. Some fantasies are soft and romantic, others are violent or sadomasochistic. Studies conducted in the past decade have shown that men's and women's fantasies are becoming more alike, with women reporting more graphic and sexually aggressive fantasies than they had in the past. Most people have "favorite" fantasies, those scenarios that can arouse them over and over again. Fantasies, whether violent or repetitive, are a concern only if they inhibit healthy sexual expression or the development of intimacy with a partner. Most fantasies don't.

Should you then worry about your fantasies? Most likely not. Recurrent violent fantasies can be indicative of deep-rooted emotional problems. The need to use the same fantasy every time during mas-turbation or lovemaking may indicate relationships issues or other problems. But for most people, no matter their age, fantasies serve many useful purposes. They enhance masturbation, create a mood conducive to lovemaking, sometimes facilitate orgasm by helping block out intrusive worries or concerns, and allow people to explore "taboo" activities such as sadomasochism, group sex, or affairs. Indulging in fantasy is a way of widening sexual experience without taking any risks. Even fantasizing during intercourse is not indicative of a relationship problem.

At midlife, fantasies can become more beneficial. They are aides for people who don't have partners and want to maintain their sexual vitality through masturbation. (Yes, it can be true that, if you don't "use it," you do "lose it"—"it" being the ability to achieve arousal and orgasm.) When arousal is a frequent problem, a man or woman can begin fantasizing well in advance of the sexual encounter. And fan-tasies can make your sex life seem more interesting too.

How does aging affect sexual fantasies?

- *You may feel less guilty about having fantasies at midlife.* Many peo-ple report having less guilt about sexual thoughts and fantasies than they once did. They may be more aware now that fantasies are a "normal" occurrence shared by most of the rest of the human race. And they may also feel less threatened by their fan-tasies and less confused about what they mean. A young man, for example, might fear that the occasional homosexual or group-sex fantasy indicates he is secretly gay, while an older man under-stands his fantasies aren't suppressed desires.

- *You may be more willing to share your fantasies with your partner.* As guilt diminishes, the desire to share grows. With an accepting partner in a strong intimate relationship, secrets can be told. Many people are over 40 before they feel comfortable enough with themselves and their partners to share their sexual fantasies.

- *You may be more skillful at using fantasies.* With age comes sexual self-knowledge. You probably know what fantasy to use and when to use it to speed up, or even slow down, sexual responses. Freely indulging in fantasy, as noted in a previous chapter, is also a good way to prepare in advance for a sexual encounter. At midlife, you probably know how to turn yourself on this way and don't feel guilty about doing so.

- *You may be viewing the same general categories of "movies," but the plots may be more varied.* Studies show that people in all age groups have fantasies that can be fitted into the same general categories. In one Danish study of women ranging in age from 22 to 70, the age of the woman did not significantly impact upon the type of fantasy she had. The older women *slightly* favored fantasies including more foreplay and caressing while the younger women *slightly* favored fantasies of new experiences and partners. Similar U.S. studies show that, while fantasies vary considerably from person to person, age was not the determining factor in what types of fantasies men and women had. The fantasies within categories, however, were somewhat more varied in older people. In romantic fantasies, for example, the men and women over forty put more detail into their romantic scenarios and chose more different settings, perhaps reflecting travels they've taken.

"I have more control over my fantasies than I did when I was in my twenties so I enjoy them more," says Chan, 48. "I don't know about other men, but in my youth, I often felt a hostage to my own sexual thoughts. It was hard to turn them off sometimes. They got in the way. Really, they were too much of a good thing. Now I can call them up and consciously use them for my own purposes. If I am having trouble ejaculating, I can pull up a fantasy that does the trick for me—a woman masturbating or swallowing me or me ejaculating between her breasts."

THE TOP TEN MIDLIFE SEX FANTASIES

1. *Making love with someone other than one's regular partner.* This is the top fantasy for people of all ages. After 40, we still fantasize about supermodels and superheroes. In our fantasy scenarios, we very likely have not aged.

2. *The forbidden partner—someone from another race or class, a relative, a friend's spouse, a much younger lover.* At midlife, the forbidden partner may likely be much younger. This fantasy lover may even be someone entirely unsuitable or inappropriate, like your best friend's son or daughter. Remember, it's a fantasy, not a wish.

3. *Group sex.* The fantasy of having sex with multiple partners is common to people of all ages. Some people may fantasize a group of people their own age, while others see themselves as either younger or the age they really are but with a group of much younger people.

4. *The romantic fantasy.* Young women more commonly fantasize sex in idyllic surroundings than young men do. As they age, men become more romantic, less focused solely on genital sex. By midlife men too are fantasizing making love to their partner on a moonlit beach.

5. *The spontaneous encounter.* The fantasy of sexual serendipity appeals to men and women of all ages. Midlife boomers identify it as "the zipless" fuck popularized by novelist Erica Jong in *Fear of Flying.* In that fantasy, we meet a stranger and two bodies come together in such perfect sexual union that the clothes fall away easily from our bodies, the body parts meld beautifully together, the simultaneous orgasms are shattering. No stuck zippers. No messy details.

6. *Forced sex, sometimes called "the rape fantasy."* Both men and women, young and old, have this fantasy, which does not indicate a true desire to be raped. They enjoy the fantasy of having another person "control" their responses, "forcing" them to enjoy sex, maybe a type of sexual activity they wouldn't really participate in. Older people, especially women, are more comfortable with the fantasy, because they know it does not represent a rape wish. In one survey, many young women reported

negative feelings, including guilt, about the rape fantasy, while few women over forty did.

7. *"Taboo" sex acts, such as having sex in a public place or as some form of sadomasochistic activity.* Men and women over 40 may have more of these fantasies than they did when they were younger for two reasons: They are less likely to suppress sexual thoughts or ideas that frighten or induce guilt. And they feel more free to explore, at least in fantasy, those areas of their sexuality previously held off limits. Some men and women get a little kinkier with age.

8. *Exhibitionistic or voyeuristic fantasies, in which one is having sex while being watched or watching someone else have sex.* In a common version of this fantasy, a man watches his wife make love to another man. Like the "taboo" fantasies, and for the same reasons, they are somewhat more common after the age of forty.

9. *Homosexual encounter.* Common to both genders and all ages, the homosexual encounter is more often fantasized by the young, confusing and alarming some. By midlife, a man or woman is probably secure enough about his or her own sexual identity not to be concerned about that fantasy, which may be one reason it occurs less often.

10. *Sex with a celebrity.* One study reported that people in their twenties were most likely to fantasize sex with a celebrity. While midlife men and women do have the occasional celebrity fantasy, they may be dreaming about having sex with the President or the First Lady rather than with rock stars. In fact, the same study found that 22 percent of women over 35 had fantasized having sex with either the President or another high-ranking government figure, such as the governor or senator of their state.

SHOULD YOU SHARE YOUR FANTASIES?

There is no definitive answer to that question. Sometimes sharing fantasies ignites a couple's passions; and sometimes it douses the fire. Your fantasy may be very exciting to you, but not to your lover who considers it boring, repugnant, screamingly funny, or personally insulting. Sharing some fantasies robs them of their power to arouse. Once the fantasy is put out for discussion and analysis, it can be like a magic trick after the special effects have been exposed. The thrill is gone. Still, many couples take the risk of sharing and are rewarded in pleasure.

"My wife and I were sharing secrets one night, and I told her for 20 years I'd fantasized about what it would be like to have sex with her sister and her best friend," says Robert. "When I saw the stricken look on her face, I quickly added that I'd fantasized maybe a couple dozen times over twenty years, not daily obsessing. Not good enough. I was in trouble for months. She thought I wanted her sister and her best friend because they were 'thin' more than I wanted her because she was 'fat,' which she isn't. We didn't have sex for three weeks after my bad case of mouth diarrhea."

On the other hand, Jerry told his wife he'd "occasionally" had a "stray" fantasy about having sex with her and her best friend together; and she was aroused by the idea.

"We both agreed," Jerry says, "we'd never do it in real life, but we had a hell of a hot time in bed talking about doing it. I got my wife to say words out loud I thought I'd never hear, like, 'Now I'm taking Naomi's nipple into my mouth.' Wow!"

Five Tips for Sharing Sexual Fantasies

Before you share fantasies with your partner, keep the following five tips in mind:

1. *Think about how comfortable your partner will be discussing this type of sexual activity.* Some people might find violent, aggressive fantasies disturbing. Some might respond unfavorably to hearing that their partner fantasizes about group sex. There's nothing wrong with pushing each other's comfort envelopes, but doing that takes care.

2. *Preface your sharing with some general discussion of fantasies, what they mean and don't mean.* You might want to read this chapter out loud to your partner. At least summarize the main points.

3. *Be reassuring about your partner's desirability.* Some fantasies may make your partner jealous. A man or woman who has aging issues, such as body-image concerns or performance anxieties, may feel threatened by hearing that you fantasize making love to someone else, particularly a friend or relative in good physical shape.

4. *Let your partner know there's no pressure to act upon the shared fantasies.* You both may decide it would be fun to try fantasy acting, but sharing shouldn't turn into coercing.

5. *Remember that sharing is a reciprocal activity.* The other person has the right to say, "I don't find this erotic at all." Be receptive to your partner's fantasies, too. You aren't the only one with a secret mental life.

SHOULD YOU ACT OUT YOUR FANTASIES?

"My wife and I had both fantasized a threesome," Jay says, "but it was two men in her script and two women in mine. We met this couple in the Bahamas who were celebrating their silver wedding anniversary, as we were, and one drink led to another. We shared the fantasy with them; and, of course, no surprise, they'd had the same fantasy. 'Why not a foursome?' someone said.

"We ended up in this huge bed in their suite, all of us naked, sobering up quickly, embarrassed as well as bare-assed. We made this half-hearted attempt at groping each other's partner, the women pulled off a tepid Lesbian embrace and kiss, and we guys, dicks at half staff, fucked our own wives side by side in the missionary position. I think everybody faked an orgasm. We avoided that couple for the rest of our visit.

"'The next time we act out a fantasy,' my wife deadpanned as we were packing to leave, 'we'll go with the monkey story.' We found that terribly funny and still laugh about it. The fantasy sex was a dud, but trying it didn't hurt our relationship."

As in the question of "to share or not to share," there is no correct answer here. Acting out a fantasy can add excitement to a relationship—or be a passion fizzle. It can bring a couple closer together or start a fight, which, ironically, could bring them closer together anyway. In fantasy, everything is perfect and possible. In real life, zippers get stuck, feelings get hurt, and the steps of the Lincoln Memorial are hard and cold on bare skin in winter. Whether or not a couple can safely and erotically act out a fantasy depends on four factors only they can evaluate:

1. *Feasibility.* Ask yourself: What price a threesome with the neighbor? Can genital contact be made and sustained while hang-gliding? Would the ASPCA file charges? A fantasy feasibility study should take each partner's physical, moral, and emotional safety into consideration.

2. *Adaptability.* Acting out fantasies is like adapting a book into a film. You can't be too literal minded. In your fantasy, you are being ravished by a cruel stranger while your helpless and bound partner watches. In the bedroom version, your partner can wear a mask and behave masterfully. But some fantasies, like some books, simply don't lend themselves to adaptation.

3. *The sizzle factor.* If your partner finds the fantasy disgusting, excessively amusing, or not erotic, the acting will lack passion. Both members of the troupe need to be excited by the concept. In a two-person play, there are no walk-ons.

4. *The props department.* Would an arousing adaptation require more props than you can pull together from existing materials or buy, borrow, or rent? Some plays are too expensive to produce.

CHOOSING A SCRIPT

If you and your lover both want to try acting out a fantasy:

- Keeping the four factors in mind, write six scenarios each. Be as wildly imaginative as you like within the boundaries of feasibility and adaptability. Limit the actors to two.

- Together, pick from the lists the one fantasy you both find the most exciting. Don't pressure your partner to try something he or she doesn't find appealing.

- Adapt the scenario for reality.

EROTIC ROLE PLAYING

"Acting out fantasies has allowed my wife and me to shed some inhibitions by pretending to be different people," says Ray. "We started out with the cliché scenarios. She was the maid; and I was the lord of the manor. I was Spartacus; and she was a rich, bored, and cruel Roman wife. Then we got more creative. Last week I was Henry VIII and she was Anne Boleyn. It was the night before Anne's beheading; and in our script, Henry and Anne had sex one last time. She treated his penis with great reverence, going down on it as if she were receiving a sacrament.

"Maybe we are frustrated actors. We both did amateur theatre in college. This may sound crazy to some people, but we have had some of the hottest sex of our lives acting out fantasies. We are both interested in history and historical characters; and we like to imagine what some of these people were really like in bed."

Assuming the roles of historical figures won't be every couple's ideal scenario, but erotic role playing is an integral part of fantasy play. The most common roles are:

- *The Aggressor.* One partner becomes the sex goddess or slave master, the lord or lady of the manor, the boss. Though the scenario has been decided between the two, the aggressor appears to be in control of the action. Women are as likely as men to play the aggressor. In fact, many men fantasize being dominated by a strong, aggressive woman.

- *The Passive One.* This partner gets to be "taken" or "used" sexually by the other. Acting out the passive and aggressive roles allows a man and woman to sample the joys of occasionally being dominant or submissive. Doctor or nurse and patient, teacher and pupil are variations of the game.

- *The Stranger.* Some couples get dressed in their best clothes, go out separately, and one picks the other up at a prearranged place, preferably a classy bar. She may be sitting on the barstool with her skirt just above her knee, legs crossed, waiting to be approached when he gets there.

Erotic role playing gives a couple the opportunity to explore their own undiscovered territory. Many couples have used their fantasies and role playing games to trigger self-confrontation leading to growth. This can be an opportunity for forging a stronger connection to your partner, in bed and out. And some people keep their fantasies private, utilizing them for personal exploration that enables them to be better lovers and partners in the end.

Gerald says, "I would be a less satisfying partner to my wife if I didn't have a fantasy life apart from her. There are things about me she could never understand and probably not accept. I don't believe that we must have total knowledge of each to be happy. I've seen our son and his wife go into the bathroom together. My wife and I think some things aren't meant to be shared."

He and his wife, Deanna, were both 18 and virgins when they got married. In earlier years, his fantasies often revolved around other women, those he knew or had seen in real life and movie stars. Elizabeth Taylor was a favorite fantasy partner. As he aged, his fantasies grew more complicated and sometimes darker.

"I wasn't satisfied with fantasizing Elizabeth Taylor in the missionary position with me anymore," he says. "I wanted her to be wearing high-heeled boots, carrying a whip, and making me grovel at her feet. I traveled a lot in my job. A kinky novel I bought in a hotel gift shop inspired some wild fantasies. And, now with the variety of sexual material available on cable TV, I have a lot of fantasies Deanna would find shocking."

On an out-of-town trip a few years ago Gerald made one of his sadomasochistic fantasies come true. He answered a dominatrix's ad and paid her to verbally abuse and lightly spank him. The experience fell far short of his expectations. Rather than feeling arousal and exhilaration, even guilt, he felt "just plain foolish."

"In reality, I didn't want to be insulted and spanked," he says. "I just wanted to indulge in the occasional kinky fantasy while masturbating. What good would it do me to share that with Deanna?"

But his private life has enriched his sex life with his partner. He has asked her to initiate sex more often, to assume the female superior position frequently, and to be vocal about her desires. In behaving in a more sexually dominant way, she didn't turn into the woman of his fantasies—something he doesn't want anyway—but his wife has become a more exciting lover for him.

"We have better sex together because of my private life," he says. "Neither one of us is the type to examine our deepest thoughts for the hidden meaning. She wouldn't thank me for laying my fantasies down on the table for her to interpret. I don't want to know about it if she fantasizes having sex with animals or something."

Like Gerald, some men and women find themselves entertaining sexual fantasies that would never have occurred to them when they were younger. Men especially may get "kinkier" as they get older, but women are not immune to the erotic allure of forbidden thoughts.

Elaine, who didn't know what the term S/M meant until she was past forty, says, "My husband and I admitted to each other that our fantasies had grown wilder in recent years. We attribute that to cable TV. I find myself, for example, mesmerized by women's breasts or titillated by a spanking scene. Remember, I grew up in a time when girls didn't see each other's breasts unless they had sisters around the same age; and I didn't.

"The visual images enchange our fantasies and give us something to talk about, though neither of us wants to act out what we call our 'dirty-mind movies.' I have discovered that, if I'm not in the mood for sex, I can put an X-rated tape in the bedroom VCR during foreplay and get warmed up. After a few minutes, I don't need to see the screen. I'm running my own film."

These couples use fantasy to enhance their sex lives—without "sharing" or "acting out." If you don't want to have the full-blown fantasy discussion, use your sexy scenarios in your own way to generate excitement. Keeping a fantasy private is not the same thing as withholding information a partner may be entitled to have.

But what if you want to encourage a reluctant partner to participate in your fantasy life in some way?

SEVEN STEPS FOR CONNECTING FANTASY TO REALITY

One of the common themes running through the sex questions people ask is: How can I get him/her to do what I want? The young may stumble over the issues surrounding this central question more than the rest of us, but everyone does occasionally find their sex life reduced to the question. If the desire is perceived to be outside the bounds of "normal," the question takes on greater power. It becomes harder to ask.

1. *Be clear about what you want.* Do you want to "share" fantasies—in other words play, "I'll tell you mine, if you tell me yours?" Do you want your partner merely to listen or to give feedback? Or, do you want to act out—or at least talk out during lovemaking—your fantasies?

2. *Differentiate between the elements of fantasy that could be made real and those that should probably not be.* If your fantasies run toward heavy S/M, for example, it's unlikely that you really want to act them out. You may want to talk through them during lovemaking or adapt them in softer ways to real sexplay. Make the difference clear to your partner or you may risk scaring or offending him or her.

3. *First, introduce your desire as a subject rather than a request.* Maybe you haven't ever discussed bondage, spanking, making love in the pool, or whatever with your partner. Bring up the subject. Gauge the reaction. Move carefully from there.

4. *Anticipate the difficulties.* Your partner may feel jealous, threatened, repulsed, or amused by your innermost erotic thoughts. Be prepared for that. Don't overreact. In other areas of life, we can stand to hear, "What a silly idea!" or "I'm not interested in that at all!" When sexuality is on the line, many people get defensive.

5. *Remember that telling doesn't necessarily lead to action.* Your partner will probably need to mull over your erotic thoughts before making a decision about participating actively in them. It may seem as if you've waited a long time for this great fantasy moment, but you have to remember: It's news to your partner. And news takes time to digest.

6. *Be receptive to change.* After studying your fantasies, your partner may want to edit them. Be open to the possibilities suggested. Compromise is part of lovemaking as well as of life.

7. *Remember what fantasies are—and aren't.* Look upon them as an arousal tool in your erotic kit. Maybe they don't, and never will, work for your partner. They have to work only for you. Don't read too much meaning either into having fantasies—or having them rejected.

OVERCOMING A NEGATIVE FANTASY EXPERIENCE

Remember Robert, whose wife refused to have sex with him for three weeks after he shared his fantasy about having sex with her sister and her best friend? Here's my prescription for avoiding that outcome:

1. *Prevention.* Sometimes a shared fantasy simply fails to excite the other or causes unintentional hurt. In some cases, however, lovers share fantasies with malice aforethought. They flaunt their fantasies to wound their lovers or at the least to get a reaction. Bad idea. You might receive momentary satisfaction, but you'll pay a long-term erotic price for that fleeting moment of venomous glory.

2. *Develop a thicker skin.* Granted, it doesn't feel good to hear that your beloved craves the neighbor. You can retreat behind wounded pride or take a more mature view of human sexuality. Your partner's fantasies will not always include you, even if you're Christie Brinkley. Develop a stronger sense of your erotic self, one that is not entirely dependent on your partner's desire.

3. *Don't withdraw.* What about your partner's fantasies is so disturbing? Talk about it. Insist he or she listen without being defensive.

4. *Appreciate your lover's honesty.* She/he deserves credit for taking an emotional risk. Sharing something as intimate as our sexual fantasies takes some courage. Whether you can appreciate or accept those fantasies, you can admire the honesty.

5. *Get perspective.* Remember that fantasies are only thoughts, not actions, not wishes. Focus on how your lover acts toward you sexually and how your actions affect his or her responses. If you've acted out a fantasy and found the experience disappointing, put it behind you. Some thoughts are better enjoyed in the head than in the bed.

Sizzler # 7

MY SECRET SIN

Wanda closed her eyes and slipped into the cool waters of a blue lagoon. Floating on her back, she felt the gentle waves lapping at her breasts and penetrating her labia like liquid fingers. The gardenias pinned behind each ear gave off a delicious scent, filling her nostrils. She was alone and intensely happy. Her lover, a Hawaiian body builder, would soon be joining her in paradise. Meanwhile . . . her hand drifted to her genitals.

With her orgasm, the lagoon, gardenias, and expected lover fell away. Wanda was alone on her bed in a comfortable suburban home. Her children were away at college, her husband off on a business trip. And like the fantasy Wanda was alone, but intensely happy.

My fantasies are my own business, she thought. She didn't add: As long as I use them only when I'm masturbating. But she might have. Wanda felt guilty about having fantasies during love-making with her husband. She feared becoming "dependent" on them. Did the fantasies mean she didn't love him? That she wasn't happy in her marriage? Because she was afraid they meant exactly that, she banished them from her mind. Surely they were the "dirty thoughts" she'd been warned about many years ago in a Catholic girls' high school.

Wanda separated her private sex, masturbation, from the sex she shared with her husband, Anthony. Then one day he turned her sex life upside down. Anthony told Wanda that he had fantasies too.

"I did something naughty while I was out of town," he said. She raised her eyebrows and smiled at him encouragingly, expecting him to confess he'd put an expensive purchase on one of their credit cards or had consumed a series of high-fat, high-cholesterol meals. "I rented one of those X-rated movies on the hotel TV."

"Will it show up on your bill?" she asked. "Will your boss find out?"

"It will show up only as a pay-per-view charge," he said, laughing at her. "My boss won't question an in-room movie charge, honey. It's not as if I threw a party in my room."

"Oh," she said. Suddenly the significance of what he had done struck her. "An X-rated movie. Aren't those things disgusting?"

And didn't his renting one mean he was dissatisfied with her in bed?

"You would have liked it," he said. "It was told from a woman's point of view. She was masturbating to a fantasy of sex with a man of a different race, and suddenly he appeared, like a genie out of a bottle."

Wanda blushed scarlet. He knew. Her husband must have guessed.

"Wanda?" he asked. Anthony hadn't know before, but he knew now. "You have a secret life?" Tears sprang to her eyes. Laughing, he grabbed her to him in a big embrace. "My darling wife, we all have fantasies. There's nothing wrong with that."

He begged her to share her fantasies with him, but she wasn't ready for that. Maybe she never would be. He agreed not to push her for details. Their conversation did have a big impact on their sex life, perhaps unbeknownst to him. A week later, while they were making love, she let her mind run free.

As Anthony's tongue circled her clitoris, she put her arms over her head and grasped the bars of her antique brass bed. She imagined her wrists were chained to them. A captive sex slave, she was being deliciously tormented by her master. Ownership wasn't enough for him. He wanted more than her grudging compliance. He wanted her pleasure.

"If I can make you come, I will know I truly own you," he'd whispered in her ear as he chained her to the huge bed in his luxurious suite.

"Never," she'd said, writhing, as he twisted her nipples cruelly between his fingers.

"Never," she repeated more weakly as he lovingly lashed her genitals with his tongue. "Oh, no," she gasped. Groaning and writhing, she tried at first to pull away from his mouth, but she couldn't. He held her thighs firmly apart. In the morning, she would have bruises where his fingers had been.

When she could hold out no longer, he abruptly took his mouth away.

"Oh, please," she begged. "Please."

"Call me master," he insisted; and she did.

The fantasy dissolved in a series of rippling orgasms. When at last they were finished, she looked into Anthony's eyes. For several minutes, he'd truly been her master, and he seemed to know it.

GETTING IN SYNC WITH YOUR PARTNER AGAIN

"Sometimes I feel overwhelmed by Kevin's need for physical affection and attention," says Belinda. Both in their midfifties, Kevin and Belinda have been married for 30 years. They have two teenage children, two busy careers, a large suburban house, the requisite dog and cat, cars, gym memberships, friends, and extended families. "In bed at night he wants to hold me and be held. He craves cuddling and intimate chats. Often I'd rather read a book on my own side of the bed, with him reading a book on his side, or have him downstairs puttering in the den like he used to do.

"The sex is still good. I'm not complaining about the sex. I just wish he didn't need so much attention from me when we aren't having sex. Last week after we'd made love one night, I wanted to get up, go pour myself a glass of wine, sit alone in the living room and sift through a pile of magazines I hadn't had time to read. He wanted afterplay.

"Ten years ago, the situation was reversed. I wanted more affection, more cuddling, more time talking about feelings. He had limited tolerance for all that. I had to learn how to cope with the differences between us. Now he comes to me brimming with emotion and expects me to be delighted with his soulful outpouring. I'm not, but I try not to show it. Will we ever be in sync?"

When a couple are "out of sync," one partner wants a more intimate relationship while the other wants more time for self. When men and women are young, she is typically the partner who wants more "intimacy." Kissing, caressing, embracing, and cuddling may be more satisfying to her than intercourse. At midlife, as she develops a need for self-fulfillment that makes intimacy less important to her, she also has increased sexual self-confidence and finds greater satisfaction in intercourse. Orgasm, more easily achieved, may take on a new significance in her erotic life. And now, inspired by his changing physiology, *he* wants more tenderness in their lovemaking, more shared confidences in their afterplay. Intimacy has become more meaningful and important to him. Early in the relationship, she may have complained he doesn't have enough "we" and too much "I." Now she is reveling in her "I" time, while he is craving more "we."

This sexual role-swapping is common, if perplexing to the couple who find themselves suddenly in opposite emotional positions. A recent study found 61 percent of women under 35 named "love" their primary reason for having sex. Only 38 percent of woment 36 to 57 said that. For men, the results were reversed. Only 31 percent of the younger men cited "love" as the primary reason for making love, but more than half the older men did. Another study found that women over forty placed a higher priority on erotic pleasures such as swimming in the nude and watching X-rated videos than other women *or* men in all age groups.

There are, of course, other contributing reasons for a couple being out of sync. They may be in different developmental phases, with one, for example, thriving in the workplace while the other is floundering. One may have a better relationship with teen or adult children than the other does. Or one may be in the emotional throes of dealing with ill or disabled parents while the other's parents are in good health. In some couples, one has significant aging issues while the other seems to move easily into a new life stage. What's common to all these situations? One partner needs more comfort and safety from the marriage, while the other, in a personal cycle of growth and stability, needs less.

ACCEPT BEING OUT OF SYNC

In every long-term relationship, the partners will almost surely experience some out-of-sync time. Balancing one partner's greater need for intimacy against the other's desire for self-fulfillment is an ongoing process. Here are some hints for doing that:

- *Don't expect the relationship to meet all your needs.* Sometimes everyone has to provide his or her own comfort and solace in the face of disappointment, sadness, frustration. People find that comfort in many different ways including long walks with the family dog and hobbies such as golf. Some people turn to religion. Friends and relatives can also provide support. An intimate partner is more than a source of succor and not the only person whose companionship can make your burdens seem lighter.

- *Acknowledge your own (or your partner's) inner strength.* Most people are not as fragile as they think they are during emotionally needy times. Recall how you have handled difficult situations or crises in the past. You are strong and resilient. (Or, your partner is strong and resilient; stop worrying so much about his or her temporary need for attention.)

- *Realize that being out of sync with your partner is "normal," not a problem.* Couples who expect to be soulmates on the same wavelength for life have unrealistic expectations. Long-term intimate partners may connect intensely or feel like two very familiar ships passing in the night. Both synchrony and time spent out of sync are necessary for healthy interaction.

- *Use the out-of-sync time for personal growth.* This is a positive, useful time for both partners, not a traumatic event. Out-of-sync periods encourage couples to expand their individual coping skills and increase their ability to comfort themselves and develop personal hobbies and interests. Sometimes friendships and other family relationships are strengthened.

HOW BEING OUT OF SYNC AFFECTS SEX

"Molly and I went through a period a few years back where we weren't connecting sexually or otherwise," says Dan. "I was stagnating in my middle-management job, and she was very happy with her work as a school librarian. In addition, she'd gone back to college part time to work on her masters degree. Every day to her was filled with excitement; and every day to me was another day at the same old grind. I hated my job and simultaneously was terrified of losing it one day to corporate downsizing. And I resented her, because my income made it possible for her to do what she wanted to do. Thanks to me, she had it all.

"I wish I could say I manfully resolved my issues through solitary soul searching, but I didn't. I punished her by withdrawing sexually just at the point where she wanted sex more often. She was the initiator, and I was the one with the headache. One evening she stood in front of the television set wearing high heels and a black-satin nightgown, and I craned my neck around her to see the set. We had a big blow-up that night after I'd rejected her. It cleared the air, and we began to talk. She hadn't realized how stifled and trapped I felt in my job. It was my fault she hadn't because I'd never told her. We agreed that we had to work toward equity in the marriage, something that wasn't in our initial agreement when we got married. At 22, I thought I'd always want to be 'the man,' carrying the family's weight. Now I'm back in school, too, taking courses to prepare me for a switch to self-employment. We alternate semesters because we can't afford the cost of both of us going at once, and we can't leave our young teenagers on their own that much either.

"Our relationship has definitely improved. Sexually, it's never been better. We are making love more often now than we were ten years ago when the kids were preschoolers. Last summer when they were at camp, we made love in the pool. It was fantastic."

Being out of sync may affect a couple's sex life in one of the following ways:

• *A decline in lovemaking.* Like Dan, many men and women who perceive themselves as being the partner shortchanged in life or in the relationship react by withdrawing sexually. That may be a subconscious desire to punish the more positive partner who wants to make love more often or more fully. It may also be the direct result of mild depression. Little is more sexually debilitating than depression.

How to Handle: Meeting him at the door dressed only in rolls of saran wrap isn't likely to solve the problem. If the unhappy partner doesn't or can't initiate a dialogue, the other one has to do so. Start talking, but not about sex. Don't say, "Why don't you want to make love anymore?" Ask about what's going on in the rest of his or her life.

• *An affair.* One or both partners may have an affair. The one who wants more sex in the relationship feels cheated and justified in looking elsewhere. The other partner feels misunderstood, used, unloved by his or her mate, and also justified in looking elsewhere. When couples are out of sync with each other, they can often make a good argument for an affair in their own minds.

How to Handle: If you're thinking about having an affair, weigh the risks carefully. When people get involved in highly charged emotional affairs, they almost always experience pain and conflict. Even a casual affair can be damaging to a relationship.

What if your partner is having an affair? First, try not to say anything you really don't mean, like threatening to walk out. That only puts you in a weaker position. Sometimes a brief separation helps. On the other hand, it may only culminate in an illusory resolution with the straying mate's apology being accepted by the aggrieved partner with neither examining the underlying causes for the affair.

If both partners want to heal the relationship, the affair will most certainly have to be ended. Counseling is useful in helping couples deal with feelings of guilt, anger, and resentment, and helping them establish communication and eventually trust again.

• *Arguments about how often and how to make love.* Typically the partner who is feeling less emotionally needy wants to make love more often or in more creative and inventive ways than the other does. The average out-of-sync couple tries to resolve the differences through argument. It doesn't work. The partner who wants less sex may be depressed or despondent and is probably experiencing a decline in libido that is not likely to be elevated by a good logical argument for more sex.

How to Handle: Stop arguing. Be more attentive to your partner when you do make love. Don't pressure by being overly seductive. Be more subtle when you do attempt to seduce or initiate, more gentle and generous when you decline. If you're the less interested partner, don't automatically say "no." Instead, say, "maybe"; and maybe you'll change your mind. If you're the more interested partner, remind yourself that your partner isn't rejecting you. His or her current lack of interest in sex is an attitude subject to change.

• *Hotter sex.* A woman's midlife sexual awakening can be the spark that ignites a smoldering sexual fire in a longtime relationship. If a man is not caught up in his midlife issues, he may be responsive to her taking the sexual lead now. He wants more intimacy; and to most men, that does include more sex. Her increased interest in lovemaking may flatter and arouse him. And her increased responsiveness may free him from concerns about pleasing her in bed or "giving" her sufficient orgasms.

How to Make it Happen: Each partner can take some cues from the other's previous sexual behavior in a role-swapping situation. She once appealed primarily to his genitals when she wanted to make love. By wearing erotic clothing, setting a seductive mood, touching him in certain ways, she let him know what she wanted. Now he can approach her in the same way.

Twenty years ago, he seduced her with romance. Now he could use a little romance, too. Many couples think "romance," like "foreplay," is what men do for women to get them into bed. Even women who are savvy enough to understand their man's increased need for erotic touch fail to appreciate his corresponding desire to be treated in a romantic way. At midlife, he will at least fully appreciate the romantic notes, flower- and scent-filled bedroom, candlelight dinners, and other little touches he noted only in passing as he headed straight for the genital connection when he was younger.

"Woo him," advises Jeannette, 52, who has been married for 32 years to Daniel. "Men reach a point in their lives when they are tired of being in charge of the love and romance department. Send him flowers. Compliment his appearance. Touch him with pride when you're out in public. Curl up next to him on the sofa, massage his neck, and ask how his day went. Listen to him attentively. After 20 or

30 years, women stop listening. Reach him through his heart and soul, and his penis will follow.

"When our lovemaking began to decline a few years ago, I pestered Daniel about it. Then I remembered a similar period in our marriage when the kids were toddlers, ages one and three; and I was too tired and stressed for sex. He brought me back to erotic life by wooing me. So I pitched some woo, and it worked beautifully."

THE RELATIONSHIP-SYNCHRONY QUIZ

Each partner should take the quiz separately and compare answers when finished. This isn't meant to be a "test," merely a tool for helping couples recognize where their synchrony lies—or doesn't.

1. Do you look forward to rejoining your partner at the end of the day?

2. What aspect of your life gives you more pleasure or stimulation: relationship, work, children, hobbies, or other?

3. Describe the five aspects of your relationship that are most pleasing. Now, the five least pleasing.

4. Is your sex life satisfactory? If not, what would make it better?

5. Have there been recent occasions when you wanted to show affection to your partner but didn't? Why not? Give the full details, including your feelings.

6. Recall three instances in the past month when either you have annoyed your mate or vice versa. Give the full details, including your feelings.

7. What was the reason for your latest quarrel? How was it resolved?

8. Name five enjoyable activities you've done together and five you've done alone in the past month. Which did you enjoy more? Explain.

9. Would you prefer more time alone? Or more time with your mate?

10. Was there a period in your marriage when you were more accommodating to your mate's request or desires than you are now? And vice versa?

HOW TO USE YOUR RESPONSES

- *Look for patterns.* Do the two sets of responses indicate the relationship is a greater source of satisfaction for one than the other? Is there a repetition of resentment, feelings of loneliness, anger, hurt?

- *Empathize with your partner's responses.* Empathy doesn't require agreement with the other's viewpoints. The most refined form of feeling-oriented communication, empathy is an effort to understand the other's beliefs, practices, and feelings without necessarily sharing or agreeing with them.

- *Don't play blame and counterblame.* Assigning blame to a partner for being out of sync with you is counterproductive. Some couples make blame a major part of their relationship. Resist that trap. Just accept that each is in a different place.

- *See where compromises and exchanges can be made.* Could one partner get more time alone by giving the other a greater role in choosing shared activities? Is it possible for each to be more accommodating of the other without relinquishing autonomy?

- *Negotiate compromises.* Make an appointment with each other for a compromise-exchange discussion. Each partner should state specifically what he or she would like and should avoid vague generalities. For example, "I would like greater closeness" is too broad, but "I would like to eat dinner with you four nights a week" is specific. Don't try to negotiate feelings. And be patient. Compromise takes time.

COMMON MIDLIFE SITUATIONS THAT GET IN THE WAY OF SEX

The following typical midlife situations can have an impact on sexuality. In each situation, there is often an out-of-sync element adding to the couple's problems.

Raising Teenage Children

Research has shown that the most stressful time for a marriage is when the children are teenagers. For parents confronting their own midlife issues *and* raising teenagers, as many people are today, the level of difficulty climbs in geometric proportions. To be the midlife parents of a 15 year old is to live on the horns of two sets of major life-stage dilemmas, all complicated in many cases by the lack of synchrony between the partners. A sudden and precipitous decline in lovemaking often occurs in these marriages. If the relationship was close, warm, and intimate, it will survive a sexual drought or two. The partners will find their way back to each other.

The obstacles to sex in this situation are created by adult attitudes and fears as much as by the stresses of raising teenagers. A midlife father may contrast himself to his teenage son, bursting with sexuality, the constant reminder of his own (perceived) dwindling ability. Some men have affairs, probably with a younger lover, out of the need to prove they aren't "over the hill" sexually.

The midlife mother of a teenaged daughter has her own issues. Coping with wrinkles, gray hair, and sagging breasts, she is reminded of her own "fading" looks every time her daughter walks past her. Compounding the problem, her husband, this girl's father, may be so uncomfortable with his daughter's emergence into womanhood that he is suppressing all sexual feelings. He avoids his daughter and his wife, leaving them feeling rejected and confused. Overwhelmed by the youth in front of them, parents in these situations may let themselves go physically and withdraw sexually.

Sometimes power issues between father and son put the mother in a difficult position. He is so busy trying to prove he's still in charge that he antagonizes everyone, including his wife. Either one parent or both may regress and behave like teenagers themselves. They are rebelling against their own perception of how they are expected to be. In all these scenarios, one parent may likely be experiencing more difficulty with raising teenagers than the other, creating an out-of-sync element.

Caring for Aging Parents

The term "middle age" may have been adopted because it accurately describes where people are at this point in their lives: caught between the needs of their maturing children and their aging parents.

Both are demanding, leaving the midlife adults in the middle struggling to meet everyone's needs simultaneously. Aging parents are also a reminder of their own coming decline.

The death of a parent makes almost everyone more conscious of mortality, and some more aware of their blessings, others of their discontents in the face of time running out. They may want more from their relationships, including more and better sex. With a critical or authoritarian parent no longer looking over the shoulder, a man or woman orphaned at midlife can feel the pressure to change and improve, even if that means getting a divorce or having an affair. Old issues, such as premature ejaculation, routine sex, infrequent sex, or orgasmic difficulties may loom as problems that can no longer be tolerated.

The out-of-sync element comes into play when a partner understandably doesn't have the same life-changing response to the parent's death.

Fear of Declining Sexuality and Other Age Issues

Fear of impotence looms large in many men's minds. If they have one experience of impotence, they fear it is the beginning of the end of their sexuality. In other words, they "catastrophize." Some men become quietly frantic, either withdrawing from sexual expression or behaving in a hypersexual way with other, probably younger, women. Other men seek medical help for what is really a minor psychological problem: fear of aging, fear of loss, fear of death, all displaced onto the penis. Often all they need to do is confess their fears to their partners, thus building intimacy and making it possible for both to bring transition to a higher form of lovemaking.

Menopause can be a woman's excuse for shutting down sexually. Religious views encourage some women to stop being sexual when procreation is no longer possible. If a man buys into the menopause myth about her declining interest in sex, she may interpret his caution as disinterest and may retreat. It's easy for a couple to get out of sync when one is unhappily immersed in aging issues and the other is handling them more easily.

Living in the Empty Nest

When the kids leave home, a couple may have the hottest sex they've had in years. After decades of being careful not to alarm the children, they can have sex in the afternoon, make noise during love-making, walk around the house naked. With greater privacy, more time for intimate conversation, and less accountability to other family members, partners in a good relationship may find their sexuality blooming.

But the masquerade is over for those couples whose relationship revolved around kids. They probably fall into one of the three types of sexually challenged relationships:

1. *The conflict-related couple.* They live to fight. Conflict is so much a part of their lifestyle that their grown children, other family members, and friends can't think of them any other way except trading verbal blows.

2. *The devitalized couple.* They were in love once, but have grown apart. A low-energy couple, they seem apathetic rather than conflict-ridden. Passive but congenial, they would probably consider themselves happy.

3. *The convenience couple.* They are similar to the devitalized couple with one exception: The spark was never present in their relationship. Their emphasis is not on the marriage, but on other things, such as money and property, civic and social involvements, family, friends, careers, and hobbies.

When the partners in these relationships are out of sync, they have a much harder time connecting than other out-of-sync couples.

Health Problems

The effect of diabetes, high blood pressure, heart problems, and other chronic illnesses on sexuality will be discussed at length in Chapter 14. When one partner is suffering from a debilitating illness, the other, no matter how sympathetic, is probably not as needful of emotional comfort within the relationship. This particular out-of-sync situation can be more difficult than some others.

Anti-Sex Myths

By age 60, a man isn't deemed sexual in our society unless he's wealthy, well-preserved, and sporting a beautiful young woman on his arm. A woman that age has to be Joan Collins or Lauren Bacall to be considered a sexual being. The ideas of beauty and sexuality in our society are not as sophisticated as they are in European societies, where style, experience, and character hold their own with fresh skin and tight bodies.

In America adult children are uncomfortable imagining their parents as people who have sexual needs. They want Mom and Pop to be stereotypical aging parents, soft pot-bellied grandparents. The job description excludes sex appeal. An older couple can become seriously out of sync if one accepts society's sexual limits on aging and the other doesn't.

Retirement

Some couples now retire at 50. If they share interests and leisure activities, they can have fun together and will probably find their sex lives improving. When a man retires and his wife doesn't, there may be a power shift in the marriage, with both feeling differently about his role and importance. Some men become depressed and anxious after retirement, which can lead to impotence. In general, men and women who were happily sexual throughout their lives understand and accept their changing sexuality, are more imaginative in bed, and can enjoy the satisfactions of age without being tormented by the sexual ambitions of youth.

Various studies show sexual desire continuing in the majority of men and women throughout their seventies and beyond. The psychoanalyst Eric Erickson, a pioneer of research in sexuality during various stages of the life cycle, found that older people experience a more generalized sexuality, as opposed to specific sexuality. In other words, they may become more sensuous while having intercourse less often. Again, a couple becomes out of sync when one is in transition with relative ease while another isn't.

HOW TO RECONNECT IN BED

"Jeff made a lot of money in a high-profile, high-pressure corporate job, so much money that he could afford to retire on his fiftieth birthday without us having to give up any of our lifestyle," says Diane, an artist who has a studio at home. "I was a little concerned about his retiring, because I was so used to his being gone, working 12-hour days, traveling for days, even weeks at a time. We had separate lives, and suddenly we were going to put them together. I was afraid he'd get bored playing golf and would drive me nuts looking for attention. Surprisingly, he was fine. He became involved in volunteer projects, began doing a little consulting work, and by the time he'd been 'retired' six months was so busy and happy in his new life, I felt left behind.

"He was more interested in lovemaking than he'd been since we were first married. I was always pushing him off, telling him I was too busy with my work or too tired. One afternoon he came out to my studio with a picnic basket, including a bottle of chilled champagne and two glasses. I started crying and couldn't stop. He insisted I make an appointment with my doctor."

After her internist could find no physical reason for Diane's mild depression and lack of libido, she recommended counseling. In therapy, Diane quickly came to terms with her problem: She felt old because her husband was "retired." And "old people" didn't "have sex."

"My mother was 65 and my father was 69 when he retired," she says. "When Jeff retired, I was suddenly catapulted into old age. I hadn't realized how many negative attitudes I had about aging until then. It took me a while to be comfortable with Jeff's increased sex drive and my own suppressed sexual feelings, but now I am. We celebrated the first anniversary of his retirement by taking a romantic cruise. This may sound like a cliché, but we had the best sex of our lives."

THE FIVE STEPS FOR GETTING IN SEXUAL SYNC

1. Become more verbally intimate

If you want more affection, a certain type of caress, more oral sex, more frequent lovemaking—*ask*. Many people find it difficult to ask for what they want sexually because they believe their longtime partners should "know." They don't always. Would you like to add a degree of wildness to your lovemaking? Talk about your fantasies and secret wishes. The more verbal you can be about your erotic desires, the more likely you are of realizing them.

2. Learn how to say "no"

It is possible to say "no" to sex or a certain sex act without rejecting your partner or feeling guilty. Hearing an unqualified and unexplained "no" can feel like being hit with a weapon. The recipient is wounded; the refuser is guilt ridden-or angry at being "made" to feel guilty. Explain your refusal even if you aren't quite sure of the reasons yourself. "I don't know why I'm not in the mood for lovemaking, but I'm not," is preferable to "no."

Some people say "no" in nonverbal ways, like his repeatedly being unable to get an erection or her being unable to reach orgasm in encounter after encounter. These are hurtful and damaging ways of denying a partner.

3. Respond to a partner's emotional needs

Take care of the often unexpressed feelings; and the sex will follow. The best way to a man's (or woman's) heart may not necessarily be the stomach, but the best way to his or her genitals certainly may be the heart. You probably can't use reason to bring the out-of-sync (and sexually detached) partner around to a more positive way of thinking, but you can help him or her "feel" the way back to erotic life.

What are your partner's emotional needs? And what can you do to help meet them?

4. Check your attitudes

Do they need some readjustments? Go back to Chapter One and read again.

5. Mix up your lovemaking styles

There are four basic lovemaking styles. Too many couples at midlife have fallen into a rut, making love in one, perhaps two different styles. When they are out of sync in other areas of their lives, lovers especially need to vary their styles. The change may jolt them out of their individual spaces and help them reconnect.

The four styles are:

1. *Quickies.* Quickies are brief episodes of sex centered around intercourse. Sometimes there is an aura of stealth surrounding the encounter. A couple may have a quickie in the bathroom while the children are watching television in the family room. They may snatch the erotic time from the middle of a busy work day in a "nooner," or while his visiting mother is on the phone making plans with other family members, or in a semi-public place such as their own backyard at twilight. The urgency and excitement inherent in the brief sexual encounter make it a stimulating and pleasurable experience for both partners, whether orgasm is achieved or not.

More relationships don't have enough quickies. Lovemaking need not always be a production. Sometimes the needs of the higher-sexed partner can be met through an occasional quickie. At midlife, a man may be capable of having an erection, sustaining it through intercourse, yet not needing or wanting to ejaculate. His partner, on the other hand, may be able to have an orgasm more easily than she ever did. She may come to the quickie aroused from fantasy or minimal foreplay and ready for release. For them, an occasional quickie can give her what she wants and needs, while making him feel like a great lover.

COMMENTS: A 52-year-old woman says: "Fast and frantic sex is energizing. About once a week we have a quickie in the shower in the morning before work. If one of us doesn't want to come, that's fine. We're more charged for lovemaking the next time around."

2. *Garden-variety lovemaking.* In this style, the couple employ trusted methods of arousing each other, use their favorite positions, and typically continue lovemaking until both reach orgasm. The encounter may last 15 to 30 minutes and almost always takes place in the bedroom at the same time of night or perhaps early morning. Garden-variety lovemaking is comfortable, predictable, and emotionally safe. During times of stress and anxiety, couples find solace in their familiar sexual pattern.

If this is the only way a couple have been making love for a while, however, they need a change. Sometimes making love a different way, like a change of scenery, can bring people closer together. If nothing else, it will probably open up communication. To do something different, you have to communicate.

COMMENTS: A 49-year-old man says: "We have a basic lovemaking pattern that is like an oasis for me when I need it. Our sex life has always been active, creative, and inventive. But the old standby—foreplay, oral sex, her orgasm, missionary position, my orgasm—is my shelter, my church, my rock. If I've had a performance problem, if we've had some relationship problems, if she hasn't come the last few times we've made love, this is the way we need to do it to get back to our sexual selves."

3. *The long romantic encounter.* Lovemaking at a leisurely pace with great attention to seduction and loveplay may last 45 minutes to an hour or longer. Like a special dinner, it is likely the end result of some advance planning. Perhaps one or both partners staged a romantic scene. Preliminaries may include a shared bubblebath or shower, an erotic massage, a candlelight dinner at home or in a restaurant, or the donning of special clothing.

Couples tend to plan these long romantic encounters more often early in their relationships. At midlife, they may have fallen out of the habit. If you add one long romantic encounter to your lovemaking agenda every month, you'll be surprised at the benefits reaped, including a richer enjoyment of the other sexual styles. One such session can sustain intimacy for days or weeks.

COMMENTS: A 51-year-old woman says: "When our youngest left the nest last year, we made a list of things we were going to do for ourselves that we had stopped doing while raising the kids. Romantic dinners topped the list. After our first candlelight dinner we had a wonderful lovemaking session. Now we plan one every three or four weeks. We take turns planning and shopping and do the cooking together. The dinners inevitably end in long lovemaking sessions. We block out the whole evening for just us. We turn the phone off and let the answering machine pick up. It's heaven."

4. *The sexual adventure.* Some people have never or rarely used this lovemaking style. Adventurous sex adds elements of play and risk to the encounter. A couple may try an unusual position, use sex toys, share or act out their fantasies, watch erotic films together or add props or elements such as food or ice to their lovemaking. Where does the risk come in? The adventure may be wildly erotic or embarrassingly funny. An idea that sounded arousing may in execution by merely silly.

The sexual adventure adds *variety* to lovemaking. Without an occasional trip down a less familiar erotic lane, the average couple will find it hard to reach a level of high energy, excitement, and passion in their other lovemaking styles after years of being together. And being playful in bed will help you feel young.

COMMENTS: A 50-year-old man says: "My first wife never wanted to do anything out of the ordinary in bed. Oral sex made her a little uncomfortable. Without some changes in the patterns, sex gets boring. My second wife understands that. She likes to play. We've been together 15 years now, and I still find her exciting. I know there isn't anything I can't say to her about sex. We've done some crazy things, like pulling over to a rest stop area on an interstate to have a quickie in the car. We have a box of sex toys and costumes under the bed."

HOW TO USE AFTERPLAY TO IMPROVE YOUR RELATIONSHIP

For the out-of-sync couple, afterplay may be their best opportunity for reconnecting. During that period of cuddling, caressing, and sharing intimate thoughts after lovemaking, men and women are more vulnerable to each other than they are at other times. Tender and affectionate afterplay will probably make them feel in sync again, at least temporarily. No, the other problems and issues won't go away, but the lingering feelings of caring and understanding will make them seem less insurmountable.

Some hints for making the most of afterplay:

- If there has been a sexual problem, don't address it now. Afterplay is not time for a sexual postmortem. Don't obsess on what went wrong. Use this time of warm acceptance to make each other feel better. Don't allow your nonsexual problems into the bed while you're cuddling either.

- But it is okay to express sexual thoughts and feelings. If you haven't told your lover how much you enjoy certain touches, you can do so now. Inject a note of playfulness into the conversation by suggesting something lighthearted and fun you want to do together.

- Spend at least five minutes, and preferably longer, on afterplay. Fifteen is better than five.

- Say "I love you." The words have a special meaning in tender moments and can be balm to a sore ego.

Sizzler # **8**

MAKING TIME FOR LOVE

When the sex was over, he let go of her reluctantly. Gloria was satisfied with weekly lovemaking, but David wanted more. More sex, more caressing, kissing, cuddling, and afterplay, more affection, more time spent alone with his wife. When he retired at age 55, he looked forward to sharing long walks in the woods and on the beach, preparing gourmet meals together, making love in the hot tub. He had romantic plans. She, on the other hand, had a job she loved.

Seven years his junior, Gloria had taken a dozen years out of her work life to be a full-time mother. At 48, she was finally coming into her own professionally. She had friends of her own, new interests, and less time for David than she'd ever had. Often she gently pushed him away when he was being affectionate with her. When he suggested things they could do together, she countered with, "That would be lovely, darling, but you don't need me tagging along to enjoy yourself."

The waitress at the coffee shop where he sometimes had a late breakfast alone was beginning to look good to him. He flirted with her and wondered what it would be like to have an affair. Some mornings he took the thought further. What would it be like to leave Gloria and start over again with someone new, a woman more interested in him? But the waitress rebuffed him, and he felt dejected.

Predictably he took his frustration out on Gloria, the real target of his resentment. He accused her of being "selfish, so absorbed in her own life" that she didn't have time for him anymore. That made her angry, and she said, "You're the selfish one. I arranged my life to suit the needs of you and the boys for years. Now it's my turn, and you're jealous. Nobody said you had to retire. You could find part-time or consulting work. You could volunteer. Take up a hobby. You could get a life!"

Her word stung. But after he stopped smarting, he realized she'd scored some points. In a few weeks' time, he'd begun laying the groundwork for a part-time consulting career, signed up for a French class, and joined a poker group. He still wanted more sex. How to persuade Gloria?

David saw his wife as a woman in near perpetual motion. To seduce her, he'd have to slow her down. "What could I do to make your life easier today?" he asked her casually one morning as she was hurrying to get dressed. Surprised, she was at a momentary loss for words and finally suggested he could pick up her suits at the drycleaner. He did, and she was grateful enough to hug and kiss him warmly that night. The precedent was set. He, who had more time, handled the bigger share of household chores, particularly running errands. Their evening meals became more leisurely.

One soft, late-spring evening, after enjoying a dinner that he'd prepared, they took their coffee onto the deck. The air smelled of lilac and freshly mown lawns. She inhaled deeply and sighed happily. He lifted her feet into his lap and began to massage them, one foot at a time, beginning with the toes and working up to the ankles. When he was finished, she wiggled her toes in his lap, prodding his semi-erect penis.

"Don't cut me off at the ankles," she teased.

He kneaded and massaged her calves, then worked his way up her thighs. He felt her flesh growing warmer beneath the thin cotton fabric of her slacks.

"I'm warm," she said. "Would you take off my pants?"

He took off her pants, kneeled before her, and pressed his face against the hot cotton triangle of cloth covering her pubis. She moaned, then giggled. Reading her mind, he whispered, "It's almost dark." Their deck was relatively private anyway. Through his fingers pressing lightly into her flesh, he felt her acquiesce. With one hand, he pushed the cotton aside and began stroking her labia with his tongue. When her juices were flowing, he raised his face. She kissed him with more passion than she had in years.

Wordlessly, they tore off clothes until they were both naked below the waist. His penis stood firm and proud. She opened her legs and beckoned to him with her hands. He sat on her chair, his legs astride her, and she guided him inside her. They kept their eyes open while they made urgent love. He felt her orgasm as intensely as he felt his own.

9
STRETCHING YOUR SEXUAL BOUNDARIES

"Before my fiftieth birthday, I realized I was living in a series of connecting boxes," says Thomas. "Every area of my life was circumscribed by somewhat arbitrary rules. I wanted to be that kid who colored outside the lines again. It's easy to see how many men, and women too, go off the tracks at midlife. They need to shake something up, so they shake everything up. I didn't want to do that. I didn't want an affair, a divorce, a new career, but I really wanted, needed something to change.

"Sex is where I put my initial focus for change. We weren't having as much sex a I wanted. Our lovemaking routines, though satisfying, weren't exciting. When I tentatively broached the subject to my wife, June, one night, she surprised me by saying how much she'd been thinking the same things.

"'We should be getting more out of life now, not less,'" she said. "That became our rallying cry. Together we began coloring outside the lines. It started with sex. For several years she'd been having fantasies about trying anal sex and had been too embarrassed to tell me.

We went to a sex emporium to buy anal condoms, special lubricant, and a book on the subject. Just being in there got us so excited, we were groping each other in the car in the parking lot afterward.

"When we got home, we read the book together, getting more and more aroused. I performed cunnilingus on her to bring her close to orgasm. She lay across my lap moaning and writhing in pleasure while I gently played with her anus, inserting first one well-lubricated finger, then two. By the time she was in position and I had the head of my penis pressed against her anal opening, she was more than ready. It was an awesome, powerful, life-changing experience. We were both astounded at how profoundly moving and passionate anal sex was for us.

"After that day, we were closer than we'd ever been; and I felt freer than I'd felt in years."

MEASURING YOUR SEXUAL BOUNDARIES

What are sexual boundaries? Those erotic lines you and your partner have become afraid, embarrassed, or too lethargic to cross. For some couples, the boundaries are the limited times of sexual activity, for example, only at night or in the morning, only on the weekends or no more than twice a month. Some couples use only one or two lovemaking styles. Others don't participate in oral sex or share their fantasies or make love outside the bedroom. They have sex in the same way every time as if lovemaking were a Thanksgiving-day menu, not subject to change. And many couples have sex only when both are "in the mood," the mood being specifically erotic. Sad or angry, silly or mournful are not "sexy" moods. A significant number of couples have sex only a few times a year or not at all, perhaps because their boundaries kept shrinking until there was no remaining space for sexual expression.

As Thomas and June once did, many midlife couples contain their sexuality within a set of boundaries that didn't exist for them in their youth. They didn't get together one day a decade ago and say, "Let's put some limits on our sex life." The boundaries developed over time, a product of repetitive routine lovemaking, maybe some unsatisfactory encounters, and the failure to communicate to each other about their changing needs and desires. Other factors, many of them covered in previous chapters, also play a role in the establishment of sexual limits. They include those familiar villains negative attitudes, repressed anger and resentment, and untreated depression and anxiety, among others.

How are your boundaries drawn? Think back over the past year. Honestly evaluate how your sex life has been defined by the following criteria.

THE SEXUAL-BOUNDARIES QUIZ

FREQUENCY

1. Did you have sex more often during some weeks or months than others? Or do you maintain a steady rate of sexual activity, a rate that may be lower than one or both would actually prefer?

2. Does that rate represent a precipitous drop-off over lovemaking of previous years?

MOOD

3. Are you sticklers for making love only when both are "in the mood"? Or can you adapt your mood to one or another style of lovemaking?

4. Have you recently tumbled into bed on a gale of laughter or been carried there on a flood of tears?

TYPE OF SEXUAL ACTIVITY

5. Do you always have intercourse when you make love?

6. Is the pattern of loveplay culminating in intercourse predictable?

7. Or do you sometimes make love without intercourse, without desiring orgasm?

8. Is "lack of variety" one of your sex-life complaints?

LOCATION OF SEXUAL ACTIVITY

9. Do you always make love in the bedroom? Or have you experimented with lovemaking in other rooms of the house or outdoors?

10. How long has it been since you planned a weekend getaway or vacation mainly to make love in a different setting?

Your answers indicate where you've been drawing the sexual lines. Moving outside those lines, stretching your boundaries, may feel uncomfortable initially, but the rewards are certainly worth a little discomfort. If you thought you were too firmly entrenched in that rut to get out of it, you wouldn't be reading this book.

How to Have More Sex

"My wife delighted in finding statistics proving we were not having as much sex as the average couple in their fifties," Harry says. "I had lost almost all interest in sex. All my excuses—tired, busy, stressed—seemed like the real thing to me. When she pressured me to have sex or explain why I didn't want to have sex, we ended up in an argument.

"Maureen tried every seductive trick to get me interested again. Finally she said, 'I'm not ready to take a vow of celibacy. If you aren't interested in sex anymore, you have two choices. We can get a divorce or we can stay married and I will take lovers, discreetly, of course.' I wrote her comments off to female histrionics.

"I didn't believe she meant it until I saw her go into action at a party one night. She had a younger man hanging all over her. Watching them together, I saw her through his eyes. She is still a beautiful woman who has kept herself in excellent shape and has a charismatic personality. I saw the exchange of business cards, and I had no doubt she meant to schedule an intimate lunch with him. It was a blow to the solar plexus. I took her home and made passionate love to her. For the next few weeks, we were very emotional together, alternately fighting and making love and crying because we realized how close we had come to losing each other.

"I feel like a man who walked away from a bad accident with only a few scratches. Did I learn something? You bet. My wife is a fascinating woman who had really grown into being her own person right under my nose. I hadn't been putting any energy into our relationship, and now I am."

Desire is the erotic urge preceding arousal. Low sexual desire is the number-one sex problem in America today, especially among people at midlife, and few of them will have the same eye-opening experience or the same response to it that Harry had. Many men and women don't feel the urge to make love, they blame their low libido on fatigue, stress, the demands of jobs, growing children and aging parents, and lack of time for lovemaking. If one partner would like to make love more often, she/he may stop initiating lovemaking after several rejections. While there is no "normal" rate of lovemaking frequency, a standard that must be met, for couples at any age, most people have a "normal" rate of frequency for themselves. When they are feeling good about themselves and connected to their partners, they typically want to make love on average a certain number of times per week or month. One partner's loss of desire may be confusing, disappointing, and hurtful to the other who has maintained the same, or an increased, level of sexual interest.

Frequency is a problem when:

- One partner feels continually frustrated by the other's lack of desire.

- Both partners have lost desire, feel disconnected from each other, and are unhappy about having infrequent sex.

- Couples fight about how often or when to have sex.

Some people have naturally low sex drives. In their youth, they were less interested in sex than other people their age, and at midlife, they may have only occasional desire. Obviously this isn't a problem if they're not in a relationship or married to someone with a similar low sex drive. Disparate sex drives often do create tension in a couple. If the woman suddenly blossoms sexually at midlife, the unexpected disparity can be more troubling to both partners than it would be if it had existed throughout the marriage.

The reasons for low desire are complicated. Almost everyone goes through some phases of low desire in their lifetime, typically at crisis points, such as major illness or some kind of loss or following the birth of a child, and the phase is a temporary one. Some medications suppress desire (see Chapter 13) and, particularly at midlife, excessive smoking, drinking, and eating can have the same dampening effect on libido. In some people, low desire is a function of low hormone levels (see Chapter 11). When inhibited desire is a chronic condition not explained by physical factors, the causes are often rooted in unresolved relationship issues. Sometimes, like Harry and Maureen, a couple have grown apart because one or both neglected the relationship. Passion doesn't thrive inside a marriage of convenience or a financial and parenting partnership.

TEN STEPS FOR INCREASING DESIRE

There are many good reasons for wanting to make love more often. Sex is not only a way of sharing pleasure, it is also one of the primary means a couple has of building, maintaining, and reinforcing emotional intimacy. When a man and woman are satisfied with their sex life together, their bond seems stronger.

1. *Start building sexual bridges to each other.* Touch more frequently. When frequency becomes an issue, some couples stop touching each other altogether. They may fear a hug, a held hand, a caress could be misconstrued as a sexual signal.

2. *Set aside nonsexual time for each other.* Spend more time together. Do all or most of your evenings out involve friends, business social obligations, family functions, or civic affairs? Get to know each other as interesting people again.

3. *Agree not to make frequency a control issue.* The partner who wants more sex will agree not to be overly seductive or demanding. The partner who isn't interested in sex very often will take the responsibility for letting the other know when he or she is feeling desirous.

4. *Don't expect your partner to gratify all your sexual desires.* Masturbate. Fantasize. Indulge your sensuous nature.

5. *Don't expect your partner to be responsible for turning you on.* If your libido is low, encourage and nurture your sexual fantasies. Read and watch erotica. Masturbate, but not to orgasm. Give yourself more sensuous treats, such as clothing that feels good against the skin.

6. *Separate sex and romance.* Have you stopped being romantic because you're afraid a romantic gesture will be construed as a sexual invitation? Romance can, but doesn't have to be, a prelude to sex. It can be an end in itself.

7. *Speak freely.* Frequency is in your minds whether you discuss it or not—and may, in fact, become a bigger stumbling block if you don't. Without blaming each other, have a conversation about desire. Be specific about how often you feel desire, what it feels like to you, what seems to instigate those feelings.

8. *Examine your issues.* Now might be a good time to go back over some of the material previously covered. Do you have unexpressed resentment toward your partner? Unresolved anger? A low level of desire could also reflect a lack of optimism, enthusiasm, or passion in your life in general.

9. *Make a nondemand sex date with your partner.* You can be sexual without having intercourse or achieving orgasm. It may be enough to hold and stroke each other. Or perhaps the partner with less desire would enjoy bringing the other to orgasm.

10. *Move straight to arousal.* You don't have to feel desire to experience arousal. A man who thinks he has no interest in lovemaking can get an erection when stimulated by his partner. Being aroused does not mean you have to complete a sex act. Like romance, it can be an end in itself.

HOW TO PUT THE SEX BACK IN A SEXLESS MARRIAGE

Catherine and Ben are an enviable couple. In their early fifties, both are attractive, physically fit, and successful in their respective careers, advertising and computer sales, the parents of a handsome teenage son who has caused minimal family strife, and the adult children of four parents in good health into their seventies and eighties. Not caught as are many of their contemporaries in classic midlife stressful situations, they look like a couple who probably enjoy a good sex life.

"We haven't had sex in over a year," Catherine says. "People we know would be shocked by that. Our friends think we're a 'sexy' couple. My women friends envy me because Ben always treats me with such courtesy, tenderness, and chivalry in public. We have genuine feelings for each other. There are no big issues, no looming problems between us. I would like to make love more often. Ben puts so much of his energy into sales that he's depleted by the time he gets to bed."

Does Catherine really believe that two healthy, fit, attractive, and sexy people who have "genuine feelings" for each other haven't had sex in a year because his energy is depleted by his work?

When pressed, Ben admits there are "a few issues, one being Catherine's shopping habits. If I am feeling aroused at night, all I have to do is look around the master suite or, God forbid, open one of the doors to her two walk-in closets to lose my erection. We'll never be able to retire, but maybe we'll open a clothing museum."

When couples stop having sex altogether, the reason is frequently blocked anger. Short bursts of anger can clear the air and ignite passion because that anger is recognized and acknowledged. Long-term anger, unacknowledged and unresolved, builds up and blocks sexual expression. The sex problem won't be resolved until the anger problem is.

If you and your partner are not having sex:

- *Acknowledge the problem.* At midlife, if a man abstains from sex for long periods of time, he will likely have trouble with arousal when he does try to make love again. A woman may also have difficulties with arousal and orgasm under the same circumstances. Someone has to say, "We haven't made love in months (or years). There's something wrong."

- *Make schedule adjustments so you can spend intimate time together.* A couple who aren't making love need to open a dialogue about the issues surrounding their sexual shutdown. Often they plan their lives carefully so they are too busy to talk in anything other than brief updates. See hints in previous chapters for opening intimate dialogues.

- *Incorporate as many of the aforementioned ten steps for increasing desire into your life as possible.* Do what you can. Holding hands while walking together could be the beginning of a bridge back to each other.

- *Consider counseling.* You and your partner may both need a little help to define and resolve the underlying emotional or relationship issues causing the problem. That can often be accomplished in a surprisingly short time.

You *can* put the sex back in a sexless marriage, but the sooner you begin, the better.

HOW TO GET IN THE MOOD FOR LOVE

"Carrie used to tell me over the phone, 'I'm not in the mood for sex, don't come over,'" says John of his companion of twenty years. "I sometimes teased her by responding, 'So what's the mood for sex? I can have sex with you in any mood.' Often I could cajole her out of her not-in-the-mood-for-sex mood and get her to invite me to spend the night."

John and Carrie have an unusual relationship. Neither has ever been married or lived with another person after shedding their college roommates. An archaeologist based at a Midwestern site, he has spent as long as two years at a time in Egypt in a time zone hours away from St. Louis, where Carrie is a professor of anthropology. Yet they have maintained a "close and monogamous relationship" by both accounts.

"We need more privacy than most people," he says. "Being a solitary person has made me more observant, not less, of people's moods. I can read Carrie's moods and flatter myself that I respond in a productive way most of the time."

When they met, Carrie says, she "suffered from having read too many romantic poets in my girlhood. I was given to exaggerated fits of grand passion or periods of sweet tenderness with my lovers. When I was feeling otherwise inclined, I told the lovers, 'no.' I had never laughed in bed before John. What a revelation. I remember having a tremendous orgasm and looking dead into his eyes when he *laughed!* 'Whatever do you find amusing?' I asked after I'd caught my breath. He said, 'I just feel happy and you have such big serious eyes.'"

Whatever mood you're in, you can be in the mood for love. Life is full of moods. One day you feel good, the next bad, and between those two poles are compressed all the joys of love and the anguish of loss. Practically any mood can lend itself to lovemaking. Think of eating. How many of us eat only when we're hungry? Few, indeed. We eat when we're sad, joyful, frustrated, resentful, anxious, or for no reason at all except a meal is being served. Food comforts us.

Why not consider sexual contact in the same way? Reach out for your lover when you need comfort or feel giddy. Take the mood, whatever it may be, and direct its energy into some form of lovemaking. You may be surprised at the effect this has on your erotic creativity.

Chapter 9

EXPLORING ALTERNATIVE FORMS OF LOVEPLAY

Close to the top of most sex wish lists is the ubiquitous word "variety." What does it mean? Almost anything that takes a couple out of same-time, same-place, same-way mode of lovemaking. Implementing some of the suggestions already offered in this book will add variety to your sex life. A move as simple as turning on the lights can create change. Like spices in cooking, some people respond to a hint and others need a large dollop before they experience a new sensation.

Some less conventional forms of loveplay than those already covered in other chapters include:

Heterosexual Anal Sex

Anal intercourse takes place when the penis is inserted into the anus rather than the vagina. This has to be practiced with full consent and special care, including the use of anal condoms and copious amounts of a water-soluble lubricant such as astrolube or KY jelly. Unlike the vagina, the rectum does not produce lubrication. An oil or petroleum jelly product can cause condom breakage. The practice should be limited to monogamous couples because it is a high-risk activity for HIV transmission. Why use condoms then? To prevent bacteria present in the rectum from entering the man's urinary-tract system through his urethra.

According to various studies, approximately 40 percent of heterosexual couples have tried anal sex at least once. The anus, like the vagina, has sensitive nerve endings. Some women become highly aroused both by the sensations and the psychological connotations of anal penetration. Men are excited by the tightness of the anal opening, the forbidden nature of anal love, and the idea that a woman would surrender herself to them in this fashion.

Anal intercourse requires mutual trust, good communication skills, and patience on the man's part. Here's how to proceed:

- He should make sure his partner is very aroused (and well lubricated) before he approaches her anus.

- The woman should concentrate on relaxing the anal muscles, not tensing them, and should expect some initial discomfort.

- Entry should be effected carefully and with her cooperation, followed by short, shallow thrusts.

- Once movement is established, he won't be able to thrust as vigorously as he would during vaginal intercourse without risking damaging delicate tissues.

- The experience will probably be pleasurable for both as long as he is prepared to move slowly, follow her lead on depth of penetration, and stop at any time she requests.

COMMENTS: From a 48-year-old married woman: "As a young woman I was intrigued by sexual variations. I read about anal sex, bondage, and spanking and wanted to try those things. I found some old magazines in the attic of the first house we bought. Now I know the beautiful brunette in the bondage layouts was Bettie Page, the fifties cult model. Then I only knew I was excited by the pictures. I fantasized about a man tying me over a vault and fucking my ass. Just saying those naughty words in my head turned me on. Twenty years later I told my husband about the pictures, my fantasies, my desire for experimentation. It blew him away. We had anal sex that night. It hurt a little more than I thought it would, but only at first. I felt like I had completely surrendered to him, giving him something more precious than my virginity had been. Why did it take me so long to get over my modesty and tell him what I wanted?"

Bondage

Bondage is erotic restraint, the sensual experience of safe captivity. Light bondage, or "tie and tease," may be the most common sex game couples play. One partner ties the other, either lightly binding wrists together or binding wrists and sometimes ankles to the bedposts. The bound partner is then "helpless" and must submit to the other's sexual ministrations. The object of the game is intensifying pleasure through delaying gratification. The one in charge teases the other to the brink of orgasm, pulls back, teases again.

How to proceed:

- Using silk scarves or ties or Velcro restraints (purchased in a sex toy catalogue or store), loosely bind your partner's wrists and/or ankles. If she/he is comfortable with it, add a blindfold.

- Check the bindings to make sure they are not constricting blood flow.

- Kiss, caress, stroke, and fondle your partner's body, avoiding the genitals.

- Using the oral techniques on pages 52–56 and the manual techniques on pages 56–60, stimulate him or her to a level of high arousal.

- Abruptly stop genital stimulation.

- Again kiss, caress, stroke, and fondle his/her body, avoiding the genitals.

- Repeat the stop-start method of genital stimulation until your partner begs for an orgasm.

- Remember even light bondage can lead to muscle cramps. You don't want to sustain the experience so long your partner is begging for a muscle massage, not an orgasm.

COMMENTS: From a 54-year-old man: "My wife and I love to play 'tie and tease' occasionally. Both the dominant and submissive roles in this game have their own joys. To be in charge of the other's pleasure, the withholder and dispenser of the orgasm, is a potent experience. Seeing your bound partner panting, sweating, and writhing is a real turn-on. She likes to leave on a silk teddy or camisole and panties. After a while, they're plastered to her body. Very erotic. But I also enjoy being bound and tormented. The sense of being controlled is freeing. I don't have to perform. She has to make me come. We didn't start playing sex games until later in our marriage, after the kids were gone away to school; and it's brought us closer together. At a family reunion, she whispered in my ear, 'What would they think if they knew what I did to you last night?'"

Spanking

Erotic spanking is the administering of blows to the buttocks for the purposes of arousal. In less politically correct times than our own, spanking was regarded as a form of lighthearted sex play between partners. The *Kama Sutra* offers detailed instructions on administering the four kinds of blows to produce the eight kinds of sounds. On television in the fifties, Ricky spanked Lucy. Their bedroom set was required by network censors to hold twin beds, not a double, but spanking was permissible. In the movies from the thirties through the fifties, Tracy spanked Hepburn, and Cary Grant spanked many women and they were not alone. Today spanking is a taboo activity, but an astonishing array of magazines, books, and newsletters devoted to the practice are available in this country. A good number of people are at least fantasizing breaking the taboo.

Spanking as foreplay is typically a part of an erotic role-playing scenario in which the naughty girl or boy is disciplined by an authority figure. The hand is most commonly used, but spanking implements can range from a kitchen spatula to a specially purchased lightweight whip. If you and/or your partner have administered the occasional light slap during intercourse to favorable response, you might enjoy an occasional spanking game. Here's how to proceed:

- Agree on the terms beforehand. How many slaps? With hand or what instrument? How hard?

- Make sure your partner is fully aroused before the hand meets the ass.

- Start with a very light touch. Gentle slaps bring blood to the surface, minimizing bruising.

- Carefully monitor your partner's response.

- Have a "safe word," which when spoken by the spankee means STOP. Saying, "Oh, no, don't spank me," may be part of the script. Make the safe word something like "peanut butter." Don't use "no."

COMMENTS: From a 50-year-old man: "My partner and I take turns spanking each other occasionally. We had never thought about adding this to our repertoire of sexual tricks until we saw a video that included some spanking. She said, 'I can't believe how much this is arousing me.' I lied and said it didn't arouse me. She put her hand around my erection and said, 'Oh, no not much,' then with the other hand slapped my ass. What a feeling! Delivering the slap and receiving it are both strong sexual sensations. A well-timed blow can make my erection hard again if it's beginning to wane during intercourse."

Light S/M

More theater than pain, light S/M (sadomasochism) games are erotic power exchanges between consenting partners. They sometimes involve costumes and props and nearly always include role playing. One partner plays the dominant, the other the submissive, character in an erotic drama. The dominant "controls" the action by administering light doses of physical pain and/or verbal abuse and making the submissive do his or her sexual bidding. The submissive is really in charge, however, because it is understood between the players that the game doesn't go any further than the submissive desires.

The word "sadomasochism" is derived from combining "sadist," who enjoys inflicting pain and/or humiliation, and "masochist," who enjoys receiving pain and/or humiliation. People who take the behavior to the extremes are a small minority. For them, the exchange of pain has almost or entirely replaced sexual activity. They refer to S/M as a "lifestyle," because it does define how they live their lives. The vast majority of people who dabble in S/M, however, use it as an occasional form of erotic play to intensify arousal and orgasm, and they are "switch" players, alternating the dominant and submissive roles.

If you want to play:

- Don't underestimate the importance of costumes and props. Certain items of clothing, types of fabric or other material, and special accoutrements have S/M connotations. Visit a sex-toy shop or browse a catalogue for ideas. Generally they include tight-fitting leather or rubber garments, the color black, bustiers, corsets, garter belts, stockings, very high heels on pumps or boots, masks, nipple clamps, bondage gear, and spanking implements.

- Work from a script. You don't have to write down the dialogue, but you must have the plot worked out before beginning. Talk about what you want to do in detail with your partner.

- Set limits and stick to them. A velvet-covered whip can sting. So can words. Be clear about how far is too far to go, both verbally and physically.

- Use a safe word. The submissive should be able to stop the game at any time by saying the safe word. Again, don't use "no." It's too confusing.

- Remember that a little goes a long way. You may fantasize giving or receiving a level of rough treatment that would be a turnoff in real life.

- Be sure your partner is aroused before you administer pain, and be sure she/he continues to be aroused by the action.

- Switch roles the next time you play.

Comments: From a 45-year-old woman: "Playing with S/M brings emotions to the surface for us. I'm not sure it would be a good idea for couples who have hidden anger. One might lose it while dominating the other. But for us it's been a healthy way to express latent feelings of dominance and submission. We take turns being the master or the slave. The last time he was master he ordered me to crawl across the floor on all fours and suck his 'dick.' I haven't been so aroused performing fellatio in a long time. I really wouldn't want to be sexually enslaved, but it's fun to pretend for a little while. It's just as much fun to play mistress when it's my turn to make him serve me."

Exhibitionism/Voyeurism

An exhibitionist has sex in public places. The average couple can get their own illicit thrill by making love in a semi-public place such as their hot tub on the deck or by making out in the car in the parking lot at the mall. Voyeurs become aroused by watching other people have sex. Again, the concept can be adapted for home play. A couple can, for example, make videos of themselves having sex and watch them together.

True exhibitionists and voyeurs take big risks to get what they need for arousal because they can't be sexually excited in a variety of different ways like most people. Their focus is very narrow. Erotic dabblers have a wide range of arousal choices, and they don't put themselves and their partners in dangerous or illegal positions. Just remember:

- The thrill comes from the *possibility* of discovery, not the likelihood of it. Making love in your own swimming pool on a summer night imparts an erotic edge because the neighbors might see or hear. But it's still your pool. If you make love in a public pool after hours, have bail money in the car.

- If you take nude photographs of each other, use a Polaroid camera unless you have a darkroom. Keep compromising photos and videos under lock and key.

- Employ the tricks of the trade. Use soft lighting for your erotic photography. Shoot his penis from "up and under," as they do in the business. In other words, have the camera slightly beneath his erection, the lens tilted upward. Mist her labia with water for that dewy look.

- Adapt your fantasies for reality. Making love in Central Park could get you killed. How about on the living room floor behind the palm tree with the drapes open?

COMMENTS: From a-58 year-old man: "At 54, my wife still has beautiful breasts. She's full and voluptuous like Elizabeth Taylor. I like to take her out wearing low-cut gowns, almost cut to the nipple line. She looks magnificent, like a goddess. Men of all ages, and women too, admire her. I get very aroused by that, and so does she. Sometimes we can't wait to get home. Our daughter, who wants her to start dressing 'her age,' disapproves of her 'exhibitionism.' We pay the girl no mind on this issue."

How common is "kinky" sex? Anywhere from 10 to 30 percent of people have experimented with some form of kink (excluding anal sex, a separate category) at least once in their lives. Americans have probably gotten kinkier in the past decade for several reasons: the prevalence of media imagery celebrating bondage and S/M images; the availability of sex information as well as erotica about kinky practices; a greater level of social tolerance for sexual variations, especially among more educated people; and the aging of the Baby Boom generation. As people grow older, they are more comfortable with expressing long-held desires and more likely to need variety to maintain their sex lives in a satisfactory way.

TEN PLACES TO HAVE SEX OUT OF BED

Location is the fourth factor defining sexual boundaries. If you never make love anywhere except a bed, you are missing opportunities for variety. Try some of the following ideas:

- *Shower.* Great for oral sex. The water gently trickling over the head and shoulders of the partner kneeling at the other's genitals adds to the pleasure.

- *Living room.* You can have sex sitting in a chair, on the sofa, the floor, maybe the coffee table. A fireplace in winter adds ambiance, but candlelight works too.

- *Kitchen.* Floor, table, counters. If he is tall, they can have intercourse with her sitting on the counter while he stands.

- *Dining room.* Chairs, table, floor. The association with food can make sex more interesting, especially if the table hasn't been cleared.

- *Garage.* Have you ever made love sitting on a parked riding mower? Look around the garage for other ideas. Improvise.

- *Deck.* An obvious choice for warm nights, even cold ones under a down comforter.

- *Pool.* Another obvious choice.

- *Other bathrooms, not your own.* There is nothing like a quickie in a friend's bathroom or public restroom to energize a relationship plagued by routine sex.

- *Car.* Not for teenagers only.

- *The great outdoors.* Every couple should make love on the beach or the lawn at least once in their lives.

Phone Sex

If you haven't looked at a sex magazine—or "girlie" magazine as they were known when we were younger—in recent years, you would probably be more surprised at the pages of phone-sex ads than at the nude layouts. Men have always been aroused by sex talk so graphic it creates strong visual images in the mind. The phone-sex industry was developed to fill an unmet need.

On a slightly higher level, phone sex was in the news during the White House sex scandal known as "Lewinskygate." The young intern who allegedly had some kind of sexual relations with the President also allegedly bought from a local bookseller a copy of *Vox*, a novel about phone sex by Nicholson Baker. On the strength of this reported bit of gossip alone, the book went back into print.

If either you or your partner travel on business—or even if you don't—phone sex is a way to generate exotic enthusiasm for the coming reunion. Here's how to play the game:

1. *Warm up by leaving erotic messages on his or her voice mail*—assuming no one else has access to the messages, of course.

2. *Don't feel guilty about "talking dirty."* Nice girls weren't raised to say "bad words." That's what makes them so exciting when they come out of your mouth for only his ears. Your voice is an arousal too, just like mouth, lips, tongues, hands, genitals.

3. Learn some new words. Erotic novels are filled with euphemisms for genitals and their interactions. The steamier romance novels are another good source of inspiration.

4. *Practice.* If the words don't come easy to you, say them out loud when you're alone. Get used to the feel of naughty words in your mouth. Like learning a foreign language, "dirty talk" takes some practice.

5. *Rent movies you consider erotic—and listen to them.* Close your eyes so you won't be distracted by the visual content of the film. You'll be surprised at how much the words, tone of voice, and inflection contribute to the experience.

6. *Read erotica out loud to each other.* You may find it easier to be creative on your own after reading other scripts. Choose novels with a lot of dialogue.

7. *Now you're ready for phone sex.* Choose a scenario that you know will be particularly arousing to your partner. Phone-sex operators say that anal sex, oral sex, and female-domination scenarios are the most popular with their callers. Remember to be specific. The heat of phone sex is in the details.

8. *Add sound effects.* Heavy breathing, panting, soft moans add a note of similitude to the experience.

9. *When you're more comfortable with the game*, create scenarios out of your own unexpressed desires and hidden fantasies.

10. *Make a ruling about whether masturbating to orgasm will or will not be "permitted."* Why wouldn't it be? If you're going to see each other within a day or two, you may want to save the orgasms for then. A certain level of mental excitation can be sustained if phone sex doesn't end in orgasm.

Sizzler # 9

THE BONDS OF LOVE

Ian suggested "the game" as a joke. Marta, his partner of ten years, had become more dynamic and forceful after fifty, while he had grown more patient and easygoing. She saw aging as time running out, while he saw it as time slowing down. He often told her that she "had a habit of cutting off [his] sentences before the verb," especially if she thought she knew what he was going to say. She did, she conceded, frequently interrupt him while he was talking, but, she countered, she did know what he was going to say on those occasions because he said the same things over and over again.

"I should tie you to the chair and put a gag in your mouth when I need you to listen," he teased.

"Would you waste an opportunity like that by talking?" she countered.

Their eyes met, and each recognized a devilish glint in the other's gaze. They began teasing each other more readily. The mock threat of binding and gagging was invoked when one expressed an opinion contrary to the other's—or when Ian retold an oft-told story. Erotic tension, which had been largely absent from their relationship for years, bubbled beneath the surface again.

"Would you like to play a game?" Ian asked Marta. She was seated at her dressing table, fresh from a bubble bath, a gray cashmere robe loosely belted around her waist. He put his hands on her shoulders; and she set down the jar of face cream she was holding in her hand. "I think about this game every time I see you sitting in that chair now."

Wordlessly, she nodded her head. He had her complete attention for a change.

"Don't move," he said gently, but firmly.

While she waited, heart beating fast, he took four silk ties from one of the racks in his closet. Their eyes met in the mirror when he returned to the bathroom, ties in hand. He hadn't seen that eager yet shy expression on her face since their earliest days together. He smiled.

"Spread your legs," he said, "and put your hands behind your back."

She complied. He fastened her ankles to the chair legs with two ties and secured her wrists with another. She was breathing heavily, her breasts rising and falling seductively inside her robe. Holding her face in his hands, he kissed her, gently at first, teasing her lips with playful licks of his tongue, before thrusting it forcefully into her mouth. She surrendered to the kiss, and he pulled way. He wrapped the fourth tie around her mouth, gagging her.

"You're my captive audience," he said.

Eyes flashing mischievously, she squirmed in the chair. He pulled open the robe, exposing her breasts and her pussy. She arched her back and twisted her torso, throwing herself into the game.

"Are you ready to listen?" he teased. She shook her head from side to side, a negative. "Oh, you're going to be feisty? I'll have to do something to make you more receptive to my words."

He took her breasts in his hands and massaged them. An urgent sigh formed in the back of her throat. She arched her body forward to let him know she wanted a stronger touch. He got the message. As his hands moved down her body, her gyrations increased. When he inserted two fingers into her vagina, she rocked the chair back and forth, riding him.

"Do you want me to lick your pussy?" he asked.

She nodded a vigorous "yes." He brought her to the brink of orgasm with the skillful use of fingers and tongue, then abruptly stopped. She squealed in protest.

"You have to do something for me before I give you an orgasm," he said. "Will you do it?"

She nodded that she would, and he removed her gag. As she sucked in big gulps of air, he unzipped his pants to expose his erection. He put his hands on the sides of her head as he had when he'd kissed her and guided her toward his penis. The position wasn't comfortable for her, he knew, and in this situation, that added to his pleasure. She fellated him to orgasm.

Marta looked beautiful to him, with traces of semen around her lips and sweat on her brow. He knelt before her and licked and sucked. She didn't have to tell him not to stop after her first orgasm; he knew.

10

THE UNLIMITED POTENTIAL
OF MIDLIFE ORGASM

"Everything I thought I knew about orgasms after 40 was wrong," says Mark, 51, a practicing internist in Maryland. "I remember an older man, a colleague I admired, telling me when I was in my late twenties that I should enjoy my orgasms while I still had 'real' ones. He said after 40 the male orgasm was a pale shadow of its former glory. That's not true at all.

"The mature orgasm is richer, more varied in depth and intensity than the youthful orgasm. When you're young, you want to ejaculate purely for the release. Every orgasm feels pretty much the same. There is a physical urgency in the last stage of arousal that you may not feel, at least all the time, in maturity. But the orgasm now is more deeply and diversely felt. Beginning in the genitals, it radiates out into other parts of the body. Sometimes I feel it in my elbows and my toes.

"If I were explaining this to a younger man, here is what I would say: 'In your twenties you drink more wine; by age 50 you drink less, but the wine is better, and your ability to appreciate it has grown a hundredfold. At my age, son, you know a good bottle of wine.'"

THE MIDLIFE ORGASM

In both men and women an orgasm is a series of rhythmic contractions triggered by intense physical and psychological stimulation and typically lasts 3 to 20 seconds, with intervals of less than a second between the first three to six contractions. Some women experience spasms for a minute or longer. The contractions are centered in the genitals, including the vagina and uterus in women, and the rectal sphincter. At midlife, men especially may experience fewer contractions. Women may have the same number of contractions into their sixties or early seventies. This diminishing of the number of spasms was once thought to signal a decline in the quality of the orgasmic experience. If an orgasm were only the release of sexual tension and primarily a genital event, perhaps losing a spasm or two over the years would qualify as a diminishment.

But an orgasm is more than the sum of its contractions, especially at this point in your life. The orgasmic potential of midlife men and women has been underestimated by doctors, therapists, and lay people until recent years. In the late 1980s the sexologist Dr. Herbert Otto studied a group of people over 40 who were able to experience a fuller range and depth of orgasmic sensations than they'd ever known through the use of "shaping and developing" techniques. Using the following methods, you can expand your own orgasmic experience too.

Why might you want richer, fuller, deeper orgasms? The reasons include:

• *Some health benefits of orgasm have been documented by researchers.* Orgasm promotes cardiovascular conditioning, imparts a healthy glow to the skin, and improves overall body tone. Recent studies have shown that breast-cancer survivors who experience orgasm—through lovemaking or masturbation—recover more quickly than those who do not. In addition, orgasm triggers the release of chemicals in the brain that can help relieve headaches and other minor aches and pains.

• *There are real psychological benefits associated with orgasm.* In 1940 famed psychologist Wilhelm Reich in his groundbreaking book, *The Function of the Orgasm*, broadened the definition of orgasm beyond the genitals. He was the first sexologist to say that a person's emotional health was related to his or her capacity to experience orgasm. Reich thought orgasm was a whole-body event, a belief he shared with the Eastern sexologists and one that was largely ignored by Western authorities on the subject until recently.

   • *Orgasm during lovemaking builds intimacy.* Orgasm has relationship-bonding power. After orgasm, men and women often feel closer to their partners, a feeling that has in part a physical basis. The chemical oxytocin, released in the brain upon orgasm and nicknamed the "cuddling hormone," inspires feelings of attachment. Women, not surprisingly, produce much larger amounts of oxytocin than men do—until midlife, when the percentages are more nearly aligned.

The Orgasm Quiz

This quiz will help develop more awareness of your orgasmic experiences. The first step in increasing orgasmic potential is understanding where you are now. This is not a test, and there are no "right" or "wrong" answers.

1. List all the ways you are orgasmic, including via oral sex, masturbation, manual stimulation by your partner, intercourse, or other.

2. Do you experience orgasm differently, depending on the way it was achieved? Can you explain the differences?

3. How frequently do you reach orgasm during lovemaking?

4. Have you ever had or do you sometimes or often have multiple orgasms?

5. Have you ever experienced an extragenital orgasm, or an orgasm achieved with stimulation to areas other than the genitals?

6. Have you ever felt an orgasm in parts of your body other than the genitals?

7. Be as specific as possible in describing exactly what kinds of stimulation, including pressure and amount, bring you to orgasm.

8. How do your emotions and your feelings toward your partner affect your orgasms?

9. How does your partner's orgasm affect yours?

10. Do you have a particularly sensitive body part (aside from the genitals) that, when stimulated at the same time your genitals are being stimulated, affects orgasm?

Orgasm is a blend of physical, psychological, and emotional factors. In youth, the physical element often takes precedence over the others, especially for men. As people mature, the psychological and emotional elements take on greater importance, again especially for men. At any age, the orgasmic experience varies depending on many factors, including the type of sexual activity, the closeness felt toward the partner, and other physical, emotional, and psychological conditions.

Your answers to the ten questions will help develop a better awareness of how you reach orgasm, differentiate the feelings of orgasms achieved using different methods of stimulation, and assess how much you may have been limiting orgasmic potential by attitudes and behaviors.

HOW TO BUILD NEW PATHWAYS TO ORGASM

Even if you are not interested in pursuing extended orgasms, multiple orgasms, extragenital, spontaneous, and full-body orgasms, you can experience orgasm more fully and deeply than you do now. What could stop you? Two things: thinking you can't, and using exactly the same approach to masturbation and lovemaking as you've been using for years. It's time for a sexual shake-up.

Here's how to build those paths:

Masturbate

Orgasms attained through masturbation feel different from those reached during lovemaking with a partner, but masturbation encourages greater sexual self-awareness. With no emotional distractions, you can assess how a certain method works. To gain knowledge about your sexual responses, practice the techniques you'll learn in this chapter during masturbation and transfer them to lovemaking. Allow sufficient time for self-pleasuring. Create a sensuous and comfortable environment by using the soft lighting or music, scents, candles, or other accessories you save for special lovemaking times. If you don't own a vibrator, buy one.

Most important, alter your solo style. Don't fall back on the trusted habit to bring you to orgasm after a few minutes of being adventurous. Many people are more comfortable about trying something new with a partner after they've experimented privately on their own bodies. Begin the sexual shake-up with you.

Focus on parts other than genitals

Devote a masturbation or lovemaking session almost exclusively to one area of your body that brings you intense pleasure when fondled, but hasn't led to orgasm. This may be a woman's breasts, a man's nipples, a hot-spot area, the inner thighs, or some other place. See how much more sensitive the area becomes when you use different techniques for stroking and massaging and continue stimulating it past the point where you would have shifted to genital stimulation.

But don't make orgasm a goal. If you reach an irresistible level of arousal and want to have an orgasm via clitoral or penile stimulation, fine. Does the orgasm feel stronger or deeper than usual? In other masturbation or lovemaking sessions, focus on different areas.

Focus on Genitals

Now focus your erotic attention exclusively on the genitals during a single masturbation or lovemaking session. Without being distracted by touches or caresses to other body areas, you can see exactly how using the following techniques will influence arousal and intensify orgasm. But, again, orgasm need not be a goal. If you don't feel like having an orgasm this time, don't worry about it.

Add Special Effects

During a masturbation- or lovemaking-focus session, add the vibrator and other sex toys if desired. Continue stimulating the same area but alternate the manual (or oral) stimulation with the vibrator. How do the sensations change? Does orgasm happen more quickly? Feel different?

Create Fusion

When most people are close to orgasm, they continue stimulating the genitals in a certain way, faster and harder, in highly focused movements. They may kiss their partners at the same time, but other than the kiss, which is more an intense mouth lock, they connect only at key genital points. Typically during intercourse the man maneuvers so that the head of his penis receives the greatest friction, while the woman tries to angle her body to receive clitoral friction, which she may or may not augment with her own hand or his.

Using techniques that worked during single-area focus sessions, stimulate your own (and your partner's) other hot spots, breasts, nipples, or inner thighs simultaneously while creating the primary genital friction. An orgasm achieved from stimulation to more than one site is called a "fusion" orgasm. Many people experience it as more intense and widespread than orgasms reached via stimulation of the primary genital areas.

Keep an Orgasm Diary

At first this may be difficult to do and perhaps seem rather foolish. Try anyway. What you record in your diary will help further expand and develop your orgasmic potential. During the afterglow, write down everything you can remember about this orgasm in the following categories:

- *Body sensations.* How many orgasmic contractions did you feel? Where were they located? What were the different feelings in various parts of the body? Did you feel waves of warmth in other body areas? Tingling sensations in certain parts? Describe where, how, and how intensely you felt the physical sensations of orgasm.

- *Emotions.* What were your feelings as you reached orgasm?

- *Images.* Did you see colors or images at orgasm? Were you involved in a fantasy that culminated in orgasm? Did a scrap of a fantasy or remembered real-life scenario come into your mind at orgasm?

COMMENTS: A couple in their early fifties who were initially reluctant to employ these methods for learning new pathways to orgasm eventually did so because "we were in such a rut that orgasm didn't feel that good anymore."

After six months, she says, "I am more orgasmic than I have ever been. The orgasms are more varied. Sometimes I have light, fluttering orgasms that seem to skip across my clitoris and send delicious chills up my spine. And other times I have these deep shuddering emotional orgasms that defy description. One night I cried as I came."

And he says, "When I was young, I felt orgasm throughout my penis, into the base, and the surrounding area including the anus. A few years ago I noticed the orgasmic sensations were more limited to the head and first third of the penis, with the other parts feeling minimal tingling. Now I feel orgasm throughout the entire genital area and beyond. Orgasm is often a very intensely emotional experience for me now too."

EXTENDING YOUR ORGASM TIME

For young men, orgasm is an almost certainty, while for young women it may be a sometime event. At midlife, women get more "sometimes" and men don't always find orgasm inevitable. Both are ideally suited now to experience extended orgasms, something a man probably can't master in youth and a woman might not have the confidence to try.

Strong PC muscles are required to extend an orgasm beyond its minimal seconds. Go back to page 78 and review the Kegel exercises. If you haven't been practicing them, start now. Once the PC muscles are strong, use them to extend orgasm.

- The man pumps his penis in time with the contractions by squeezing his PC muscles.

- The woman squeezes her vaginal walls in time with her contractions.

- Begin squeezing with the first contraction.

Repeated use of the method gradually extends orgasms and, for many people, makes the initial contractions more intense.

COMMENTS: A couple who gave themselves face lifts for their fiftieth birthdays, which were six weeks apart, also began doing Kegel exercises when they were recovering from surgery.

He says: "It was the only workout I could do for a while, so I thought why not. My expectations were minimal, and I was really surprised by the results. Using the PC technique for extending orgasms has worked very well for me. I have more contractions and feel them more strongly."

She says: "I have a physically fit vagina for the first time in my life. Any woman who thinks that doesn't have an effect on the quality of orgasms doesn't have one. It's a huge difference. Yes, I can make my orgasms last longer and feel stronger. The contractions continue gently subsiding for several minutes afterward. It's like having earthquake aftershocks going off in my vagina."

MULTIPLE ORGASMS AT MIDLIFE

Multiple orgasms occur when a woman (or a man, which is less likely) has a second, third, or more orgasms without completely returning to the resolution phase. In other words, a level of excitation is maintained between orgasms; the woman or man is not starting the climb over again from a low point on the arousal scale. Probably all women are capable of having multiple orgasms though it is estimated fewer than 50 percent ever do. Far fewer men do, and whether all can or not depends on one's perspective on sexuality.

At midlife women are more likely to have multiple orgasms than at any other time. As previously noted, her erotic responses are more rapid, her level of confidence higher, her sexual self-awareness greater. For many women, regular orgasms or multiple orgasms begin to happen now because they've finally gotten over their embarrassment about needing manual clitoral stimulation during intercourse to achieve orgasm. Once they feel free to touch themselves or ask for the touch, they become more orgasmic.

The types of multiples are:

- *Compounded singles.* Each orgasm is distinct and separated by a partial return to the resolution phase.

- *Sequential multiples.* Orgasms occur two to ten minutes apart with minimal reduction in arousal between them.

- *Serial multiples.* Numerous orgasms are separated by mere seconds or minutes at most with no diminishment of arousal. Some women experience this as one long orgasm with spasms of varying intensity.

How Women Can Have Multiple Orgasms

Mental attitude is key. First, if you haven't discarded the idea that lovemaking ends with a man's ejaculation, do so now. His orgasm isn't the signal for the end of lovemaking.

Next, a woman must be focused on her own pleasure to achieve multiple orgasms. Shut out intrusive thoughts. You deserve pleasure, and now you are going to take it.

Finally, start on warm. Prepare for the possibility of multiples by fantasizing about sex before the encounter, caressing your own genitals in the bath or shower before lovemaking, and having a glass of wine, if that works to relax you.

The Techniques

1. *Alternating stimuli*

- Ask your partner to give you the first orgasm via cunnilingus. Oral sex more fully arouses the female genitalia, making orgasm during intercourse more likely.

- After the first orgasm, he should manually stroke her to another orgasm if possible.

- If she does not reach orgasm easily by manual stimulation, revert to oral.

- After a second orgasm, he should immediately enter her, with either of them continuing manual stimulation at the same time. Some women report that intercourse at that point seems to "spread" the sensations of orgasm throughout the body.

- Maintain a pattern of varied stimulation as long as desired.

COMMENTS: From a 52-year-old woman who experienced multiple orgasms for the first time recently: "Alternating stimuli, with the first orgasm via cunnilingus, works for me. The other methods don't. In fact, I like two oral orgasms. After that, if I'm in the right mental place, I can fly. I feel myself soaring into a level of pleasure I'd never reached any other way."

2. *Manual contact*. Women who aren't comfortable touching themselves during lovemaking are less likely to experience multiples, because they have to depend on their partners to know exactly where and how to apply the stimulation that would take them from one peak to the next. Even the best lovers can't always get it right.

- Stroke yourself during cunnilingus or intercourse.

- Vary the stimulation to the clitoral area.

- When you feel orgasm approaching, move the stimulus from the clitoris to the area surrounding it to "spread" the orgasm.

COMMENTS: From a 54-year-old woman: "I can have multiple orgasms in a variety of ways. I'm one of the lucky women. Manual stimulation is the surest way for me to get there. From masturbating, I know exactly when, where, and how to touch myself to bring on the spasms. My husband of 29 years is an excellent lover, but he can't pinpoint the site and pressure changes I need to take me from one orgasm to another as fast as I can. Besides, he loves it when I touch myself."

3. *Repeated direct stimuli*. While some women are more likely to have multiple orgasms using alternating stimuli, others have a better chance of doing so if their partner (and they) repeatedly stimulate the clitoral area in the same way. A few women need constant, concerted stimulation at the focal point to have multiple orgasms. Many women, however, find the clitoris too sensitive to sustain this pattern of stimulation.

COMMENTS: From a 50-year-old woman: "I can keep having orgasms if I or my partner continue stimulating the clitoris throughout and beyond the first orgasm. Sometimes the clitoral area gets so sensitive, I think I can't bear the touch. If I don't pull away, the acute sensitivity passes. I move into a place where I sometimes feel like I could come forever."

4. *The flame.* Some women can have multiple orgasms only during cunnilingus. This technique, following the other suggested strokes on page 166, often works. The directions are for him.

- Pretend the tip of your tongue is a candle flame.

- In your mind's eye, see the flame flickering in the wind.

- Move your tongue rapidly around the sides of her clitoris, above and below it, as the candle flame moves.

COMMENTS: From a 53-year-old woman: "This is nirvana. I don't know where my husband learned it. He said from a book. Wherever he picked it up, I'm glad he did. After the second or third orgasm this way, my whole body feels like it's convulsing. I'd never had multiples until he pulled this little trick out of his bag."

5. *G-Spot multiples.* Some women can have multiples only when they are receiving both clitoral and vaginal stimulation in the area of the G spot. Here's how a man can make this happen for her:

- Using the come-hither gesture with a finger or two, a man should stimulate the G spot area as he performs cunnilingus.

- Or, during intercourse in a position she considers favorable for G-spot stimulation, he should stroke her clitoris.

COMMENTS: From a 51-year-old woman: "This works for me, especially in the rear-entry position where I get the best G-spot stimulation. One reason the position works is that I stimulate my own clitoris. I still like to have the first orgasm via cunnilingus, then switch to rear-entry intercourse and manual-clitoral stimulation."

HOW MEN CAN HAVE MULTIPLE ORGASMS

The refractory period—the time following ejaculation before a man can have another erection—does increase with age. As little as minutes in young and virile men, the refractory period can last days in a man in his seventies or older. By midlife, the refractory period may be as much as 24 hours. How are multiple orgasms possible under those circumstances?

According to many Western authorities, male orgasm and ejaculation are the same thing; and multiple orgasms are rare in men. According to Eastern belief, male orgasm, like female, is a psychosexual event that, unlike female, typically includes ejaculation, but not always. In other words, orgasm, the pleasurable sensations of the rhythmic contractions, and ejaculation, the release of semen, are separate events. Those who subscribe to this view of male sexuality say men *can* experience multiple orgasms and are far more likely to do so at midlife when they have greater control of the ejaculatory process and are able to differentiate between orgasm and ejaculation.

Stan Dale, who has a doctorate in Human Sexuality from the Institute for Advanced Study of Sexuality in San Francisco, is often credited with popularizing the concept of male multiple orgasms through his workshops and the national media attention they garnered. Dale discovered his own multiple-orgasm capability at midlife and quite by accident. He says he discovered the difference between ejaculation and orgasm when he was required to ejaculate into a small jar for the obligatory sperm-count test a month after his vasectomy. After 15 minutes of "the most unsensuous masturbation" of his life, he produced the required sample. As he was walking back to the nurse's station, he thought to himself, That was a nonorgasmic ejaculation.

This discovery led him to the study of Eastern erotic arts. The following techniques are adapted from those exotic sources.

The Techniques

1. *Three-Finger Draw.* Practiced in China for five thousand years, the three-finger draw is a simple and, according to Taoist practitioners, *effective* method for inducing multiple orgasms. Similar to the perineum massage, the three-finger draw uses three curved fingers

to apply pressure to one spot on the perineum, rather than the whole area, at the point of ejaculatory inevitability.

- Locate the pressure point midperineum, the area between the anus and the scrotum.

- Use three slightly curved fingers to apply pressure, not too light and not too hard, to the perineum point as soon as you feel ejaculation is imminent.

- Repeat as often as necessary until you can experience a nonejaculatory orgasm.

COMMENTS: From a 47-year-old man: "I recommend practicing during masturbation because it's not easy to find the right spot. After you find the spot, don't expect a miracle. This takes time and patience. After much practice, I have made it work. Was it worth the trouble? Oh, yes. Sometimes I have multiple orgasms and sometimes a single orgasm without ejaculation. Either way, I am ready for lovemaking again sooner than I am after I ejaculate. My wife loves it."

2. *The Big Draw*. This technique requires—yes, again—strong PC muscles.

- When you feel ejaculation is imminent, stop thrusting.

- Pull back to approximately one inch of penetration, but do not withdraw entirely.

- Flex the PC muscle and hold to a count of nine. Alternately, flex the PC muscle nine times in rapid succession instead of holding the count.

- Resume thrusting with shallow strokes.

- Repeat as often as necessary until you experience a nonejaculatory orgasm.

COMMENTS: From a 54-year-old man: "Mastering the art of orgasm without ejaculation separates the men from the boys. It took me several months to develop my PC muscles and make the big draw work for me, but it was time well invested. I feel erotically powerful now. I can come without ejaculating; I can come and come again and again. I am at the top of my sexual game at a point in my life where I had anticipated being on the slippery slope downward."

3. *The art of brinkmanship.* Some men train themselves to experience orgasm without ejaculation fairly easily using the art of brinkmanship: pulling back at the last possible second before ejaculation.

- Practice while masturbating.

- Continue stimulation to the point of imminent orgasm.

- Then stop. Don't resume stimulation until your arousal level has declined.

- Repeat as often as possible. With practice, you should be able to experience the contractions of orgasmic release without ejaculating.

COMMENTS: From a 50-year-old man: "When I was young, we called this coitus interruptus, and it was something you did to avoid ejaculating inside a girl so as not to make her pregnant. As a callow youth, I had so little control that I was coming by the time I sensed I was about to come. The message doesn't make it to the brain in time for the body to react. As a mature man, I have exquisite control, and I have learned to use this technique to prolong, increase, and multiply my orgasms. I really believe any man can do it; and the only thing stopping most men is ignorance."

4. *The Valley Orgasm.* According to the Taoist master Mantak Chia, who teaches workshops for men, the "peak orgasm," or male orgasm with ejaculation, is "one fleeting moment of intense, even excruciating pleasure, then nothing." On the other hand, the valley orgasm, without ejaculation, is "a continual rolling expansion of the orgasm, a greatly heightened ecstasy." To the men who experience them, the valley orgasm feels like a rolling series of orgasms without ejaculation. Here's how to experience one:

- First, make love using the nine shallow, one deep method (page 169).

- Stop thrusting when you feel near orgasm.

- Use the big draw—or the five-finger draw if you aren't the master of your PC muscles yet—to delay ejaculation.

- Hold your partner in a close, comfortable embrace.

- Continue shallow thrusting.

- Each time you feel ejaculation is imminent, use the big draw.

- You will experience the sensations of orgasm, though more diffuse, without ejaculation.

COMMENTS: From a 48-year-old man: "My wife got me involved in Tantric and Taoist sexual practices and teachings. At first, I was skeptical, but I went along to make her happy. Gradually, I realized our sex life was improving. It took me a while to master the art of having an orgasm without ejaculating, but once I did, I was in love with the concept. The valley orgasm isn't going to happen every time or even very often for a man, but when it does, it is incredible. I feel like a born-again lover."

How to Have an Extragenital Orgasm

An orgasm achieved with no genital contact is an extragenital orgasm. Fewer than 10 percent of women—and even fewer men—can reach orgasm simply from kissing passionately or by having their breasts or nipples kissed or sucked, their thighs caressed or licked, or their ears or neck nuzzled. How can it be done? Women and men who experience extragenital orgasms are able to excite themselves through erotic thoughts and fantasies to the point where any form of physical stimulation sends them over the edge into orgasm. In men, the phenomenon most frequently occurs in the "wet dream," a nocturnal orgasm and ejaculation following an erotic dream. Anywhere from 10 to 20 percent of women have also had a sleep orgasm, the female equivalent of the wet dream.

If you want to try experiencing one:

- Have a more traditional orgasm first. Some women and fewer men can experience an extragenital orgasm after they've had an orgasm through clitoral or vaginal stimulation.

- Either caress or have your partner caress your genitals until you are on the verge of another orgasm.

- Switch the stimulation to a nongenital area such as breasts or thighs.

- Alternate from genital to nongenital stimuli until you are so close to orgasm that a simple touch like running a finger down the inner thigh could induce it.

COMMENTS: From a 44-year-old woman: "I rarely have a nongenital orgasm, but when it happens it's always at the end of a prolonged and intense lovemaking session that produced multiple orgasms. The first one occurred shortly after my fortieth birthday, what a gift! There's an element of serendipity in these occasions. Much depends on how I am feeling physically, mentally, and emotionally, and how closely I am relating to my husband. When it does happen, it happens during afterplay. My husband will be holding and caressing me, perhaps massaging my breasts, and unexpectedly I am coming again."

HOW TO HAVE A SPONTANEOUS ORGASM

The ultimate no-hands solitary sex experience, a spontaneous orgasm occurs with *no* physical stimulation at all. According to limited research on the subject, a few women actually can think themselves to orgasm. In her book *Women Who Love Sex*, Gina Ogden, Ph. D., not only interviewed women who claimed to have this experience but measured their physical responses in a clinical setting and proved their claims had merit.
     How do they do it?

- First, relax. Take a bubblebath, have a glass of wine, put on some music, light candles.

- Create a lush, passionate, and emotional sexual fantasy. Really move into it.

- Breathe. Lying on your back, knees bent, feet spaced well apart, start with deep breaths. Pull your breath into your body so deeply you can feel your diaphragm expanding and can imagine air going all the way down to your genitals. When you breath out, pull that air all the way out, again imagining you are draw-ing it up through your genitals into your body.

- Pant. After a dozen or so deep breaths, pant. Breath rapidly from your belly with your mouth open.

- Now use the *fire-breathing* technique. Begin with relaxing shal-low breaths. Then breathe deeply. Inhale through the nose, exhale through the mouth. Make the breathing continuous or circular. Imagine a circle of fire beginning first as a small circle, nose through mouth, then expanding to include chest, belly, and finally genitals. Feel the erotic heat moving in a circle through-out your body as you breathe.

- Flex the PC muscles either alone or in combination with the breathing. Coordinate your flexing with deep breathing. Switch to panting, then back to deep breathing, finally to fire breath-ing—all the while flexing the PC muscles.

- If you don't have an orgasm this way, don't despair. Most people won't. But use the technique during masturbation or intercourse and see how much stronger your orgasm is.

COMMENTS: From a 52-year-old woman: "I am easily orgasmic, multiply orgasmic, capable of extended and whole body orgasms, but I couldn't make this one quite work. I could get to the point where just touching my clitoris a few times brought me to orgasm. However, I recommend the exercise, simply because it leads to an incredibly intense orgasm when you finally give up and touch yourself."

HOW TO HAVE THE ULTIMATE ORGASM: A FULL-BODY ORGASM

Sexual ecstasy, or high sex as it is known in some Tantric circles, is a way of making love that expands arousal and orgasm beyond the genitals and extends the time of orgasmic response—giving lovers both extended and whole-body orgasms. A whole-body—or total-body—orgasm is an orgasm that seems to be felt throughout the entire body. Many people experience this kind of orgasm only when they are feeling a strong emotional connection to their partners. Some can have a whole-body orgasm when they are feeling particularly sensual, sexual, or both. For most, the experience is a complex blend of emotional, sensual, and sexual elements.

The whole-body orgasm is more possible in midlife than earlier. If you want to experience one, try the following:

- Practice the techniques for extending orgasm until you are able to do so.

- Practice the techniques for spontaneous orgasm until you are able to become aroused almost to the point of orgasm through fantasy and breathing alone.

- Practice the techniques for multiple orgasms until you are able either to have them or to continue a state of arousal past orgasm.

- Combine the skills you've mastered in a lovemaking session with your partner when you are feeling very emotionally connected.

- If you do not experience a whole-body orgasm, you will almost undoubtedly have a wonderful time together.

COMMENTS: From a 53-year-old woman: "My husband and I sometimes experience whole-body orgasms, I more often than he. We have taken workshops in Tantra and put the principles to work in our lives as a whole, not just our sex lives. A whole-body orgasm occurs for me when I'm really in tune with my body and his, with my soul and his, and when I am rested and in a good emotional space. It feels like the orgasm will blow off the top of my head and push out the ends of my toes at the same time."

The point of this chapter is to encourage you to expand your orgasmic potential, not set orgasm goals or measure your "performance" against those of the people quoted here. The exercises are all worth doing, whether they result in extended, whole-body, extragenital, or multiple orgasms, or not. They will improve the quality and perhaps the quantity of the orgasms you're having now. And that, in turn, will give you physical, psychological, and emotional benefits, as well as help strengthen the intimacy bond with your partner.

Some couples still believe that the ultimate expression of sexual intimacy is the simultaneous orgasm. In films and novels that were popular when men and women over 50 were forming their sexual ideas and ideals, the lovers almost always appeared to come at the same time. Their ecstasy at the same moment left little room for alternative interpretations. Women—the consumers of more romantic fiction—particularly believed mutual climaxes were better than separate but equal ones.

In fact, the simultaneous orgasm is more serendipitous than typical. The belief that they should climax when their partners did led some women to fake an orgasm at the propitious moment, then feel secretly angry and dissatisfied afterward. In real life, men, especially when younger, reach orgasm before women do, and women are far more capable of multiple orgasms than men are. Modern lovers have adjusted the mythology to their own reality. Often the man performs cunnilingus or manual stimulation on his partner to bring her to orgasm before initiating intercourse.

Clearly, simultaneous orgasm can't, and shouldn't, be the "ideal." Some couples like to experience it occasionally because they enjoy the special intimacy that coming together brings to lovemaking. A mature couple has a much better chance of making the following technique work than a younger couple does because their response cycles are more closely matched.

With a little attention to timing and advance planning, you can make this technique work.

The Simultaneous-Orgasm Technique

1. Time your response cycles so that you know approximately how long it takes for each partner to reach orgasm during your most typical lovemaking pattern.

2. Assuming it takes her longer than it does him, let him stimulate her alone until she reaches the point where she is the same distance away from climax as he will be when stimulation begins for him.

3. Assuming it takes him longer than it does her, let her stimulate him alone, using a stop-and-start pattern of stimulation until he is approximately the same distance from orgasm as she will be when he begins stimulating her.

4. Communicate with each other. If one of you is moving faster toward climax than anticipated, say, "slow down."

IS ONE ORGASM BETTER THAN ANOTHER?

Perhaps because we are such a competitive society, men, and women too, frequently want to know if they are having the "best" possible orgasms via a particular method or at a certain point in their lives. Cultural theories about orgasm have added to confusion. Most of us are old enough to remember when the clitoral orgasm was considered inferior to the vaginal orgasm for women. That thinking was seriously challenged by the work of Dr. William Masters and Dr. Virginia Johnson in the sixties. The clitoral theory was challenged again by the G-spot proponents in the seventies. The female orgasm achieved through G-spot (vaginal, again) stimulation was deeper and more intense than the clitoral orgasm, they maintained.

When we were young, we thought the youthful orgasm was better than anything our elders might be experiencing. And now that we are the older generation, we think we have once again discovered erotic bliss of the sort another age group can't comprehend. Well, some of us do. Others pine for the golden days of their youth when the penises were hard as blue steel and the orgasms flowed like jug wine at parties.

There really is no "best" orgasm. Whether the orgasm seems to originate in one place or another makes no difference in measurable responses. A woman may not be able to have an orgasm via intercourse alone, or if she does, only by delaying penetration until she is on the brink of climax. A man may not be able to have an orgasm every time he makes love now. However and whenever they occur, orgasms are joyous events. And so is lovemaking without them.

Sizzler # **10**

COME AGAIN

Elaine was amused and a little puzzled when she discovered her husband, George, immersed in a book with a distinctly New Age title and cover illustration. Was this a harbinger of midlife crisis? Curious, she picked up the book to see what was inside as soon as he was out of the room.

"Tantra?" she asked when he returned with a fresh cup of coffee. "Isn't that some kind of Eastern religion?"

"More like sacred sexuality," George said. He took the book from her hand, flipped a few pages, and read out loud an excerpt from a chapter on orgasms. Looking up from his page, he noted how closely she was paying attention and grinned. "Shall I read further?"

"Oh, please," she said, patting the sofa cushion beside her. "And get comfortable while you do."

Like many Western readers of Eastern philosophy, George and Elaine paged past the sections pertaining to spiritual development and went straight for the sex advice. He, she was surprised to discover, had purchased the book because he wanted to improve the quality of his orgasms. The nagging feeling that they once were, and could be again, "better" kept him from fully enjoying lovemaking in what they both jokingly referred to as their "golden" years.

"My orgasms are better than they were when I was young," she retorted. "I don't know what's wrong with yours."

"Maybe they are," he said. "But wouldn't you like them to be still better?"

Heads touching, they read. The language wasn't erotic, yet they were both aroused. Could they use the techniques described to prolong George's arousal phase and delay his orgasm? Could Elaine have multiple orgasms on a frequent basis?

"What have we got to lose?" George asked; and Elaine acknowledged they had nothing to lose and much to gain.

They began "orgasm training" as they laughingly called it together. That training consisted of Kegels and other physical as well as breathing exercises—activities they could have done separately as well as together. When they were able to influence their orgasms by using their newly strengthened musculature and breath control, they added some new techniques. Soon Elaine was having multiple orgasms whenever she wanted them. More surprising, George experienced his first set of multiples too. When it happened, they were both surprised and delighted.

Elaine particularly enjoyed one part of the "training." Helping him delay orgasm. That prolonged lovemaking, turning sex into a leisurely experience that made her feel wanton and pampered. She had to be closely attuned to his arousal level to help him prolong the intensity he craved by varying or abruptly stopping stimuli during intercourse, and she grew deft at gently squeezing the head of his penis to stop ejaculation.

She played with his penis as she'd done when they were young lovers, but with greater assurance. Together they could control this magical organ in new and wonderful ways. Frequently they made love with the caveat that George could not come. Elaine could have as many orgasms as she wanted. After a session or two of nonorgasmic lovemaking, he was desirous of release, and even she could feel his ejaculation was stronger inside her than it had been for decades.

"I want to come," he told her on a rainy Sunday afternoon. They were lying in bed, reading. She allowed him to arouse and satisfy her, before she said, "No, you can't come today. I think you should wait another day or two." He was exasperated, but she remained firm. "As your orgasm coach," she said, "I think it's time to push your training up a notch."

A few days later he initiated sex. "I'm coming this time," he said, and she replied, "We'll see." Concentrating more on his pleasure than her own, she repeatedly brought him to the brink of orgasm, then helped him hold back until he couldn't restrain himself.

She felt him inside her, his penis throbbing in the familiar rhythm, with each jolt more intense. But he did not ejaculate. Gasping, he told her, "I came, but I didn't come!" He pulled his penis from her vagina. It was slick with her juices, none of his own, and erect. She guided him back inside. Within seconds, he was coming again. He experienced several orgasms before finally ejaculating explosively.

"Thanks, coach," he whispered when he could talk.

11

SEX AND HORMONES

"After I developed the first symptoms of menopause, hot flashes and night sweats, I was inundated with advice from family and friends on whether or not to ask my doctor for hormone-replacement therapy," says Jill, 52. "Everyone had a position, and they sent me books, newspaper, and magazine articles backing their position. I was in a quandary. Finally, my husband suggested I talk to my doctor, a woman I trust, and ask her *advice*, rather than asking her for medication. He rather gently added: 'Tell her you aren't interested in making love anymore, and see if she thinks there is a hormonal link.'

"My doctor said there very well could be a hormonal link to my lack of interest in lovemaking, but it could also be caused by other factors, including relationship issues, my own attitudes about aging, any number of things. As for the hormones, she said she never just writes a prescription for them. She orders blood tests. If the blood tests show the estrogen is very low and there are no medical reasons for not doing so, she puts the patient on hormone-replacement therapy, HRT, and monitors the progress. She gave me reading material to take home.

"The tests showed my estrogen level was very low. I went on HRT. The hot flashes, night sweats, and low libido disappeared. I'm not saying that HRT is a sexual panacea, but it was what I needed. Women should make informed choices, based on their own research and their medical doctor's opinion, and not be influenced by others."

HOW HORMONES AFFECT SEXUALITY

Controversy surrounds both testosterone replacement for men, and increasingly women, and especially hormone replacement (estrogen or a combination of estrogen/progesterone) for women. This chapter examines only the effects of hormones on sexuality. It will present the options without endorsing one particular approach. To make an informed decision about taking hormones, you need to consult your medical doctors and take into consideration the available research, constantly being updated, on side effects and health benefits as well as sexual benefits. An article you read two years ago may be out of date by now.

In general, it's wise to view with a critical eye any authority who takes an extreme position, saying in this case either hormones should never be prescribed or conversely that they are always the answer. It's also smart not to trust a doctor or therapist who sees you in only physical or psychological terms. Especially at midlife, the answers to our questions seldom lie in one area alone. Hormones are one part of the physical component. It is wise to seek out a health practitioner who knows your history and will follow your progress as you age.

Two hormones directly affect sexual desire and performance. As men and women age, they produce lesser amounts of these sex hormones. In men, the decline of testosterone is a very gradual process. Beginning in young adulthood, a man's testosterone levels begin to fall gradually, dropping to about a third to a half of their peak by the age of 80. In women, menopause at an average age of 51 precipitates a dramatic decline in levels of estrogen and progesterone, but has far less impact on her production of testosterone, the male hormone responsible for sex drive also present in smaller amounts in women. The effects of hormones on sexual desire and performance follow.

In Women

Estrogen

- When the amount of estrogen drops, so does the growth of new cells in the vagina, resulting in thinner vaginal walls. That can lead to irritation, even tearing, during intercourse. In addition, the vagina may become less elastic, and the vaginal lips lose some of their firmness, perhaps contributing to some discomfort or self-consciousness during lovemaking.

- Since estrogen promotes vaginal lubrication in addition to stimulating cell growth, a lack of the hormone leads to vaginal dryness. Again, that can make intercourse painful.

- Estrogen promotes blood flow through the arteries. Declining estrogen levels also means the flow of blood to the vagina may decline. When that happens, the vagina doesn't become as engorged with blood as it did, decreasing vaginal sensitivity. For some women, that may lessen the pleasure of intercourse.

- Low estrogen levels can also cause a change in touch perception in some women. Nerve endings may be affected. It may take longer for a woman to become aroused or reach orgasm.

Progesterone

In combination with estrogen, progesterone regulates the menstrual cycle. It prevents cells of the uterine lining from growing in a disorderly fashion, causing them to slough off at a certain point in the cycle. In HRT, the two are often used together, but progesterone alone has little if any impact upon sexuality.

Testosterone

On the plus side, many women find their interest in sex increases when estrogen levels drop because the ratio of testosterone to female hormones is now greater, creating a stronger sex drive. Some women's sex drive is unchanged by menopause. Only about 30 percent of women actually report a significant decline in libido associated with menopause. For those women, hormone-replacement therapy is a valid treatment unless contraindicated.

In Men

Testosterone

- The surge of testosterone at puberty is responsible for the development of such male characteristics as beard and body hair, a muscular physique, and the genitals.

- Throughout a man's life, testosterone fuels the sex drive, or libido.

- Testosterone also affects sexual potency, which includes quality of erection and erectile endurance.

- *But*, the good news for men is that testosterone decline doesn't have the same impact on their sexuality as estrogen loss does on a woman's. For most men in good health, testosterone levels, though lower, remain adequate for sexual functioning into old age.

Conquering Common Hormone-Related Sex Problems

"When my wife's interest in lovemaking declined at menopause," says Curt, 54, "it never occurred to me that there might be a hormonal reason for it. I thought she was going through a psychological crisis about aging. To me, menopause was a woman's midlife crisis. For her part, she was too embarrassed to talk to her doctor about the problems we were having in bed though she knew they had a physical basis, and I didn't.

"She had been avoiding sex because intercourse, even with a lubricant, was painful. After her doctor put her on HRT for other reasons, our sex life improved. She told me then she'd been suffering pain, but the pain was gone. I insisted she mention it to the doctor because I was concerned the pain would come back. The doctor said her vagina had been showing signs of atrophy, which was corrected by HRT.

"We were lucky. This is how people give up on sex. They are too embarrassed to talk openly to each other or even to their doctors about their problems. So the woman suffers in silence until she withdraws sexually, which the man accepts as the nature of life."

Some people do experience sex problems associated with hormone loss. According to one survey, 14 percent of women reported fewer orgasms after menopause and 16 percent had some pain or discomfort during intercourse. In another report about a third of women over 65 found intercourse painful because of changes that have occurred in size, firmness, and lubrication of the vagina. After a doctor has performed a vaginal examination and had blood tests done to determine estrogen levels, he or she can make a diagnosis of hormone deficiency in a woman with some confidence. Determining whether men's reported problems can be attributed to testosterone loss is less clearcut. (See Chapter 12 on impotence.)

These are the sex problems associated with hormone loss with suggestions for treating them:

Vaginal Dryness

Some women have almost no diminishment of lubricating ability, especially if they are thoroughly aroused, while others have significant problems with dryness. Vaginal dryness is a signal a woman and her partner can easily misread. Because they are accustomed to measuring her arousal level by the amount of her secretions, they may equate dryness with lack of desire. A simple misunderstanding can cause both of them to pull back from initiating sexual contact.

How to Handle: There are several ways of dealing with dryness. They include:

- Use of the simple remedy, K-Y jelly or another water-soluble lubricant. Replens is a lubricant that can be used daily, not just in preparation for intercourse, to nourish and maintain the vaginal area. Often this is the only treatment necessary.

- More frequent sexual activity, which helps regulate estrogen levels and promote greater production of estrogen even in menopausal women.

- Add more soy products to your diet. (See following)

- Avoid as much as possible substances that dry your membranes, such as antihistamines, diuretics, alcohol, and caffeine. They also dry the lining of the vagina. Drink eight glasses of water a day.

- Use an estrogen cream. You can purchase a natural, plant-based estrogen cream, OstaDerm-V, made by an Oregon company and found in many health-food stores, in conjunction, or not, with a natural progesterone cream. Or your doctor may recommend a transdermal estrogen formula, which contains a much smaller dosage of estrogen than is contained in pills or even patches.

- Or, *if other symptoms indicate its use*, HRT will likely solve the problem.

COMMENTS: "Vaginal dryness made me feel old," says Kate, 52. "It was like the wrinkles on my forehead. It got to me. I knew the problem could be solved with K-Y jelly, and I knew younger women often need to use lubrication, too. Logic didn't help. I had never needed additional lubrication; and now suddenly I did, and I felt old.

"My doctor suggested Replens, a lubricant I could use on a regular basis, not as a preparation for intercourse. That made all the difference for me. If I could consider it an addition to my beauty routine, like alphahydroxy lotions and sunscreen, I could live with it. Pulling out a tube before intercourse was too humiliating. We all have to do it our way, don't we?"

Vaginal Atrophy

"Vaginal atrophy" is the name for the condition of the aging vagina with thinning walls, which has shrunk in size and lost its elasticity and firmness. Typically, there is some narrowing of the vaginal opening and shortening of the vaginal canal. One woman who suffered from atrophy before taking corrective measures (which in her case included masturbation with a dildo, natural estrogen creams, and Replens, not HRT) described it as "feeling shriveled and dried up."

HOW TO HANDLE:

- *Enjoy more frequent sexual activity.* The best prevention of vaginal atrophy is an active sex life. If you haven't been sexually active for a while, you can restore the vagina through some of the suggestions listed earlier under vaginal dryness, a related condition, and those to follow.

- *Masturbate.* If you don't have a partner or aren't having regular relations with your partner, use a penis-shaped vibrator or dildo (available in sex-toy shops or through mail-order catalogues) to get your vagina back into shape.

- *Consider HRT, if other symptoms indicate its use.*

- *Do Kegel exercises.* Kegels strengthen and tone the vaginal muscles. Doctors recommend them for use after childbirth because of their restorative powers.

- *Use an estrogen cream as previously suggested.* In addition to promoting vaginal lubrication, these creams can thicken tissues. Follow directions on labels or consult your physician.

- *Use vitamin-E oil or cream or supplements taken by mouth.* Some evidence indicates that vitamin E may be beneficial in reducing the symptoms of vaginal atrophy. Again, consult your doctor.

- *Eat more soy products.* Soybeans contain phytoestrogens, which have been shown to rebuild and moisturize thinning vaginal walls. Soy flour, soy milk, tofu, and many other soy products can be found in most health-food stores. A cautionary note: Read labels. You may need to consume more soy products than is palatable to attain the benefits.

COMMENTS: From a 60-year-old woman: "I went for five years without a sex partner after my husband died. I had been on HRT for five years when my doctor decided it was no longer necessary. She gave me dietary recommendations and advised the regular use of estrogen creams and lubricants as well as the continued practice of Kegels. On my own, I figured out that masturbating with a vibrator to simulate intercourse would help. When I met a man and became sexually active with him, I had no problems. If I hadn't kept my vagina in shape, I would have had. I know other women in my age group who've been through similar dry spells and experienced pain, even bleeding, during intercourse because they hadn't kept in shape."

Loss of Sensation

Some women don't respond to genital touch in the same way as a result of low estrogen, which causes diminished blood flow to the area. Often there is only a small degree of change in sensation. A woman can compensate for that by asking her partner for a firmer or more extended touch. Women who experience significant loss of sensation should consult a doctor for advice.

HOW TO HANDLE:

- If this is your only sex problem caused by low estrogen levels, consider changing your lovemaking style to include more vigorous thrusting, more active foreplay.
- Follow the aforementioned guidelines.

COMMENTS: From a 50-year-old woman: "I realized I wasn't responding to touch in quite the same way about the same time I began having some of the minor symptoms of menopause. I didn't connect the touch issue with the other stuff. I thought my husband didn't excite me as much as he once did because we'd been together so long. With my doctor's approval, I wanted to try handling my hormone situation naturally. It didn't quite work for me, and she put me on HRT, with the proviso that we would evaluate every six months whether I would stay on or go off. Almost immediately I felt the difference. We were making love, and I realized I experienced his touch in the same way I once had. I was more quickly aroused, and my orgasms came more easily. Women need to hear about the sex benefits of boosting estrogen. We get a lot of the other information, but not this."

Loss of Libido

There can be many reasons for loss of libido. Low estrogen is one of them. If you're suddenly less interested or completely disinterested in lovemaking, have your estrogen levels checked before you assume the cause is rooted in the relationship. Your libido may be a temporary casualty of hormonal imbalance, nothing more.

How to Handle:

- If testing shows your estrogen levels are low, see all the afore-mentioned suggestions under "vaginal dryness," "vaginal atrophy," and "loss of sensation."

- And if estrogen is not the culprit, examine your attitudes about aging, your lifestyle, and your relationship. The problem lies in one of these areas; and the solutions are elsewhere in this book.

Comments: From a 50-year-old woman: "I did experience the classic hormone-related loss of libido. My husband and I had the classic response: We blamed the marriage, not hormone loss. We went to see a marriage counselor, who never said a word about physical causes. He didn't suggest we have medical evaluations as a prelude to therapy. Ironically, an article on HRT that I read in a magazine in his waiting room alerted us to the possibility there might be a simple physical cause for my lack of interest in sex. I made an appointment with my doctor. Tests showed my estrogen level was way low. I went on HRT, and my interest in sex returned. Now I tell everyone: Don't trust a therapist who doesn't want a medical evaluation before she or he starts taking your marriage apart."

Evaluating Hormone-Replacement Therapy

There are arguments for and against HRT. Proponents cite its positive effect on preventing osteoporosis, the loss of bone density in women that leads to stooped shoulders and fragile bones in old age, and protecting against heart disease. Antagonists say that estrogen increases the risks of breast cancer, a claim that has been challenged, particularly with the development of "designer" estrogens, refined versions of estrogen targeted exactly to the physical needs of the patient. Recently, a large study involving 2,800 women in a randomized treatment/control group questioned the heart disease protection of estrogen. A larger study is underway. Again, each woman has to make her own decision about HRT with the help of her doctors.

The Sex Benefits

The HRT debate has been narrowly focused on the breast-cancer versus heart-disease issue, but there are real and important sex benefits to be derived from the therapy. Depending on a woman's needs and her lifestyle, many of these benefits can also be gained through other means, including the previously mentioned suggestions and those that follow.

- For some women, cessation of hot flashes and night sweats is a sex benefit. They may have been avoiding sexual contact because they couldn't predict when a hot flash would make them feel uncomfortable and unattractive.

- With HRT, the vagina becomes more elastic, the walls thicken, and natural lubrication returns, making intercourse more comfortable.

- Blood flow to the genitals during arousal is increased, creating stronger sensations during lovemaking.

- Nerve endings become more sensitive, restoring the familiar sense of touch in the genital area.

COMMENTS: "There is an active school of thought now telling us that menopause is a natural event and shouldn't be medicalized," says Noreen, 51, an OB-GYN nurse who is on HRT. "These are the same people who said childbirth is a natural event and shouldn't be medicalized. I have assisted women in giving birth for more than 25 years. I've watched women go through agonizing labors for hours on end without so much as a painkiller because they thought they had to give birth 'naturally'; and I've assisted other women who turned to pharmaceutical help as needed. When it was over, there was a healthy mother, a healthy infant, because, when something did go wrong, painkillers were not the cause of it. Why did one mother have to endure so much pain to get there? Why is it women are the gender who are supposed to endure every suffering 'naturally'? Who tells men not to take a painkiller when they're in pain? Who would dare tell men to suffer the irritations and miseries of menopause without help if they went through the kind of sudden testosterone withdrawal that we go through in estrogen withdrawal? HRT makes it possible for me to enjoy life, enjoy sex more than I have in a long time. And by the way, when I gave birth, I had a little help from some drugs."

And from Carolyn, also 51: "My doctor told me that not all women need HRT. A lot depends on whether you have slightly low or very low estrogen levels, your bone density, and your lifestyle. I had slightly low estrogen levels. That had no noticeable effect on my sexuality. I was able to use natural supplements (see the following) combined with weight training exercises to bring up my estrogen level. If I'd needed HRT, I would have taken it, and I think women who need it for sexual functioning should consider that as important as other needs. But if all you require is a slight boost, why do it with drugs when you can do it naturally?"

The Mitigating Factors

Your doctor may advise against estrogen if you have certain risk factors. Be sure you include any of the following in a medical history:

- Abnormal or unexplained vaginal bleeding
- Liver disease
- Sickle-cell anemia
- History of embolism, heart attack, or stroke
- History of breast or uterine cancer
- Fibroid tumors
- A heavy smoking habit

The Side Effects

Some women experience side effects with HRT. Caused by a deficiency of B vitamins, they include:

- Fatigue
- Depression
- Mood swings
- Loss of libido

Adding a B-vitamin supplement to your diet should clear up the side effects. But, if you're taking HRT and experience a loss of libido, talk to your doctor about it. Rule out medical problems. Then look for the emotional and psychological reasons that may be the underlying reasons for lack of interest in sex.

WEIGHING THE ALTERNATIVES TO HRT

Your doctor is the best source of information for alternatives targeted to specific medical conditions, such as bone density. If HRT is not an option for you for any reason, use the aforementioned suggestions for other ways of getting the sexual benefits of estrogen. In addition, investigate herbal remedies. Rather than asking a health-store employee for guidance, which could prove costly, do some research before shopping. When in doubt, check with your doctor. Some herbal remedies have serious side effects when taken in large doses or in combination with medication, alcohol, or certain foods. Unlike drugs, herbal and other "natural" remedies aren't controlled by the FDA. One manufacturer might be reputable and another not. Last, read the fine print. Not all menopausal remedies provide sex benefits. Chasteberry, for example, is said to reduce libido.

Herbs that *may* be helpful in relieving hot flashes, vaginal dryness and atrophy, and decreased libido include:

• *Black cohosh.* Available in capsules, tablets, drops, and powders, black cohosh has been available under a reliable brand name Remifemin in Europe for decades and in the United States since 1996. Remifemin has been approved for the relief of menopausal symptoms by Germany's Commission E—their version of the FDA—in 40-milligram-a-day doses. More expensive than HRT, Remifemin doesn't take effect for three or four weeks after the initial dosage. Side effects may include nausea.

• *Ginseng.* An effective stimulant, ginseng is reputed to improve sexual functioning during menopause by boosting energy and overall sense of well-being, thus stimulating libido. The research on Ginseng has been conducted primarily in Europe and is very promising. Ginseng is an ingredient in some health-food-store menopause remedies. The chief side effects, occurring in a small percentage of people, are restlessness and sleep disruption.

• *Licorice root.* Containing high levels of phytoestrogens, compounds that act like weak estrogens in some parts of the body, licorice root would seem to be nature's own HRT. Unfortunately, there are reported side effects associated with regular use of the herb. It can raise blood pressure and lower potassium in some people. Don't use it without consulting a doctor who is knowledgeable about herbs.

Many people who shop in health food stores are under the false impression that "natural" is always safer and better. That's not necessarily true. Because so many of the products in these stores aren't regulated by the FDA, you have to use more, not less, caution when shopping. You may be paying more money for an HRT alternative that puts you at greater risk than estrogen would. Read labels. Buy trusted brands. And do your own research.

TESTOSTERONE-REPLACEMENT THERAPY

"I just didn't feel sexy anymore," says Carole, 53, describing the state of her libido only a year ago. "I had sailed through menopause without problems. My marriage was in good shape, no problems at work, no problems with the kids, my parents, or his family. I'd stopped having sexual fantasies and wouldn't have thought about sex at all if it weren't for my husband who was still thinking about it. Medical tests turned up no reason for me to feel the way I did.

"My doctor said, 'There's a controversial new treatment. I'd like to try it on you. Have you heard about testosterone-replacement therapy for women?' I had visions of me growing a beard, talking in a low growl, and losing my breasts. She laughed. I thought, What have I got to lose? I didn't tell my husband exactly what it was. I just said, 'a little hormone.' No point in scaring him.

"That little pill put my sex drive back in gear. I couldn't believe the difference it made in my life, almost overnight. It's rejuvenated our marriage. We're planning a second honeymoon. My husband couldn't be more delighted, though he still doesn't know my little hormone is the same one fueling him."

Sexual desire is only partly biologically driven, of course, but testosterone, "the hormone of desire," is the primary biological component, fueling the sexual engines of both men and women. In women, it is produced in the ovaries and adrenal glands and in trace amounts in the uterus. The woman's total testosterone production is less than one-twentieth of the average man's of the same age. For most women, the slight decrease in testosterone production accompanying menopause does not create a libido problem. As noted earlier, some women report stronger sex drives after menopause when the ratio of testosterone to estrogen is higher than it was. But for a significant minority of women like Carole, a low testosterone level seems to be the cause of libido loss.

British studies have shown that the addition of testosterone to estrogen-replacement therapy is more effective than estrogen alone in boosting libido, particularly in women who have undergone a total hysterectomy, including removal of the ovaries. Testosterone is no more a libido wonder drug than estrogen is for women who have lost interest in sex because of psychological, emotional, or relationship issues. In fact, British studies have shown that 50 percent of women who take testosterone report no increase in sexual desire. Because testosterone is relatively new in the United States, no significant body of research exists.

Will testosterone therapy increase your sex drive? If you can trace loss of libido to the beginning of menopause, maybe. Blood tests can determine if estrogen levels are within the normal range. Testosterone is more difficult to measure, because amounts vary widely from one woman to another. One woman's low may be another woman's adequate to high. It's unlikely you will be given testosterone unless you are or have been on HRT anyway. Testosterone isn't the first sex hormone of choice for doctors; they'll try estrogen replacement first. Make the libido-loss timeline clear when you discuss the problem.

WHAT WOMEN CAN EXPECT FROM TESTOSTERONE-REPLACEMENT THERAPY

If your doctor prescribes testosterone-replacement therapy:

- Your cholesterol levels should be checked first and monitored regularly during treatment. Testosterone can decrease HDL (good) cholesterol levels.

- Dosage may be given in pill, injection, subcutaneous implants of small pellets, or transdermal patches. Generally, patch users report fewer side effects and better results.

- You will have to keep your doctor informed about whether or not the therapy is boosting your libido. If it works, you can probably continue indefinitely.

- You may experience a few unpleasant side effects, such as oily skin or acne, unwanted facial hair, and in rare cases, a lowering of the voice.

- And you may enjoy an unexpected bonus, increased clitoral sensitivity.

TESTOSTERONE-REPLACEMENT THERAPY FOR MEN

"My testosterone level was in the low-normal range; and my sex drive was below normal," says Ted, 56. "My doctor prescribed testosterone replacement with the warning that it might not have much effect. It did. The additional hormone in my system was like a libido jump-start, all I needed to get me going. Once I regained interest in sex, I started making love to my wife more often. The sex got better, and my interest grew.

"My wife and I are back in sexual sync now. We both give a lot of credit to testosterone replacement. If you need a little push, get the push. Don't be proud."

Testosterone plays a major role in a man's desire, arousal, and ability to get an erection and ejaculate. The hormone is produced in the testes, and production begins declining at midlife. Many factors influence sexual response and performance in addition to hormones. How a man feels about his partner and other emotional and psychological issues become increasingly important (at the same time testosterone production slows down). Variety, frequency, and the quality of love-making skills, both the man's and his partner's, impact desire. Blood supply to the penis—affected by blocked blood vessels or nerve damage caused by smoking, drinking, medications, and some illnesses—also influences arousal and performance. Testosterone is an important part of male sexuality, but not the whole story.

Can testosterone replacement reverse the effects of flagging libido, erection disorders, even impotence? The male testosterone pill is not a magic cure either. A lack of good research data led doctors to prescribe testosterone indiscriminately to any man with an erection problem when the pill was first available, with largely disappointing results. Replacement therapy is now more likely to be prescribed for a man in his sixties or seventies than in his forties. Most doctors won't automatically prescribe it for impotence or erection problems unless the man also has low a testosterone level. Otherwise, the treatment won't restore potency. Only a minority of impotent men have a true testosterone deficiency.

WHAT A MAN CAN EXPECT FROM TESTOSTERONE TREATMENT

If your doctor prescribes testosterone replacement:

- The hormone may be given in conjunction with other erection-improving medications.

- You may be given the hormone in pill or tablet form or via injection or patch. The injection should last a minimum of two to three weeks and in many men, a month. Some people learn to administer them at home.

- After treatment, you should notice improvement in your erection within two weeks. The level of desire may increase sooner than that. (Or, conversely, you may see minimal to no benefits.)

- Remember that increased libido does not necessarily lead to improved sexual performance or increased pleasure.

- Side effects may include water retention, high blood pressure, or headaches, and, less often, enlarged prostate.

Both men and women should view hormone-replacement therapy as one of the options available to them for increasing desire and improving sexual performance and satisfaction. Neither a panacea nor a medical evil, hormones may or may not provide sexual benefits for you. Be an informed consumer; and keep your doctor informed of their effects while in treatment.

Sizzler # 11

YOUNGER LOVE

One lovely spring morning Emily realized she had metamorphosed into a woman of a certain age. Clamping a wide-brimmed straw hat onto her head, she walked out into her garden where the daffodils and tulips were in bloom. She took deep breathes of the soft fresh air. In her mind's eye, she could see herself as she moved, walked, breathed. Not long ago she would have seen a younger, more buoyant version of Emily in her mind's eye. The hat would have symbolized romance, the tulips possibility.

Now the woman she saw was matronly, one of the older characters in a Jane Austen novel. She had been feeling older than her 52 years for many months. And now she looked older too.

"Emily!" her husband Alex called from the house. "I'm leaving now. See you tonight!"

See you tonight. Raising her arm to wave at him, she remembered when the words "see you tonight" conjured erotic visions. She sat on a garden chair and surveyed her domain. The tender young leaves on the rosebushes taunted her. They were yellow roses, once her favorite flower. How long had it been since she'd brought bouquets of roses into the bedroom, even sprinkled rose petals on the bed, in anticipation of Alex's making love to her?

Sighing, she made a mental list of the day's obligations. First, she had a doctor's appointment. Routine check-up. And from there, to the supermarket.

Fast forward four weeks. Emily, straw hat at a rakish angle, dashed into the pharmacy to pick up a refill of her HRT prescriptions. She engaged in mildly flirtatious banter with the pharmacist, who'd been a classmate of hers in high school. From there, she ran a series of errands, arriving home in time to clip the first yellow roses in anticipation of the evening ahead.

Alex came into the kitchen as she was arranging the flowers in vases, one for the dining-room table, another for the night table on her side of the bed. He nuzzled her neck. Her heart beat faster. She turned in his arms and lightly brushed her lips with his.

"We're having your favorite dinner," she said huskily.

"As long as I'm having my favorite dessert," he responded, "anything is my favorite dinner."

They had cocktails on the patio. She kicked off her shoes, reached across the space between them with her leg, and ran her foot up and down his inner thigh. He captured her foot in his hands and held it against his crotch as he massaged her instep. Sighing, she closed her eyes and leaned her head back. The breeze lifted the ends of her hair. She felt her nipples harden.

Their foreplay continued over a candlelight dinner. While feeding her a spoon of lobster bisque, he spilled a drop on her neck. He licked it off. Later, as she served him chicken and rice, she grazed his back with her breasts. By the time they walked hand in hand to the bedroom, both were glassy-eyed with desire.

Slowly, they helped each other undress while embracing and kissing inside the bedroom door. By the light of two dozen votive candles, they lay down together, the scent of yellow roses wafting over them. He took her in his arms; and she thrilled to his touch.

In a full-body embrace, they kissed deeply until she felt his penis stir against her. She reached down, took it in her hand, and held it firmly. He responded by putting his hand to her genitals. She was wet already.

"Oh, Emily," he whispered.

Her desire ignited his. Eagerly his tongue explored her mouth as his fingers sought out her clitoris. As her breathing grew harder, so did his. She moved her body against his hand. Everything fell away. The room, the bed, the reality of their lives all disappeared until there was nothing but Alex doing wonderful things to her body and the scent of roses in her nostrils.

Guiding her hips, he pulled her over on top of him. She mounted him easily. Her wet swollen vagina embraced him. They made love, love the way they had made it before the long dry spell.

Emily was no longer a woman of a certain age. She was young again.

OVERCOMING IMPOTENCE

"I thought I was becoming impotent two years into my second marriage," says Alan, 56. "I panicked. Four years after I lost my first wife to cancer, I married Dee. In the early days of our relationship, I had erections and enjoyed the lovemaking tremendously. Then sometimes I wouldn't be able to get an erection or sustain it through intercourse. Dee was very understanding. She said I was pressuring myself to be a great lover for her and I should relax. I didn't tell her how frightened I was about becoming impotent, but I made an appointment with a therapist.

"We talked through my performance problems. He said I was applying very strict standards to measuring my erections. True, I wasn't getting many spontaneous erections, but that, he said, was a natural change accompanying aging. I needed stimulation to get erect, and, of course, I'd been embarrassed to ask Dee to stimulate me to erection. I thought I had to be erect when I approached her. And I wasn't really 'losing' an erection during intercourse either. Sometimes

I don't need to have an orgasm. I can sustain intercourse for quite a while, long enough to satisfy Dee. Then my erection subsides.

"Once I understood what was happening, I stopped worrying. I ask Dee to get me hard; and she's very enthusiastic about doing that. If I hadn't talked to a therapist, I might have worried myself into becoming impotent."

By the time they are 40 years old, 90 percent of men have experienced at least one erectile failure. This is a normal occurrence, but many men "panic" at the first sign of erectile problems. Now they are likely to run to a urologist and ask for the highly publicized impotence pill, which they may not need and may or may not find effective. Being in a new marriage at midlife might have intensified Alan's responses to his perceived erotic failures. He could have been experiencing some guilt about having a second lease on sex life with another woman following his first wife's tragic death. On the other hand, the very newness of his relationship with Dee probably inspired a level of sexual performance he wasn't able to sustain. Isn't that true of new lovers at any age? These circumstances combined with his lack of knowledge about the sexual aging process to set him up for performance problems. That might have led his wife to blame herself for his lack of interest in making love and caused her to withdraw from attempts to initiate sex. If he hadn't received good advice and reassurance from someone he trusted, Alan might have "worried himself into impotence."

WHAT IMPOTENCE IS—AND ISN'T

Impotence is the chronic or ongoing failure to get or sustain an erection. A man at any age can fail to achieve a desired erection or lose an erection during lovemaking. In youth, the situation is embarrassing, maybe confusing. Most men, however, know that the occasional erectile problem is typically linked to fatigue, overconsumption of food or drink, or a relationship issue. At midlife, a man may read a lot more into a bout of impotence. He may see his future in a failed erection. How he and his partner handle these occurrences helps determine how frequent they will be.

These common changes in sexual response at midlife aren't indicators of impotence:

- A man probably needs direct penile stimulation to have an erection, and he may no longer be able to get an erection just from thinking about sex or seeing his partner in an alluring pose.

- It may take him longer to achieve erection.

- He may require more time for ejaculation and may not need to ejaculate every time he has intercourse. After a period of intercourse, he may find his erection subsides. After ejaculation, he also may find his erection subsides more quickly than it did.

- His erection probably won't be as hard as it was when he was a teenager.

- The refractory period, the recovery time between ejaculations, will be longer.

The changes are gradual, and you shouldn't be frightened by them. Changing response patterns enable a man to be a better lover than he was because he is now responding at a pace more similar to his partner's. Lack of knowledge and refusal to accept the aging process as an erotic opportunity can prevent him from seizing the sexual moment. Anxiety also plays a major role in creating an impotence dynamic. If a man misinterprets his responses and becomes anxious about his potency, he will be tense and fearful about lovemaking and convey those negative attitudes to his partner.

Some men do experience erection difficulties that are more serious than the normal changes associated with aging. Psychological factors ranging from performance and stress issues to intimacy conflicts can contribute to erection disorders. Physical problems can also cause impotence. Illnesses such as diabetes, vascular disease, urological or neurological conditions, and others, can lead to impotence. Heavy smokers and drinkers may suffer extensive damage to the small blood vessels in the penis, again leading to impotence. For some men, impotence stems from a combination of physical and psychological factors. They need to be treated from a multidisciplinary health-care perspective, with a therapist and medical doctors involved. Injections or pills alone won't solve their problem.

If you have concerns about erections, the following questions will help determine whether or not you have a problem and if that problem is physical, psychological, or a combination of the two.

THE SEXUAL-RESPONSE ASSESSMENT

1. *Do you have an erection at least once a week when you wake up in the morning?*

The answer to this question is important because it influences whether your problem is psychological or physical. In one investigation conducted at the University of Chicago Sexual Dysfunction Clinic, 32 men who said they were impotent were asked about morning erections. They were also given a thorough urologic exam, including specialized tests designed to evaluate erection disorders. Eighty-six percent of the men whose exams indicated psychogenic impotence reported having morning erections. In contrast, 100 percent of men who were found to have an organic basis for impotence did not have morning erections.

If you have morning erections, your problem is most likely psychogenic in nature and will respond to therapy.

If you don't have morning (or nocturnal) erections very often, or not at all, or if those erections are very soft, more a swelling than an erection, you may likely have a physical impairment to erection.

2. *Are you able to get an erection firm enough for intercourse under some circumstances, for example during masturbation or with a different partner?*

There are "situational-" and "global"-erection disorders. A man with a situational disorder can get an erection in some circumstances but not in others, for example with one partner but not another, or during masturbation but not with a regular partner. If you are able to stimulate yourself to erection, you are probably capable of having an erection with your partner. Erection difficulties are likely psychogenic in origin in these cases. For the most part, physical conditions don't discriminate. If you have a physical problem, you will probably be unable to get an erection in any situation. In medical terms, you have a global-erection disorder.

3. *Did something in particular happen that seems to have triggered your erection difficulties?*

If your erection difficulties started with the beginning of a new job, moving, retirement, loss of a loved one, or any similar emotional upheaval, the problem may be a response to stress. Should the difficulty persist several months beyond the event, you may be caught in a self-perpetuating cycle of erectile failure. Stress leads to erection failure. The episode of impotence creates anxiety, which leads to another failure, and so on. Anxiety and the anticipation of failure interfere with sexual responsiveness.

4. *Do you get a firm erection but usually lose it when you attempt to penetrate for intercourse?*

If you are getting sufficient stimulation, that loss of firmness may signal a slowly developing physical problem. Poor diet, sedentary lifestyle, heavy smoking or drinking, and other behaviors may be catching up with you. But the abrupt loss of a firm erection upon penetration may also indicate a psychological conflict. If this happens frequently, have a urological exam to eliminate physical causes before you begin looking at personal and relationship issues. Gradually losing your erection after several minutes of intercourse is not a cause for concern. You may be tired. Or you may need to vary the sexual routine.

5. *Can you feel mentally aroused even if you have trouble with erections?*

Almost every man has had some period in his life when he didn't feel his normal desire for sex. In most cases, this is temporary, and desire soon returns. When loss of desire persists, look for an underlying physical or psychological cause. If you suddenly realize that you have lost all interest in sex or that your frequency has dropped dramatically, there may well be something wrong.

These questions can help you evaluate your situation and determine if the problem is more physical or psychological. They can also be used as talking points to open a discussion with your partner. Your erection problems affect her too.

If your erectile difficulties are minor—typical age-related situations—you can make some lifestyle and other changes that may lead to stronger erections and fewer episodes of erectile failure.

SEVEN WAYS OF PREVENTING IMPOTENCE

You can probably improve the quality of your erections, extend their longevity, and minimize the possibilities of losing an erection during lovemaking by adopting the following suggestions:

1. *Eat a low fat diet and exercise regularly.* The following chapter will go into more detail about how and why diet and exercise influence sexual desire and performance.

2. *If you smoke, stop.* Smoking causes much of the vascular damage in the penis that results in impotence. Long-term heavy smokers have a far greater probability of becoming impotent than do nonsmokers. One recent study found that men who smoked a pack a day for 20 years had a 60 percent greater chance of becoming impotent than did nonsmokers.

3. *Expand your definition of "sex."* There is more to making love than having intercourse, especially at midlife. That's been a frequent message in this book because midlife lovers won't move onto a higher sexual plane if they don't heed it. A man is also more likely to have erection difficulties if his lovemaking style is intercourse driven. The pressure to perform will be greater for him than for a man who enjoys satisfying his partner in a variety of ways.

4. *Have frequent sexual contact.* The more you make love, the more you will be able to make love. Erectile tissue becomes less supple with age. Without frequent erections, there is no regular flow of blood into the penis. After several months or a year of not having an erection, a man may have difficulty in achieving one.

5. *Don't make ejaculation a goal of lovemaking.* Once you take the pressure to ejaculate out of lovemaking, you will probably have more frequent erections, sustain them longer, and enjoy the experience much more.

6. *Share information with your partner.* Explain your changing sexual-response pattern to your partner. If intercourse has always ended in ejaculation until recently, she may think she has failed to excite you sufficiently. Let her know that your sexual patterns now more closely resemble hers. She has been able to enjoy intercourse without needing to reach an orgasm every time.

7. *Don't take medications you don't need.* Prescription drugs may have a negative effect on erections. If you keep your weight down and exercise regularly, you're less likely to develop high blood pressure, mild depression, or other conditions requiring continuing use of medications. When a doctor prescribes a drug, ask about its sexual side effects, if an alternative drug might not have the same side effects, and whether or not a lifestyle change would enable you to go off medication as soon as possible.

"Don't take your erections or your potency for granted is the message men need to hear around their fortieth birthday," says Gene who recently celebrated his fiftieth birthday. He began to have some erectile difficulties about a decade ago. "I wasn't getting hard enough often enough and I wasn't staying hard enough," he says succinctly. "I knew that some change was inevitable, but I was experiencing too much change. I had the sexual responses of a man 20 years my senior.

"At about the same time I developed erection problems, my doctor told me I had mild hypertension. He said I had two choices: Go on medication or lose 20 pounds, start exercising regularly, make some dietary changes, and stop smoking. Initially I took the easy way out. I went for the pills. The erection situation got a little worse. My wife was unhappy, and so was I.

"One night we had a big argument that ended with her crying and accusing me of cheating her out of a sex life. She said my potbelly wasn't attractive. That hurt. She also said she was worried about me. Would I cut my life short the same way I'd cut our sex life short? The next day I ordered a treadmill. It wasn't easy to make all the changes I had to make, and I backpedaled a few times in the early months. But I lost the weight, quit smoking, and generally cleaned up my act.

"The erection situation improved a great deal. I'll never get as rock hard as I did when I was twenty, but, on the other hand, I have better erections at 50 than I was getting at 40. I've also learned how to be a better lover. When I look at some of my friends who are overweight, smoking, and popping pills for hypertension, I know they aren't getting erections. I'd like to talk to them about it, but that's not the kind of thing men do."

A healthier lifestyle will most likely lead to healthier erections, but any man can expect to lose an erection during lovemaking on occasion. If he doesn't let that bother him, he'll likely get it back. The worst thing you can do about a subsiding erection is focus on it.

Four Steps a Man Can Take to Restore Sexual Function

1. *If you lose your erection, let it go.* "The first few times I lost an erection during intercourse, I grabbed my penis and started working it, desperately trying to get hard again," says James, 51. "It didn't happen. My wife commiserated with me. Sex was over. Then I tried something different. When I felt my erection going, I pulled out before she could notice or respond, and began performing cunnilingus on her. That has become my pattern now for handling the unexpected soft spots. Usually I get hard again. Even if I don't, I have satisfied her, which makes me feel good."

2. *Concentrate on pleasing your partner.* James's approach, performing cunnilingus when his erection falters, is a good one. When a man forgets his own perceived "problem" and concentrates on giving his partner pleasure, he relieves his performance anxiety. And he creates a win-win situation. Maybe he will get his erection back, but even if he doesn't, he will feel good about himself as a lover.

3. *Use a partial erection to good advantage.* Paul, 56, says: "When I feel my erection subsiding during intercourse, I pull out, take my penis in hand and get creative. Grasping my member firmly, I stimulate my wife's clitoris with the head, brushing it back and forth, often bringing her to orgasm this way. Sometimes I use the head of my penis to stroke her inner thighs or her nipples. Often I get really hard this way. We both enjoy penis play."

Some men can also have intercourse with a partial erection by holding the base of the penis firmly as they thrust. You don't need a full erection to make love with your penis. Experiment with ways of stimulating your partner with the erection you have.

4. *Don't blame your partner.* In hurt pride following an erectile failure, a man might lash out at his partner, accusing her of failing to arouse him sufficiently. Don't do that. Not only will you hurt her and invite a defensive assault, you'll only feel worse about yourself later. Once a couple have started a cycle of blaming, they'll find it hard to break free and move to a place of acceptance and understanding. Let down the barriers and share your fears and concerns with her, without blaming her or yourself.

Some men find it more difficult to talk about their erection problems than their emotions. For them, a savvy and understanding woman can make the difference between an impotent future and a transition into another, less erection-based kind of lovemaking.

How a Woman Can Help a Man Regain His Erection

- *If he loses an erection during lovemaking, let it go.* Unless he requests or indicates by his behavior that he wants you to perform fellatio or manually stimulate his penis to try to bring the erection back—don't. Focusing on his limp penis probably won't help and may hurt by intensifying his performance anxiety. Hold him. Kiss and stroke him, but ignore his penis. You don't have to prove your desirability by bringing his penis back to erotic life.

- *Ask for oral sex or manual stimulation yourself.* That will take the focus off his penis and give him the opportunity to feel like a good lover. Be responsive to his ministrations. A woman's arousal is very arousing to a man. It's possible that he'll regain his erection by losing himself in your excitement.

- *Don't be solicitous.* Show your understanding by not fussing over him. If he's feeling inadequate, don't tell him his lack of erection isn't important. A man who has been sexually humiliated doesn't want his wife saying, "Don't worry, darling, it doesn't matter."

- *Don't blame yourself.* And don't let him blame you. His erection problem may be physical or psychological. Even if it's rooted in relationship conflict, you are not the "cause" of the problem. Sex is a cooperative effort. So is relating. After an erectile failure, however, is not the right time to analyze the relationship.

A man and his partner can probably alleviate or prevent many garden-variety erection problems by following the advice given in the foregoing sections. What if the problems are more severe?

THE CAUSES OF IMPOTENCE

"I was terrified at the thought of having a penile implant," says Brian, 52, "but I'd been suffering bouts of impotence for almost a year. I thought it was probably time to do something about it, even if that turned out to be surgery."

Brian and his longtime partner, Maggie, 50, were very discouraged about his erection problems by the time he sought help from his doctor. Though he sometimes had morning erections and sometimes was able to get an erection for masturbation, he was increasingly unable to become erect during lovemaking. When he did get an erection, he would quickly lose it. Both Brian and Maggie became, in her words, "obsessed with the state of his penis." They spent so much time watching his penis when they attempted to make love that they'd turned sex into a spectator sport.

"We were both suffering from performance anxiety," Maggie says. "I was convinced I could 'make' him get and keep a good erection if only I could get it right when we made love. We both felt like we'd been tested and found wanting every time we tried to have sex."

"I felt doubly bad because I left her hanging so much of the time," Brian says. "I would offer to bring her to orgasm but she would often be too upset for that."

His doctor told him that the morning erections he "sometimes" experienced and his ability to get an erection "sometimes" during masturbation were indicators that his problem might not be entirely physical or, if it was largely physical, his condition probably wasn't as far advanced as he feared. Routine medical tests showed that Brian had very high cholesterol levels, no surprise given his diet rich in saturated fats and diary cholesterol. The same substances that clog the arteries of a man's heart, his doctor explained, also clog the arteries of his penis.

The damage done by a poor diet and high cholesterol levels had caused some problems with impotence for Brian. His response, and Maggie's, had exacerbated the condition. His doctor prescribed a diet, medication to bring down the cholesterol, and recommended several sex-therapy sessions both alone and with his partner.

Brian says, "We've learned how to make love without so much emphasis on an erection and intercourse. It's really a better, more sophisticated way of making love. We both feel closer to each other now than we did."

Maggie adds, "We shouldn't have waited so long to get help. We were both positive he would need a surgical implant or some dramatic 'cure.' He could have been on medication a year ago, and we could have saved ourselves that ride on an emotional roller-coaster."

As Brian's case illustrates, impotence has a psychological component even when the cause is physical. Repeated erectile failures put stress on a man and his partner. The cycle of failure, performance anxiety, guilt or blame is hard on any relationship. When impotence is rooted in a physical problem, the cause is likely to be:

- *Diabetes.* A major physical cause of impotence, diabetes can also accelerate other causes. For example, penile artery damage from cholesterol may become significant in a shorter period of time than it would if not complicated by diabetes.

- *High cholesterol.* Impotence research in the past several years has led authorities such as Dr. Irwin Goldstein, codirector of the New England Male Reproductive Center at Boston University Medical Center, to conclude that high cholesterol is "probably one of the leading causes of impotence in this country." The penis is a vascular organ, made up of layers of venous tissue and blood vessels. High cholesterol adversely affects erectile tissues.

- *Medications.* This is another major cause of impotence. A study reported by the *Journal of the American Medical Association* showed that 25 percent of all sex problems in men were caused or complicated by medications and other drugs. Tranquilizers, antidepressants, some high-blood-pressure drugs, corticosteroids (taken for arthritis), analgesics (for pain), alcohol, tobacco, and illegal drugs such as cocaine and marijuana affect libido and performance in men.

- *Prostate problems.* Chronic pain and swelling in the prostate area can affect sexual functioning in an indirect manner if a man finds erection or ejaculation painful or uncomfortable. Though studies show 80 percent of men can return to sexual functioning after prostate surgery, many don't, indicating a possible psychological barrier.

- *Major illnesses.* Heart disease, cancer, neurological and other diseases that don't directly affect the genitals can still cause temporary impotence from medication side effects or depression. And heart disease is an indication of blood-vessel damage, a condition that may also have affected penile blood vessels.

- *Chronic alcoholism.* Shakespeare noted in *Macbeth* that alcohol provokes desire but takes away performance. In the later stages of alcoholism, desire ebbs too. Testosterone production is impaired and penile blood vessels show considerable damage. Liver damage may lead to an increase of estrogen in a man's body. Impotence is almost inevitably a consequence of alcoholism.

When impotence is rooted in psychological issues, the cause is likely to be:

- *Anger.* Unacknowledged and unexpressed anger can sit on the end of a penis and hold it down. As noted in previous chapters, repressed anger, whether at the partner or not, has a devastating effect on sexuality.

- *Intimacy conflicts.* Maybe your penis is trying to tell you something about the relationship. Conflicts that have been ignored or papered over for years can cause sexual functioning problems now.

- *Depression.* Libido is often a casualty of depression, even low-level depression, especially if prolonged. A bout of impotence can increase a man's feelings of discouragement. While antidepressants such as Prozac may lift the depression, they may fail to lift the penis.

- *Stress.* At midlife a man has to learn stress management or face increasing bouts of impotence. When he was young, he could get and maintain an erection in spite of stress. That's less likely now.

- *Worry.* Concerns about job security, personal finances, and family issues such as problems with teenage children and aging parents can also create a psychological climate for impotence. If a man is feeling powerless in the world, he may convey that message to his penis. Generally, worry and stress are short-term situations. They may result in brief periods of impotence that can be overcome in a good relationship.

- *Performance anxiety.* One occurrence of impotence can set up the cycle of failure, anxiety, failure. In fact, performance anxiety is probably the most common contributing, or secondary, psychological cause of impotence.

In addition, negative attitudes about aging, both the man's and his partner's, can lead to impotence. If a couple have surrendered to the belief that they are "old" and no longer sexually attractive and desirable, they aren't likely to have good sex. Desire begins in the brain, and so does performance. The ability to function sexually is dependent in middle and later years on the belief that one can and will.

Impotence Remedies

"Alice and I stopped having sex five years ago," says Jeff, 52. "I had a few episodes of impotence, once unable to get an erection, once losing it as soon as I got it. She assured me it didn't matter, and, since our sex life had been going downhill for years, I believed her. I thought it didn't matter that much to me either. We kept to our separate sides of the bed. Without telling her, I masturbated once or twice a week.

"Then I had a little fling with a woman I met on a business trip. Nothing emotional, it was just a purely sexual affair. No problems with erections. I went home to Alice in an erotic frame of mind. We made love for the first time in six months. It wasn't great, but it was better than it had been in a while. I was pretty sure she had an orgasm, not faked one, but I had never been completely sure about Alice's orgasms.

"To my surprise, she cried afterward. She told me she'd missed making love to me. I was shocked. We began treating each other with a little more tenderness after that night. I had another erection problem, and we decided to see a therapist together. Therapy was good for us. We forged a closer, more intimate connection to each other than we'd had since the early days when we were struggling and the kids were babies. Once we got closer, the impotence thing didn't happen again.

"My erections are pretty good, partly because we've opened up our lovemaking style. I've never told her about the fling; I don't think it would serve any purpose to tell her. But other than that, I'm not keeping secrets from her."

For Jeff, therapy was the impotence remedy. Depending on the cause of impotence, there are several ways of treating it. They include:

- *Drug-injection therapy*. Drugs that relax the spongy tissue and dilate the arteries can be injected directly into the penis. Papverine, phentolamine, and prostaglandin E. are commonly used drugs for this purpose. An erection occurs shortly after the injection and will probably last long enough for both partners to be satisfied with lovemaking.

- *Vacuum constrictor.* A vacuum-constrictor device consists of a clear plastic tube that fits over the penis and is attached to a pump. The pump creates a vacuum, drawing blood into the penis. A rubber ring placed around the base of the penis maintains the erection for approximately 30 minutes.

- *Testosterone-replacement therapy*. Effective for the minority of men who have low testosterone levels, replacement therapy is described in the previous chapter.

- *Vascular surgery*. Vascular surgery is indicated only when erectile failure is a chronic condition and caused by penile-vein deterioration. In one procedure an artery in the pelvic area is joined to an artery or vein at the base of the penis, restoring circulation in the penis. In another type of surgery for the same condition, leaky veins are tied off, stopping the blood flow out of the penis. These surgeries are infrequently performed, perhaps because they have resulted in less than satisfactory outcomes for many men.

- *Penile implant*. A penile implant is a surgically implanted device enabling a man to have an erection. Some have inflatable cylinders containing a reservoir of fluid. By manually squeezing a pump, the man forces the fluid into the cylinders, causing an erection. And some devices have a pair of malleable or semi-rigid rods the length of the penis. Inserting a prosthesis is a radical approach to impotence, one that you probably won't want to consider unless you've exhausted other options.

- *Herbs and aphrodisiacs*. Herbs found in different forms and combinations in health-food stores may or may not improve erectile functioning. Some have side effects. The most common herbs used for increasing libido are muira puanma, also known as potency wood, chinese ginseng, and ginkgo biloba, which has been proven effective in creasing blood flow throughout the body, and the herb yohimbe. Touted for centuries as an aphrodisiac, a related product, *Yohimbine* comes from the bark of an African tree. Available by prescription, yohimbine is an FDA-approved medication for impotence. It also functions by increasing blood flow to the penis. One Stanford University study reported a 34 to 43 percent success rate among various groups of impotent men.

• *Therapy to*: (1) resolve personal conflicts and issues, (2) resolve relationship issues, and (3) strengthen the relationship by building and deepening intimacy. At least a short course of therapy is often helpful in treating even patients whose impotence is clearly organic in cause. Because impotence has such confusing and painful psychological implications for a man and his partner, they can almost always benefit from talking about their feelings and fears with a counselor. If the impotence is psychogenic in origin, therapy may be necessary for the resolution of personal and relationships conflicts and issues. A satisfying sexual relationship, one that provides mutual pleasure, isn't likely to thrive when a couple are acting out significant conflicts in the bedroom.

What can you expect in therapy? A more personalized, in depth, and detailed examination of the areas covered by several chapters in this book.

• *The Impotence Pill.* The first oral medication for impotence has recently become widely available by prescription. If you haven't heard of Viagra, the diamond-shaped blue pill manufactured by Pfizer, you must not read newspapers or news magazines, watch television news programs, or listen to the late-night talk shows where comedians Jay Leno and Dave Letterman have turned the private pain of impotence into numerous one-liners. The initial interest in Viagra was beyond intense. It's hard to imagine a man, or woman, over 50 who hasn't heard about The Pill.

Before Viagra, approximately half a million men a year sought treatment for impotence, either from medical doctors or therapists or through treatment that combines the two disciplines. Informed estimates put the number of men suffering from impotence at much higher levels, perhaps as high as 30 million. Viagra has lured them out of the closet. Men who didn't want to talk about the problem with a therapist or submit to implants, injections, or other treatments have been lured by the promise of an instant cure. Open mouth. Insert pill. Wash down with water. Become Man of Steel.

Dubbed by Erica Jong as "the perfect American medication" because "it raises the Dow Jones and the penis too," the pill of the nineties has supplanted The (birth control Pill of the sixties in the breadth and depth of media coverage generated. Former presidential candidate Bob Dole said publicly that he had taken Viagra and found it helpful. Is it the miracle drug of erections? The marriage saver? Or the threat to marriage as some opposing moralists fear? (Their theory: Formerly impotent men will leave their spouses in search of younger women now that they are studs.)

Across America, pharmacies began putting up "We have Viagra" signs on their windows as soon as the drug was released for prescription by doctors. It had the fastest "take-off," the number of initial prescriptions written, in drug history. At least 10,000 scripts a day are being written for Viagra in the United States alone. Judging by these numbers, there must be millions of impotent men in this country searching for the magic bullet. Financial analysts predict that Viagra will generate revenues of $2 billion for the company by 2001. That's a lot of erections.

Predictably, media coverage quickly shifted from the positive and glowing to the negative and fear-mongering. "Impotence pill wins rave local reviews" gave way to "Viagra associated with six deaths nationwide" in a matter of weeks. Who can blame men, and women too, for being confused about the truth behind the hype?

Here, then, are the most often asked questions about that pill:

1. HOW DOES THE IMPOTENCE PILL WORK?

First, there are actually three different types of impotence pills, each working in a slightly different way. Viagra was only the first to become available by prescription. One pill, a version of apomorphine, works completely in the brain of a man who is deemed psychologically, rather than physically, impotent.

Here's a simplified physiological explanation of erection: When a man becomes sexually aroused, his brain signals the nerve cells surrounding his penis. These cells release nitric oxide, which causes the penis to make a chemical called cyclic GMP. It widens blood vessels in the penis.

The primary ingredient of Viagra, sildenafil, enhances the action of cyclic GMP while simultaneously inhibiting the effect of phosphodiesterase 5, or PDE5, an enzyme abundant in impotent men that blocks arousal. The combined effect significantly increases blood flow to the penis. Cyclic GMP is the physical key to erection. PDE5 prevents the key from turning in the lock. By boosting the natural process through which the arteries of the penis dilate, the pill encourages the simple engorgement that is an erection.

2. HOW IS THE PILL TAKEN?

The pill should be taken approximately an hour before intercourse. Available in both 50-milligram and 100-milligram sizes, Viagra costs between seven and ten dollars per dosage. Unless impotence is associated with diabetes, spinal-cord injuries, or prostate surgery, insurance companies probably won't reimburse the cost. Some may not cover the expense under any circumstances.

Follow your doctor's orders as to dosage and frequency of use. Taking more than the recommended dosage may be harmful. As with any prescription drugs, don't take medication prescribed for someone else. Your doctor should be aware of your medical history before prescribing. A diagnosis of impotence should follow a comprehensive physical exam, blood tests, and a sexual and relationship history.

3. CAN VIAGRA ALONE PRODUCE AN ERECTION?

No. Viagra can restore erection capacity, but it has no effect on libido. A man who can get aroused but can't get or sustain an erection may be helped by the pill, but a man who has lost desire won't be. You can't take the little blue pill, sit back and watch television, and wait for the magic to happen.

4. CAN VIAGRA GIVE A MAN A BETTER ERECTION THAN THE ONE HE HAS?

No. Many older men lament the quality of their erections. They complain about not being as "hard" as they were in their youth. True, most men have more rigid erections at 19 than they will have at 49. Viagra can't change that. The erectile tissue in the penis has a finite number of receptors for cyclic GMP. If you have normal erections, the pill won't make them extra normal by creating more or bigger receptors. It can't happen.

5. WILL VIAGRA HELP A MAN LAST LONGER?

No. Viagra does not create prolonged erections. This pill, like most medications, has a very specific purpose: It increases blood flow to the penis in men who have difficulty in that area. As you'll hope to have learned by now, there's a lot more to being a good lover than getting an erection.

6. CAN VIAGRA HELP A MAN BECOME ERECT AGAIN AFTER ORGASM?

Theoretically, it could *but* recommended dosage is one pill a day. After orgasm, or the decline of arousal, cyclic GMP isn't produced in the penis anymore. PDE5 takes control and shuts the erotic system down. In young men, the shutdown is brief, while in older men it can last hours or even days. Could a man have a second erection with a second pill? The question is moot because of dosage guidelines.

7. WHAT ARE THE POTENTIAL SIDE EFFECTS?

Known side effects include indigestion or nausea, a bright-red flushing, particularly of the face, neck, and chest, and headache. Some men have reported a change in their color vision that briefly made everything look bluer. Headache is the most common side effect.

Some news stories reported deaths of men who had recently taken Viagra. There is no evidence yet that the medication alone could lead to a heart attack or other life-threatening condition. However, Viagra does interact with certain other drugs to create potentially serious problems. Those drugs include nitroglycerin (used in treating heart-attack victims), Tagamet, erythromycin, Nizoral, Sporanox, and Posicor. The reported deaths associated with Viagra included two men on kidney dialysis and four men with heart conditions. Conceivably, a man with a bad heart who takes Viagra and then has a heart episode could be in serious trouble because paramedics wouldn't be able to give him nitroglycerin.

Men who take the 50-milligram dosage are less likely to have side effects than those taking the 100-milligram pill.

NO MAN SHOULD TAKE VIAGRA OR ANY OTHER PRESCRIPTION MEDICATION THAT HASN'T BEEN PRESCRIBED SPECIFICALLY FOR HIM.

8. ARE SOME MEN IMMUNE TO THE VIAGRA EFFECT?

The success rate is reported to be around 70 percent. Men who haven't been helped by the pill include those who have poorly managed diabetes, severely blocked arteries, or high blood pressure that has been a longstanding condition. Also men who are psychologically impotent are not as likely to get an erection via Viagra.

9. CAN WOMEN TAKE VIAGRA TOO?

Studies are underway examining the effects of Viagra on women. Some doctors have already begun prescribing the pill for a few women patients. The clitoris and surrounding genital tissues, like the penis, become engorged with blood during sexual arousal. Women who don't enjoy sex after menopause typically suffer from poor lubrication and poor blood supply to the genitalia. Viagra might prove to be a boon for them.

10. WHAT EFFECT WILL VIAGRA HAVE ON RELATIONSHIPS?

For couples whose main problem has been unsatisfactory sex due to the man's diminished erection capacity, Viagra can be a blessing.

Example: John and Delores, patients of mine, have been struggling with his impotence for the last three years of their 23-year marriage. His physical problem has devastating psychological consequences for both of them.

"I blamed myself for not being able to excite him anymore," she says. "I thought I was doing something wrong in bed. And I tried everything, from new sex techniques to sexy lingerie, candles, flower petals on the bed. I tormented myself about my shortcomings. Deep down I suspected he was having an affair."

John says: "I tried to reassure Delores, but I wasn't very good at it. How can you convince a woman of her desirability when you don't seem to desire her? I knew it was my problem, but I wasn't able to talk to her about it. I thought if I laid it on the line to her, she might want to leave me or at least have an affair."

Finally, John's urologist insisted he get some help in talking to Delores. He had been diagnosed with vascular blockage in the blood vessels supplying the penis when they came to see me. Shortly after that, they tried penile injection therapy.

"I couldn't get used to sticking a needle in my penis," he says. "Dolores found it hard to handle too."

When Viagra became available through prescription, John practically stood on line to be one of the first to try it. The drug worked well for him. Dolores says they have been enjoying a "second honeymoon."

John adds: "Viagra gave me back my potency, something I thought I'd lost."

For other couples, Viagra has proved to be a mixed blessing.

Some couples in long-term relationships have accommodated to being nonsexual. The woman may be secretly relieved that her husband is impotent because she lost interest in sex years ago. Avoiding sex may help both of them avoid intimacy. They may have serious relationship issues that they've chosen to sweep under the rug. Then, along comes Viagra.

"The possibility of having sex again is unsettling," a female patient admitted to me after her husband had decided to try Viagra.

She had "handled" his impotence due to blocked arteries with grace. How was she going to "handle" his renewed potency? They had lived together like affectionate roommates for three years. She was happy with the status quo.

Other women may be more willing to become lovers again after a prolonged sexual drought, but find their bodies less accommodating. A lot depends on a woman's age, physical conditions, and, of course, her relationship. A postmenopausal woman who hasn't had a period in three or four years will not find it so easy to jump back into bed. Thinning vaginal walls and lack of lubrication may make intercourse painful. She needs to ease back into a sex life, and her husband will have to be understanding of her need for a slower pace. I've had to remind some men to "court" their wives all over again. Seduce. Don't expect or demand.

A man's sudden ability to get an erection again can also create a crisis for him.

"I don't have an excuse anymore," a male patient told me. "My wife expects me to be able to make love now that I have the pill."

Remember, Viagra restores erection capacity, not libido. A man who is depressed, stressed, hurt, or angry won't resolve those problems by taking a pill. Some men have developed psychological problems as a result of their erection difficulties. They may be too concerned about adequacy, aging, and overall success issues to feel desire For men in any of these situations, Viagra may present a new set of problems rather than help to solve the existing ones.

"I was disappointed," a male patient confided, "and so was my wife when Viagra didn't change our lives."

He and his wife expected a regained erection capacity to solve their emotional problems. Instead, it destabilized their relationship. They were overwhelmed by the possibility of regular erections. Was that bad? No. Because of Viagra, they went into therapy to resolve their issues together.

In some cases, Viagra may be blamed as a chemical "home wrecker."

Once their erection capacity is restored, some men will probably be tempted to wander. They may do so for a variety of reasons. A man who still fears sexual failure may not be able to take the risk with his partner. For him, another woman is a safe testing ground. If the pill doesn't live up to his expectations, he can tell his partner "guilt" prevented him from acting upon his desire, and hurry out of the room. With his wife, however, he would have to acknowledge the "failure." She might expect him to deal with the root causes.

Other men may realize their marriages were based on accommodation, complacency, meshing neuroses. They may come to the conclusion they'd stayed married only because their flaccid members hadn't left them with many other options. How many unhappy marriages are held together by a woman's loss of interest in sex and a man's lack of ability to perform? With Viagra, the men have, or perceive they have, choices.

Will we see a flurry of Viagra divorces? Maybe. Men who once felt too inadequate to leave may now do what they've long wanted to do. The pill may force couples to examine issues they've been ignoring. Viagra won't be the cause of their problems, but it might be the catalyst for facing them. Inevitably some couples will decide they don't want to be together anymore. Viagra could be the convenient peg on which to hang their divorce.

And for some couples, Viagra will help strengthen the marriage by forcing them to resolve relationship issue.

For some couples, like Dolores and John, whom you met earlier, the problem is a physiological one. When potency is restored, the couple happily resume sexual relations. But for other couples, Viagra opens the door to the room where they've stored all their junk. If they go in there together and clean out the junk, the relationship will become better and stronger.

Jeff and Sally are one of those couples. They were in therapy before he began taking Viagra. His restored erection capacity threw them off balance.

"His expectations are unrealistic," she groused. "He thinks we're going to have sex every day or at least five times a week. I don't want to go back to the way it was, him chasing, me giving in and not being satisfied."

In addition to working on issues of buried anger and resentment on both parts, Jeff and Sally had to learn how to become better lovers. Erections don't guarantee sexual satisfaction, particularly for women.

"I feel rejected by her," he complained.

Years of impotence had left Jeff with a fragile ego. He needed to be wanted and appreciated. When he came to the conclusion that Sally preferred him impotent, he was devastated.

Their story has a happy ending because they are working through their anger and resolving the differences that kept them on opposite sides of the bed even after Jeff added the magic pill to the medicine cabinet.

Some guidelines for a return to intimacy

1. *Express a desire for intimacy, the kind of intimacy that is fully clothed.* Some couples who have experienced a long nonsexual interlude have also lost touch emotionally. An awkward distance exists between them. They can diminish that space by beginning to tell each other how they feel.

A man who has experienced erection problems for a long time may have stopped being affectionate. Touching, kissing, holding, and stroking reminded him of his inability. Also, he might have feared arousing his wife or giving her false hope. He needs to tell her why he withdrew affection.

She has probably been hurt more by his lack of affection than by his inability to achieve an erection. Feeling hurt, angry, confused, and rejected, she has withdrawn too. She needs to tell him how she feels and listen to him talk about his feelings.

A sensitive talk will take them a long way across the distance between them.

2. Men (and women too) should get a medical evaluation after a long period of not having sexual relations. A man should never start taking Viagra, or any prescription drug, without a medical evaluation. Erection problems often signal underlying medical conditions such as diabetes, high blood pressure, or cardiovascular problems. Even if he knows he has medical problems and is being treated for them, a man should still be examined again if he hasn't had a physical within six months to a year.

A woman may suffer from vaginal thinning, lack of lubrication, or other problems she hasn't recognized because she hasn't been having sex. She should let her doctor know that her husband is planning to take Viagra and ask if there are any steps she should take to make sex more comfortable for her.

3. Take it slow. For men: Don't be too anxious to use the new erection. It will still be there in a few minutes, and you can get another one tomorrow. Be loving with your partner. Do a lot of touching, caressing, cuddling. Don't forget that she's had a long period of absence too. She can't turn on instantly.

For women: Take responsibility for your own arousal. If he hasn't made love to you in a while, he'll need your help in guiding his hands and mouth where you want them to be. Don't be embarrassed to touch yourself too.

4. Pay attention to the problems underlying erection disorders. Younger men often get into trouble by listening to their penis when they should be listening to their brain. The young penis is eager, headstrong. It can lead a man into trouble.

Mature men don't listen to their penis as often as they should. In older men, an erection problem often signals an underlying intimacy or emotional issue. Many men are not having erections due to stress, depression, or feelings of anger or hurt in their relationships.

Taking a pill may, or may not, produce an erection. If it works, a man may be able to take the pill and bypass the real problem. But that will often prove to be a costly mistake.

What does the tremendous interest in Viagra really tell us? A lot of men, and perhaps their partners too, are really unhappy with their sexual performance and probably with the state of their relationships. Perhaps Viagra is a wake-up call to action in many sexual and relationship fronts, for women as well as for men.

Sizzler # **12**

BEYOND INTERCOURSE

Robert was fired for the first time in his life at the age of 52. He hadn't seen it coming. Though his wife Donna was working, early retirement for either of them wasn't in their financial plan. For several weeks, he was in denial. Telling everyone that "this is the best thing that ever happened to me," he threw himself into the job search with gusto, and he made love in the same way. Donna, who had been prepared for the job loss/impotence link, was pleasantly surprised. Then about two months into involuntary unemployment, he failed to get a job he'd thought he'd clinched in the interview, and the predictable happened. No matter how hard he tried, he couldn't get an erection.

Donna was reassuring, supportive, sanguine. She could live without sex until Robert found a job, she reasoned. Eventually, he did find another job, a lesser position than he'd held, but his potency did not return. After a few "failures," he avoided all sexual activity.

"I want you to satisfy me," she finally told him in exasperation. "I don't care if you don't have an erection. I still want sex."

"I can't satisfy you if I can't get an erection," he countered, his face red, expressing both his shame and his anger.

"Oh, yes, you can. You have no idea how many times I've faked an intercourse orgasm. Ninety percent of my orgasms have occurred during oral sex or when you were masturbating me before or after intercourse. I usually fake another one to make you feel good."

He felt, he said, like a character in an episode of *Seinfeld*. She's taken something away from him, and he had to be alone for a while. With that, he picked up the car keys and headed for the door.

"I'm going to masturbate while you're gone!" she shouted after him, overcome with embarrassment as soon as she'd said it.

She poured herself a large glass of wine. Sipping it, she tried to conjure erotic images but succeeded only in remembering the look on Robert's face when she told him the truth about her sexual responses.

She paced the floor. Feeling alternately guilty and sad, then angry and resentful, Donna finally acknowledged that she was too "wound up" to do anything but seek release in a purely physical sensation, orgasm.

Shedding her clothes, she stepped into the big marble shower for two that had been their realization of their erotic desire when they remodeled the house. Sighing, she remembered the wonderful love-making they'd shared under the twin sprays of water. She closed her eyes and willed herself to imagine his mouth in place of her hand on her vulva.

"Pretend you're standing under a waterfall in Bali with Robert on his knees in front of you," she whispered to herself.

Slowly the fantasy began to take on life. She could almost smell the fragrance of exotic flowers in the steamy air. Her fingers raced in circles around her clitoris, the water cascading between them, increasing her arousal.

"Donna," Robert said. But of course, she was imagining his voice, wasn't she? "Donna," he repeated.

She opened her eyes and saw Robert standing in the bathroom, watching her, his eyes glazed over with longing. Reluctantly, she pulled her hand from her body and beckoned to him with it.

"Satisfy me," she begged in a husky voice.

He kicked off his shoes and came into the shower, fully dressed, moving like a man in a hurry to rescue a woman drowning. His fingers caressed her vulva as his mouth hungrily sought hers. Her mouth sobbed into his. He stroked her to orgasm, then pulled her body tight against his. Through his wet clothing, she felt his erection.

She helped him shed his pants, sodden with water, and she sank down to her knees. Eagerly she took his stiff penis into her mouth as he raised his arms to grasp the shower head. She stroked herself while she fellated him and had another orgasm, in time to his own.

SEX AND HEALTH

"What has grilled trout and steamed broccoli got to do with sex?" James asked his wife when she told them they were going on a diet and beginning an exercise program to improve their sex life.

Grilled trout, steamed broccoli, and other healthful foods don't have an aphrodisiac effect on the libido. They don't influence potency or strengthen and multiply orgasms. Yet the older you are, the more your sex life depends on maintaining good overall health habits, including diet and exercise. Studies of middle-aged and older adults repeatedly show that those in good health have more active sex lives than those who aren't. And many of the health problems suffered by people as they age are brought on by or made worse by bad health habits. In earlier chapters, you've seen the connection between smoking, heavy drinking, and the consumption of a fatty diet and the loss of desire and sexual-performance problems. If you can stay healthy, you greatly improve your odds of staying sexy.

There are several components of a healthful lifestyle. Each has an impact on sexual desire and performance.

THE SEX DIET

"The wrong foods can put a crimp in your sex life," says David, 49. "I would not have believed this was true until my doctor put me on a diet to lose 15 pounds and cut back my cholesterol levels. I eliminated a lot of fat from my diet, cut my consumption of red meat and dairy products, added more fruits, vegetables, grains, and fish. That's it. I made no other life changes. I already had a reasonable exercise routine. With the dietary changes, I lost the weight and—here was the surprise—my sex life improved a great deal.

"I lost that sluggish feeling that had been dragging me down for several years. My erections were firmer and more frequent. I had more interest in sex. My wife was so delighted with the change in me, she went on the diet too."

At midlife, what you eat does have an impact on how often and how well you make love. Dietary changes can raise libido in both men and women, improve male erections, and possibly influence the quality of orgasms. (If you have greater desire for sex and a stronger erection, you'll likely experience the orgasm more intensely.) No one food or group of foods has special erotic powers. But one food group can have a detrimental effect on sex: fats. A diet high in saturated fats has both short-term and long-term sexual consequences.

In the short term, both men and women who consume too many fats suffer from feelings of sluggishness and low energy that may impact negatively on their libidos. They are probably overweight, another factor that can pull down the libido. Because they don't look and feel their best, they may not think of themselves as sexy and desirable to their partners. The couple on the couch passing the potato-chip bowl back and forth as they watch television are probably not thinking about sex.

In the long term, a diet rich in fats raises cholesterol levels. That can, as you saw in the previous chapter, lead to impotence in men. It can have a similar, though less obvious, effect in women. When the arteries in the pelvic area narrow from the accumulated plaque of cholesterol deposits, blood doesn't flow into the area the way it once did.

Arousal feels more diffuse, less intense. Finally, high cholesterol levels lead to heart problems in both men and women.

The best dietary sex advice:

- *Cut the saturated fats.* Start basing some meals around grains, legumes, vegetables, fruits. But some fats are essential and actually healthful additions to the diet. Foods such as salmon and sardines contain omega-three fatty acids, the "good" dietary fats.

- *Get advice from a nutritionist or an internist* on how many calories you should consume daily. Take into consideration your activity level.

- *Do some background reading on vitamin supplements.* Scientific opinion is divided on the value of specific supplements as well as the amount of each that should be consumed. A multivitamin containing antioxidants and minerals is probably a good addition to the average person's health program.

- *Drink alcohol in moderation.* A glass of wine with dinner may have health benefits, but excessive amounts of alcohol inhibits desire and limits performance.

How Exercise Influences Sexuality

"Regular exercise can improve your love life, especially if you work out together," says Terry. "My husband and I joined a gym together last year. We decided we weren't getting enough exercise after we spent a weekend hiking with friends. They're a few years older than we are, and they were walking circles around us.

"After a few months at the gym, we began looking and feeling better. We were more attractive to each other, and we had more energy. Naturally we started having more sex. Energy feeds energy. Exercise was the jolt our sex life needed. One of the myths about aging is that your body has to get soft and shapeless. That only happens because people don't use their bodies, not because they age."

The physical and psychological benefits of regular exercise have been well documented. Even couch potatoes know that it promotes cardiovascular conditioning, lowers blood pressure, helps keep weight under control, and tones the body. Recent studies have shown that regular exercise also enhances sexuality. In one study, couples who exercise regularly in every age group from the twenties through the sixties reported more sexual activity than was average for their contemporaries. In another study, couples in their sixties who exercised regularly reported having more sex than the average for those in their forties. And, finally, a large study of the effects of exercise on sexuality found that 97 percent of the men and women in their forties were sexually active and 92 percent of those in their sixties were. Is that incentive to get off the couch?

- People who work out have better body images and a greater sense of well-being, factors linked to increased sexual activity.

- They have improved cardiovascular health that probably aids erections because it helps keep critical blood vessels unblocked. The vessels leading to the penis need to be unrestricted for a man to maintain a firm erection for a reasonable length of time.

- They reach orgasm more easily and more often than people who don't exercise regularly, according to research from the Center for Marital and Sexual Studies in Long Beach, California.

- And in women, cardiovascular health probably has a similar effect in the pelvic area. Good circulation creates increased blood flow, allowing the genitals to engorge fully during arousal.

THE HEALTH BENEFITS OF SEX

"The mind and body are powerfully connected," says Kate, 49, a medical writer. "And there is a growing body of evidence indicating that our brains respond to sexual pleasure in the body by influencing resistance to and recovery from disease. When my sister had surgery for breast cancer last year, I gave her articles on the link between orgasm and recovery. She was embarrassed to have her baby sister advising masturbating to orgasm as a form of physical therapy. But the research convinced her. I honestly believe that everyone can influence their health, including the outcome of illness and surgery, by encouraging sexual pleasure, if not in a relationship, then through masturbation."

A study published in the *British Medical Journal* concluded that men between 45 and 59 who had regular sex were generally healthier than were men who don't. Other studies have shown a correlation between frequency of orgasms in women and good health. In the past decade a surprising amount of research has shown how important sexual pleasure is to health.

The specific health benefits of sex include:

- Improved appearance of skin from the increased blood flow accompanying arousal and orgasm

- Diminishment of some of the genital signs of aging, including vaginal dryness and atrophy in women and poor erections in men

- Strengthening of the immune system

- Relief of mild pain, such as headache or backache, through the release of endorphins in the brain

- Release of physical and mental tension and stress

- Elevation of mood

- Mild cardiovascular activity

- Lasting psychological benefits

It may be obvious to most people that sex releases tension and elevates mood. But how does it strengthen the immune system? The state of biochemical euphoria produced by the release of endorphins at orgasm leads to the production of greater amounts of endorphins and increased levels of T cells, the white blood cells that help resist cancer and strengthen immunity. The profound sense of relaxation that people experience after good sex is an antidote to stress. And unrelieved stress takes a toll on the immune system, making us more susceptible to colds, infections, and other illnesses. Positive moods foster resistance and recovery, while negative moods, such as depression, anger, and fear of pleasure contribute to health problems. After sex, the muscles relax, tension ebbs from the body, and a general sense of well-being contributes to continued good health.

People who have satisfying sex lives are more likely to have good relationships, too. Good sex increases self-esteem and reduces anxiety. Couples have fewer arguments and feel more closely connected to each other. Some studies have shown that couples who report sharing satisfying sex lives have fewer problems communicating their needs and desires. A couple who are happy together in bed are likely to be happy together in life.

Even healthy people occasionally suffer illness or disability. What happens to their sex lives then?

THE SEXUAL EFFECTS OF ILLNESS AND DISABILITY

Many chronic illnesses and some disabilities and/or their treatments can interfere with sexual functioning. Some affect sexuality in indirect ways. When a man or woman feels ill and debilitated or is suffering pain, he or she is not usually interested in making love.

Some common medical problems and their effect on sexuality include:

Diabetes

Diabetes has the greatest direct impact on sexuality of the diseases that commonly have a midlife onset. Diabetic men have a far greater chance of becoming impotent than other men, and impotence can be the first sign of disease. In women, diabetes can cause vaginal dryness, loss of sensation in the genitals, and make achieving orgasm more difficult. It can also lead to increased possibility of yeast and urinary-tract infections, making sex prohibited for periods of time.

Patients can manage their diabetes by rigorously following the medical and dietary regimes prescribed for them. If they do, they are able to mitigate the sexual effects of the disease. Nearly half of all diabetic men suffer impotence for psychological reasons. Erectile problems early in their illness before they were diagnosed and treated may have left them feeling anxious, inadequate, and fearful of more failures.

Women who keep their diabetes well under control minimize any sexual effects of the disease. At menopause, they are particularly good candidates for estrogen-replacement therapy because diabetes often leads to lower estrogen levels and intensifies the negative impact of the hormone loss. Make sure your doctor monitors your estrogen levels carefully at the onset of menopause.

How to Handle: A sex therapist can help you get over the psychological effects of impotence. More than 75 percent of diabetic men with impotence in one study were able to overcome their problems in counseling. Various impotence treatments—see the previous chapter—have also proven successful in diabetic men. Talk to your doctor about all your options. And for women, be familiar with all the indicators of low estrogen and do everything you can to boost hormone levels.

Comments: From a 59-year-old man with diabetes: "I was impotent for almost a year following the onset of diabetes. It wasn't necessary to suffer that long. I was backward about bringing up the subject of sexual functioning with my doctor. Finally, in exasperation, my wife did. Because it had been so long, I had to use injections to get an erection for several weeks. Meanwhile my wife and I began seeing a therapist. After a few months of therapy, I was able to have an erection without the injection. I've been fine for the past two years. To remain sexually active at this age with diabetes requires two things: Following the diet-and-exercise routine and taking medication as prescribed and making love often without putting undue stress on erections and intercourse. If you don't force the erection, it will come."

Stroke

A mild stroke may have little or no effect on sexual functioning. More severe strokes obviously affect sexuality because they impair a person's ability to move freely. Even memory loss can affect sexual functioning if the patient has forgotten some aspects of lovemaking. But the mental interest in sex and the drive remain.

How to Handle: After a mild stroke, a man or woman may need more patience and tenderness from a lover. Initial lovemaking sessions may be tentative, even awkward, but that stage will pass quickly. When a stroke has resulted in some degree of paralysis, sex, rather than being a part of the past, may assume greater importance to the patient. With medical guidance and consultation with a sex therapist, find ways of making love that bring pleasure to both partners. The stroke victim may have heightened sensitivity and perceptions in the areas undamaged by the stroke. Erotic massage to the unaffected body areas may be very arousing.

Comments: From a 48-year-old woman: "After my husband's stroke, he had mild temporary paralysis and some forgetfulness for about six months. The doctor told us it would be good for both of us to resume our sex life, but he said we should put aside our performance standards for a while. When we made love, our familiar routines didn't exactly work. It was like dancing with someone who had forgotten the steps. But on the plus side, we developed some exciting new steps because we were in a sense new to each other."

Heart Attack

Many people mistakenly believe that a heart attack signals the end of one's sex life. Most heart attack patients are encouraged to resume sexual activity at the same time they begin other physical activities. Making love typically is no more strenuous than climbing a flight of stairs. Less than 1 percent of heart-attack fatalities occur during sex—and the majority of those people are in bed with their extramarital lovers, not with their spouses.

HOW TO HANDLE: The major effect of a heart attack on sexuality is psychological. People fear another attack, and they need reassurance. Regular pleasurable sexual activity may actually reduce the risk of further problems, particularly when combined with exercise and dietary and other lifestyle changes. With the doctor's approval, people who suffer shortness of breath from climbing stairs can take the usual dose of nitroglycerine shortly before engaging in lovemaking.

COMMENTS: From a 55-year-old man: "My heart attack five years ago actually gave me a new lease on life. It scared me into better health habits and made me appreciate sex more than I had in years. Initially, I was a little fearful, but I soon got over that. Sex is better now than it ever was. When you have a brush with your own mortality, it heightens your senses and intensifies your appreciation of life."

Coronary-Artery Disease

The majority of people who suffer from coronary-artery disease are able to lead satisfying sex lives. Unless angina pains are severe, unpredictable, and accompanied by shortness of breath, your doctor will probably encourage sexual activity. The emotional benefits of lovemaking are important.

HOW TO HANDLE: With your doctor's approval, you may want to put a nitroglycerine tablet under the tongue before beginning lovemaking.

Until your condition stabilizes, make love in the most familiar and comfortable patterns. Unless you have been given medical orders to abstain, abstinence is rarely part of a long-term healing process.

COMMENTS: From a 57-year-old man: "My wife was the one who feared making love after I was diagnosed with coronary-artery disease. I accepted my doctor's advice on the subject, but she was very protective of me. She had to see a counselor to get over her fear of losing me. In our first few lovemaking session, I pleasured her, giving her orgasms via oral sex."

Cancer

Both the psychological impact of a cancer diagnosis and the pain accompanying treatment can be sexually debilitating. Add to that the devastating physical effects of chemotherapy. Many people lose weight and lose their hair. It's not unusual for a cancer patient enduring radical treatment to suffer periods of body loathing. For women suffering gynecological cancer, the sexual issues are magnified. While the disease itself may not render the patient incapable of having sex, it wreaks havoc with desire and feelings of desirability, the sexual motivators.

HOW TO HANDLE: Most cancer patients and their spouses will benefit from sex therapy. They may need to learn alternative ways of lovemaking, and they almost certainly need some help with the psychosexual ramifications of cancer treatment. In the early stages, survival, not sex, may be the primary concern. As recovery progresses, sexual healing needs to take place too.

COMMENTS: From a 49-year-old breast cancer survivor: "I withdrew sexually following my cancer diagnosis. I didn't even want to be touched by my husband. He persisted in being affectionate until I responded to that. I had a partial mastectomy and reconstructive surgery so the recovery was long. And I will never look exactly the way I did. I didn't want to make love for weeks after the doctor said I could because I hated my body. My husband bought me twelve beautiful silk camisoles, very expensive ones with lace. I wore them to make love. The camisoles carried me over the worst days. Gradually I have gained enough body acceptance to let my husband see and touch my breasts during sex."

Arthritis

In a severe form, arthritis can be crippling. Even in its mildest forms, the disease can leave a sufferer with stiff joints, making some sexual positions uncomfortable. Some men and women experience cramping and slight disfigurement in their hands, which makes them reluctant to use manual stimulation fully during lovemaking.

HOW TO HANDLE: Before sexual activity, take the anti-inflammatory agents recommended by your doctor or herbal remedies to ease pain, such as yucca, ginger, and boswellin. (Again, do your own research.) Taking a hot bath or using a heating pad before sex may also help. You and your partner can share the bath as foreplay. If some intercourse positions are uncomfortable, experiment with others or adapt the favorites with the use of pillows and other supports.

COMMENTS: From a 50-year-old woman: "When I developed arthritis in my hands last year, I felt old. Every time I looked at my hands with their swollen knuckle joints, I felt like an asexual old broad. Just when my husband needed more manual stimulation of his penis, I wanted to hide my hands so he wouldn't notice them. We had always made love with the lights on, and we started turning them off. Now we light candles."

Surgery

Sexual relations following major surgery will almost certainly be curtailed for some period of time. Depending on the type of surgery and the recovery process, abstinence may extend for weeks, even months. In addition, postoperative depression often accompanying surgery can dampen libido. At midlife, regaining sexuality may be a little more difficult than it would be for a younger surgery patient.

HOW TO HANDLE: It's important for the patient to seek and the partner to give physical affection during the recovery process. Touch has been shown to have therapeutic value, and it will be easier to restart a sex life if some type of physical relationship continues. The partner of a surgical patient needs to remain sexually active through fantasy and masturbation, both for his or her own sake and for the relationship. The healthier person will probably have to take the sexual initiative. Talk to a doctor and/or therapist about how and when to resume sexual activity.

COMMENTS: From a 51-year-old man: "After a car accident, my wife needed three major surgeries, on her back and both legs. She is an enormously vital, alive, and sexual woman. When we couldn't have intercourse, we masturbated each other or I performed oral sex on her. We even played with each other when she was in the hospital. We probably made love more during the six months she was laid up than we had the prior six months because we needed each other so much more then. When we were able to have intercourse again, we used the 'love stool,' which was a gift from our best friends. It's a padded and adjustable device that straddles the recumbent person's lower abdomen. We used it to support my weight in the missionary position, because flat on her back was the most comfortable sex position for her but she couldn't stand any of my weight on her."

Chronic Back Pain

Back pain is a common complaint among midlife Americans, partly because they don't get enough exercise. Weak stomach muscles contribute to the possibility of back injury. At midlife, incorrectly lifting a heavy object can damage the back, particularly if stomach muscles are weak. Pain can limits one's sexual options by making it difficult to find a pleasurable position for intercourse. It can short circuit the libido or create enough distraction during lovemaking to quell or dull sexual responses.

HOW TO HANDLE: Stretch and take a hot bath before lovemaking. It also may help to do some muscle-stretching exercises. (Check with your doctor, of course, before doing any exercises.) Work with your partner to adapt positions to your physical limitations. The standard missionary position may be the least comfortable now. Read the information on positions in Chapter Five. The side to side, or "scissors," position may be the most comfortable one for you now.

COMMENTS: From a 56-year-old woman: "After my husband first hurt his back helping our son move a sofa, we thought our sex life was over. Every time we tried to have intercourse, he would yelp in pain, lose his erection, and that would be that. We agreed not to try intercourse for a while, but to have oral and manual sex. Then we realized we could make love in a big chair, with me on his lap, my weight supported by my folded legs on either side of him. His back has improved through regular physical-therapy sessions, and we have gradually added some more intercourse positions. Losing his gut has helped him a lot, both with the back and intercourse."

To Lessen the Sexual Impact of Illness on the Relationship

These general steps will help you and your partner restore the sexual relationship as soon as possible following major illness or surgery.

- *Share the crisis.* It's easy to let illness divide you into the patient and the other. Think of your partner's illness as yours too. If you are the one with the illness, empathize with your partner's fears and concerns.

- *Research the problem.* It helps to learn everything you can about the disease, its immediate psychological and sexual impact, courses of treatment, and side effects. Be frank about sexual concerns in talking to the doctors. Consider a consultation with a sex therapist too. Most physicians have not been trained in sexuality. When you know what to expect, you can plan coping strategies.

- *Expect a full range of emotions.* Anger, sadness, fear, and other strong feelings accompany major illnesses or surgery—for both partners.

- *Don't plan on being the sole full-time caregiver.* You need time for yourself, and your partner will benefit from being around others who care too.

- *Be affectionate with each other.* Even if you don't feel like being sexual, don't withdraw from physical affection. Both partners need closeness and physical contact through holding hands, hugging, kissing, cuddling.

- *Don't stop thinking about sex.* If your partner is too ill to make love, don't stifle your sexual thoughts and fantasies out of guilt. It's okay to have these thoughts. They keep the fire burning.

- *Masturbate.* Explore your own sexual feelings while you are waiting for your lover's recovery.

- *Remember that "sex" is more than intercourse.* Making love does not require an erection, an orgasm, or ejaculation.

- *Have a positive attitude when you can have sex again.* Don't worry about functioning. The attitude you take about your sexuality is far more important than any physical limitations you may have.

- *Look for books and articles about the lingering or ongoing physical, psychological, and sexual effects of the particular illness or disability.* In some cases, there are support groups for patients and their partners. And some associations may have helpful information, including addresses of catalogues available from companies specializing in products, such as the love stool, that facilitate sexual expression for the ill and disabled.

WHY HYSTERECTOMY DOESN'T END YOUR SEX LIFE

"Having a hysterectomy is a psychologically traumatic event for a woman because you are losing the part most closely identified with womanhood," says Donna, 49. "I had one two years ago. I believe it was necessary, and I felt better physically afterward. But I had lingering depression and no interest in sex for several months. Hormone-replacement therapy helped. My husband's tenderness really got me through the rough period. He was very romantic, as though we were newly involved with each other. Bringing flowers, making dates, writing me love notes in shaving foam on the bathroom mirror, remembering all the little things I like when he did the food shopping are just a few of the ways he courted me. I felt womanly again, and the sex followed naturally."

Though the numbers have gone down dramatically in the past decade, hysterectomy is still the surgery most commonly performed on women. In a hysterectomy, a woman's uterus and sometimes her ovaries and fallopian tubes are surgically removed. Prevailing medical thought now is that the operation has been unnecessarily performed on many women, particularly in cases of fibroid tumors that often either do no harm or respond to other forms of treatment and shrink or disappear following menopause.

For many women, plagued by pain or discomfort and heavy bleeding or other problems, hysterectomy is a relief. They find that sex after surgery is better than it was before. Other women report a loss of sex drive. Some question whether their surgeries were necessary and feel angry or betrayed by their doctors, especially if they have lost interest in sex.

Many of the concerns women have about hysterectomy are unproven. At present, there is no evidence that the surgery

- Causes weight gain. Only taking in more calories than you expend in energy causes weight gain.

- Prohibits sexual functioning, including intercourse.

- Accelerates the aging process.

We still do not know all there is to know about the impact of hysterectomy upon a woman's sexuality. Some researchers believe the uterus, which continues to produce hormones (and testosterone) in small amounts after menopause, plays an unrecognized hormonal role in sexual functioning. We do know that the removal of the ovaries and the loss of estrogen they produce leads to menopause, with attendant symptoms often including thinning of the vaginal walls, a decrease in lubrication, and general loss of sexual desire.

A woman can regain her sexual desire by:

- Taking hormone-replacement therapy, may be of particular concern if the ovaries have been removed.

- Including alternative estrogen sources, such as soy-based products, in her diet.

- Changing her lifestyle by exercising regularly, improving her diet, and shaping and toning her body.

- Using testosterone-replacement therapy, at least temporarily.

- Being honest with her partner about her feelings and asking for his support.

- Consulting a therapist.

Her partner can help by:

- Learning as much as he can about the sexual side effects of hysterectomy and about hormone-replacement therapy.

- Accepting her feelings, not trying to make her see how irrational they are.
- Being supportive and understanding, not pressuring her for sex. Let her set the pace.
- Assuring her of her desirability through compliments and gestures.
- Behaving in a romantic way.
- Seeing a therapist with her if she asks.

OVERCOMING THE SEXUAL SIDE EFFECTS OF MEDICATIONS

Often it's the medication, not the illness or injury, that precipitates a sexual problem. Prescription medications are one of the most common factors affecting erectile capacity. With over 75 million Americans taking prescription medication at any one time, drugs touch all our lives sooner or later. At midlife, many people are taking drugs to lower blood pressure, regulate heart conditions, alleviate depression, control ulcers, and treat minor infections, aches, pain, colds, and allergies. A middle-aged man with an already slightly compromised (by age) erection ability may lose that ability altogether with the addition of blood pressure medication to the equation. A middle-aged woman with some body image and other aging issues may lose her fragile libido altogether when she starts taking medication for depression.

A prescription can push a person over the sexual edge. And over 200 commonly prescribed drugs can, according to the manufacturers' own literature, influence sexual performance or enjoyment. The antihypertensives, the medicines used to control high blood pressure, have the highest incidence of interfering with erections and ejaculations, and the antidepressants have the highest incidence of inhibiting desire. Doctors rarely mention sexual side effects when prescribing drugs, and patients who don't read the fine print in the accompanying product literature often fail to connect the sex problem with the medication.

The main potential sexual side effects include:

- Decreased libido.
- Increased vaginal dryness in women.

- Impotence, or problems getting or maintaining an erection.

- Loss of sensation in the genitals.

- Difficulty with ejaculation in men and orgasm in women.

Sometimes it's difficult to determine if a sexual problem is directly related to drugs. A depressed person, for example, may lose interest in sex from the depression as well as from the drug. If you can trace the beginning of the problem to the start of medication, you have good reason to suspect the drug. What can you do if prescription medication is interfering with sexual desire and functioning?

- Talk to your doctor first. Don't take yourself off medication. Ask for alternative drugs that may not have the same side effects. If there are none, would a change in dosage help?

- If you haven't done this before, fill your doctor in on your sexual history. Be honest about the rest of your history, including whether or not you smoke, how much you drink, and what over-the-counter medications you use. All this information helps a physician evaluate the contribution of prescription medication to a sex problem.

- Make the positive lifestyle changes that might enable you to reduce dosage or go off medication altogether. Stop smoking. Reduce alcohol consumption. Take some of the fat out of your diet, and start a regular exercise program.

- Follow the previous suggestions for having more frequent sexual activity. The more you make love, the more you will want to make love. Abstinence at midlife is not conducive to sexual functioning later on.

- With your doctor's knowledge and input, explore alternative and holistic remedies. You will need to do a lot of research in this area. Look for fact-based books and articles with research statistics for backup, rather than anecdotal accounts. Remember that anyone can post anything on the Internet. Valid research pieces reprinted from reliable sources coexist with pure drivel.

Rejuvenating the Mind-Body Connection

You've read about the effects of hidden anger and resentment, depression, fear, anxiety, and other psychological factors on sexuality. How does an intense dislike of your aging body affect your sex life? For many people, the answer is: badly.

"It's hard to make love on the same day I've looked at myself in a mirror," a 53-year-old woman said ruefully. "My friends have either had or are considering having their first face lifts. My husband doesn't even want to hear about it. He thinks the whole idea is ridiculous. 'I love your wrinkles,' he says. Maybe he does, but I don't. My wrinkles are taking my libido down with them."

Whether it makes sense to the people who love them or not, some women, and men too, stop feeling sexy when their mirror image tells them they are looking "old." They will endure the pain or discomfort of face lifts, liposuction, tucks to the breasts, abdomen, and butt, hair transplants, or the cost and agony of whatever treatment promises to restore a measure of youthful sex appeal. The link between a younger-looking image and feeling desirable is a strong one in Western culture.

"Healthy and fit isn't quite good enough," a female patient in her fifties told me. "I need to look younger and *sexier* too."

For many people, the suggestions on pages 7–9 and 21–23 will help them gain acceptance of their bodies as they are now and feel more sexually desirable. For some others, nothing short of surgical intervention will jump-start their libido. As Baby Boomers age, the numbers of people submitting to plastic surgery and other forms of self-improvement more drastic than diet and exercise will continue to increase. And so will the numbers of products designed for everything from cinching the waistline to creating the illusion of hair on the bald spot via a spray can. After fifty, we may all be a little more vulnerable to the sales pitch when the promise is a more youthful appearance, a reinvigorated sex life.

If your partner is determined to have a face lift or other surgical procedure:

- Make sure your partner has researched the surgery, the doctor, and the hospital or outpatient facility thoroughly. Help her (or him) evaluate the risks and make a reasoned choice. Many people decide to have cosmetic surgery because their friends are doing it. We each bring our own set of risk factors to any medical situation.

- Walk the narrow line between being supportive and appearing to welcome the prospect with too much enthusiasm. She/he should feel free to cancel, up to the last minute. Most of us would find it hard to change our minds about surgery if we believed our partners were anxiously awaiting the new, improved us.

- Express the sentiments, "I love you the way you are, but I will love you the way you want to become too. It's up to you."

- Be loving and affectionate before surgery and during recovery.

If you are the one determined to have a facelift or other surgical procedure:

- Research the procedure, the doctor, and the hospital or outpatient facility thoroughly. Don't choose a doctor based on personal references alone. You should ask to see before-and-after photos of other patients. Also ask about the complication rate. How many patients have infections, scarring, or other complications?

- Set realistic expectations. You will not look 21 again. Traffic won't stop when you cross the street. You won't be a 20-year-younger version of yourself. Ask your doctor what it is reasonable to expect. Most people look a little younger, more rested and relaxed following a face lift. They don't look like Demi Moore or Tom Cruise.

- If you are suffering from loss of libido or some other sex problem, surgery probably won't solve it. Review the suggestions in previous chapters for increasing desire and improving sexual functioning. Talk to your doctor. Maybe HRT or some other form of treatment will help you feel young again without submitting to the knife.

- If you have reached a carefully evaluated decision, don't let anyone make you feel guilty about it. There's nothing wrong with lifting a face, inducing a bald head to grow hair, or having the spider veins on your legs "zapped" out of existence. Enjoy.

- After surgery, find ways of feeling good about yourself that aren't appearance-based. Eventually, the skin will sag again.

"I didn't want to appear vain," a male patient said about his hair implants, "but I hated my bald head. I looked in the mirror and saw my father. Now that I have a modest crop of hair, I see a virile guy, still young at 55."

"Vanity" implies an excess of pride. Most people who have their appearances changed and, it's hoped, improved via surgical or other procedures aren't excessively proud. They're worried that the way they look will inhibit their partner's desire for them.

"I can't believe the difference a mini face lift and some minor tucks have made in my sex life," says Deborah, a very attractive woman in her early fifties. "My husband will deny it to his dying day but he wasn't as interested in me sexually before the surgeries as he is after. I don't blame him. I didn't turn myself on either.

"Now when he looks at me, he sees a woman who is more like the one he fell in love with. I feel exhilarated, sexually charged. We are feeding off each other again. It's wonderful. Would I have another tuck in five, ten years? Maybe. Probably. Why not?"

Five Steps to Regaining Desire Lost to Illness, Disability, Physical Signs of Aging

As couples age, they are more likely to be confronted with illness, injury, or disability, conditions that may have important consequences for their sex lives. Also, they are more likely than previous generations to confront issues surrounding the physical signs of aging. Men and women over 50 today don't accept the same limitations their parents and grandparents did. They expect to look and feel "younger." Inevitably, their expectations will clash with the reality in their mirrors.

Some couples will stop making love in response to these situations. By regaining their passion for each other, their enthusiasm for life and lovemaking, and their erotic creativity, nearly every couple can surmount the medical obstacles to good sex. Here's how:

1. *Don't pull away from each other now when the need for touch, affection, and pleasure is greatest.* Illness can cause the sufferer to withdraw into self. Resist the temptation to do that. Reach out to your partner. If you are the healthy one, don't take your partner's withdrawal as personal rejection. It isn't. Reach out and coax your lover back to you.

2. *Review the steps for lessening the sexual impact of illness and disability.* The same advice holds true for men and women who are avoiding sex because they hate the way they look. Don't belittle a partner's dissatisfaction with an aging body. A preoccupation with sags and bags may not seem as significant as a heart attack, but it can be sexually debilitating too.

3. *Do what you can to look better—and to help your partner look better.* Studies have shown a direct correlation between the time required for a woman to resume sexual activity after a mastectomy and the effort she puts into improving her appearance, Wigs, prostheses, and special clothing are necessities, not luxuries for the recovering breast-cancer patient. Whether you're getting over an illness or making the mental adjustment to the physical signs of aging, do everything you can to look better today. A couple in their fifties who were despondent about their son turning 30 reignited their sex life by getting his-and-her makeovers.

"It was expensive," he says, "but a lot cheaper than divorce."

4. *Give yourself, and your partner, a sensual treat every day.* Take time to smell the flowers. Savor the texture of different foods in your mouth. If your home isn't filled with varied textiles, buy some, for example, a silk pillow, crisp cotton sheets, a cashmere throw.

5. *Investigate antiaging products, but don't allow yourself to be taken in by outrageous claims.* The marketplace is flooded with antiaging remedies from expensive face creams promising to eliminate fine lines to over-the-counter hormones such as melatonin, DHEA, and pregnenolone, hyped as life extenders. Manufacturers prey on the hopes and fears of an aging population with their promises, some of which are empty. Nonetheless, there are some worthwhile new products that may help you cheat time, at least by minutes, if not years.

The face-care products featuring alpha and beta hydroxy, for example, are more effective than any previous beauty aids at diminishing the appearance of fine lines and age spots. Read labels. You can buy the budget versions of these products in drugstores and supermarkets, saving significantly over the designer items marketed in department stores.

When it comes to over-the-counter hormones and similar products, do your homework. And be skeptical when reading product literature. Antiaging medicine is for the most part an idea whose time isn't quite here. But it may be soon.

Sizzler # **13**

MAKEOVER SEX

While Jim's wife, Katie, was dying of cancer, he hardly even saw himself when he looked in the mirror to shave or comb what was left of his hair. For two years after her death, he did not look at another woman. Then one bright autumn day as he was having a solitary lunch at a sidewalk café, he noticed another lone diner, a woman who must have been in her late forties or early fifties. Even in repose she looked vibrant, lively. He wondered what it would he like to make love to her.

Later at home he looked, really looked, at himself in the full-length mirror on the inside of his bedroom door. Standing sideways, he studied his profile. Potbelly. Slight double chin. Head on, he couldn't escape the bags around his eyes. The shiny pate and the fringe of graying hair surrounding it didn't bother him as much as those sagging eyes. He looked as if he would never smile again, and he was smiling when he drew that conclusion.

Jim embarked on a diet-and-exercise program. The potbelly shrank. He could discern muscles developing again beneath the fat. But those eyes. He thought of the woman he'd seen at the restaurant. She wasn't much younger than he was, probably five, maybe ten years. Would a woman like that even consider a man like him? Probably not, he concluded, because of those damn saggy, baggy eyes.

He told his friends, grown son, and colleagues that he was having his eyes fixed because the drooping flesh was narrowing his field of vision. They believed him or pretended they did. The surgery was easier than he thought it would be. After a few uncomfortable days, he healed quickly, and he was rewarded for his mild suffering with a new look. The excess flesh on his eyelids and beneath the eyes was gone. When he smiled now, he reminded himself of the actor Ed Harris. He was handsome again.

Jim went back to the café where he'd seen the woman who had turned his erotic pilot light back on. It was winter, and the outdoor tables were in storage. He sat inside at a table for one again, close to a roaring fire. She wasn't there. He made a habit of dining there two or three times a week, but he didn't see her.

Just as he was about to write off romantic fantasy, a woman asked in a soft, hesitant voice, "Do you mind if I share your table? There's not another one free."

His heart leaped. He looked up into the lovely green eyes of a woman who wasn't his fantasy, but would do. Confident of his clear gaze not obscured by folds of flesh, he held her eyes for several heart-beats. She would certainly do. Standing, he pulled out a chair for her.

"Please," he said. "I often come here and dine alone, wishing someone would join me."

"Oh, you're being kind," she said, laughing, as she took the chair he offered.

They sat together at the little table and talked through lunch, dessert, wine, and finally a selection of appetizers. He suggested a movie, followed by dinner at another restaurant. And she eagerly agreed. On that first long date, they learned a lot about each other's marital histories and tasters in food, movies, books. A widow, she had lost her husband to cancer, too.

At the end of the evening, Jim escorted her back to her apartment. At her door, he took her in his arms and kissed her, gently at first, then with growing passion. He knew they would become lovers, not tonight, but soon. When he held her in his arms, he pressed against her, just enough to let her feel the promise that he felt growing inside.

Two weeks later, Jim made dinner for her at his place. He had set the stage for seduction, and she didn't disappoint him. She came with a tote bag in place of her classic handbag. He saw something silky peeking from the top.

After a leisurely meal, he began making love to her on the sofa in front of the fireplace. The lovemaking lasted a long time. It fulfilled the fantasies he'd begun to nurture since the day he'd noticed the woman alone at the sidewalk café. The man he'd seen in his mirror that night was gone. An old man, a sad man, he had disappeared into the glass. In his place was Jim, mature, sophisticated, a lover *extraordinaire.*

The woman in his arms returned his kisses, touches, embraces. Her heart beat loudly in his ears when he lowered his face between her breasts. They were vital, alive, together, and he was going to bring her joy.

14

LOVE WITH ANOTHER PARTNER

"In the last few years of my marriage, I often felt the sex was boring, humdrum, routine," says Jackie. "It reflected the relationship. After we got divorced, I didn't have sex for two years. Then, at age 51, I met a man. It was clear by the second date that we were headed for an intimate relationship. I was excited and terrified. Would my body turn him off? Would I remember how to perform fellatio? What if I couldn't have an orgasm?

"I seriously thought about not having a third date so I wouldn't have to take off my clothes and put myself on the line. Being naked at 51 in front of a near stranger is not an easy thing to do. Parts of me have definitely gone south. When I talked it over with my best friend, she told me he was probably as scared as I was.

"'Don't you think he's worried about whether or not his penis will work?' she asked. 'Everything pales in comparison to the big penis issue for men.'

"She was right. We were both nervous. Fortunately we did it for the first time on my living room sofa by candlelight, so I didn't have to do the complete disrobing or worry about whether or not to turn on a bedroom light. He was very passionate and very tender; and his penis did indeed work. I had an orgasm. Fellatio? Like riding a bicycle. I hadn't forgotten."

Midlife couples who have been together for many years confront their own sexual issues, but people who are starting over, starting late, or finding themselves involved in late affairs have problems too. They aren't scanning lists of how to take the boredom out of the bedroom for hot tips, but they may be standing in front of the full length mirror agonizing about saddlebags and stretch marks, sagging breasts, potbellies, and prominent veins and the effect these signs of aging will have on new partners. Even people who are in very good shape may have temporarily lost their sexual self-confidence.

"It's one thing to make love to a trusted partner and another to test-drive your less-than-stalwart member with someone new," says Bruce, 50, and recently out of a long-term relationship.

If you are single, widowed, or divorced, your best hedge against first-time sexual failure is prevention.

THE SIX KEYS TO STAYING SEXUAL ALONE

Prolonged and involuntary celibacy is perhaps the most difficult sexual condition. When men or women lose a partner through death or divorce in middle age, they, particularly the women, will likely be alone longer than a younger person suffering the same loss. Nothing takes the place of sex, but if you break it down into its components, you can make sure each of the needs is being met in your life. In simplest terms, sex is warmth, closeness, physical touching, and orgasm.

It is more important now to stay in sexual shape during celibate periods than it ever has been. Regaining sexual functioning, if you've lost it, can be difficult at midlife and beyond. Don't let it go, and you won't have to worry about how to get it back when you meet your next partner.

The keys to staying sexual while alone are:

1. *Create and strengthen intimate bonds.* Find warmth and closeness with friends and family. It's important that you not get out of the habits of relating and exchanging affection. The phrase "set in his (or her) ways" is not a description often applied to a sensual and sexual person.

2. *Indulge your sensual side*. Candlelight is not only for shared meals. Bubble baths can be the prelude to self-loving as well as to love-making with a partner. Wear perfume. Buy flowers. Be romantic with yourself.

3. *Fantasize*. Don't censor your sexual thoughts because you don't have a partner and/or you think you're "too old" for erotic day-dreams. Read books and watch films that encourage sexual fantasies. Allow yourself to imagine new and creative erotic scenarios.

4. *Touch*. Take your hugs where you can get them, from family and friends, even from yourself. Put your arms around yourself and hug. When you're feeling lonely, tense, or stressed, rub your hand or arm, cheek or neck. If you don't have a pet, consider adopting one.

5. *Keep your hormone levels up*. If you're a man and you suffer from low testosterone, don't neglect treatment because you don't have a partner. If you're a woman, elevate your estrogen levels after menopause through HRT or alternatives. Keep your vagina lubricated in preparation for intercourse through the regular use of Replens or another product.

6. *Masturbate*. Regular masturbation will keep the sex organs functioning for men and women. You'll have all the health benefits of orgasm whether orgasm is achieved alone or with a lover. And you can use masturbation as a time to explore new ways of touching and stroking yourself, information you'll be able to share with a new partner.

If you follow these steps, when you meet the person who will become your lover, you'll be ready.

HOW TO BECOME SEXUALLY ACTIVE AGAIN WITH A PARTNER

"I knew I was planning to make love to Kathryn when I bought the package of condoms at the pharmacy," says Ted, 56. "I felt like an elated kid and an old fool all at once. That pretty much describes the situation when you're 'seriously dating' again after 20 years. Your emotions are up and down, up and down."

Ted had been divorced almost two years when he met Kathryn. He'd had "two casual flings of short duration" during that time. Because he did not feel emotionally involved with the women, he was able to have sex with them without worrying much about his performance.

"The first time I had sex after the divorce I felt a twinge of concern about my penis," he says, "but I told myself, 'If you have an erection failure, you just won't see her again. No big deal.'

"I knew right away it was going to be a big deal with Kathryn. I really liked her. I wanted to make love to her; and I had delayed longer than either of us wanted to wait because I was afraid of disappointing her. I could tell she was wondering what was holding me back. The day I bought the condoms was the red letter day. I wasn't entirely satisfied with my performance. My erection kept doing a disappearing and reappearing act that made me nervous. But she wasn't disappointed. She put my hand where she wanted it to be against her clitoris and had me bring her to orgasm during intercourse. I liked that a lot. It gave me confidence."

After a dry spell, becoming sexually active with a new partner can be as scary as it is exciting. Men and women share certain fears about making love to a new person at this stage in their lives. They include:

Body-Image Anxiety

One survey of single women over 40 rated "fear of being seen naked" as their number-one stumbling block to having sex again. In a society where the prevailing image of "single" is the young and beautiful cast of the television show "Friends," an older, more amply endowed woman without a partner may believe she isn't meant to have sex again. Men too have more anxiety about their appearance than they did in the past, but less than women experience. A man can think he's sexy if he's bald and overweight. It's harder for a woman in comparable physical condition to feel good about her sex appeal.

How to Handle: Being overly self-conscious about your appearance can sabotage sex. Remember, his body isn't what it once was either. To relieve some of the anxiety, start making love with your clothes on. Feeling inside clothing for the hidden flesh and groping for buttons and zippers adds to the excitement. When you are both very aroused, cellulite concerns will fade away. Until you are comfortable with nudity, keep the lights low or off and wear something lacy and filmy to bed.

COMMENTS: From a 54-year-old woman: "I bought a tube of Dermablend, a waterproof cosmetic coverup used to hide birthmarks and surgical scars. I touched up the veins on the backs of my knees and the tops of my feet. And I wore a short, sexy slip with a built-in bra that I kept on during sex the first time. The makeup and the slip gave me the confidence I needed to let go and enjoy sex."

Performance Anxiety

Women worry about whether or not their sexual technique will produce the desired results on him, and they worry about orgasms. Will she have one or won't she? In this area, a woman feels pressured to "perform." Men worry even more about women's orgasms. They fear losing their erections or, worse, being unable to get firm and disappointing her. Performance anxiety is, according to a survey of single men over 40, the biggest stumbling block to first-time sex with a new partner. Women might be surprised to learn that many men delay having sex from anxiety.

HOW TO HANDLE: He can take the relentless focus off his penis, and so can she. By making love in a less penis-centered way, they take away the pressure and add to their pleasure. He can also ask her for the manual or oral stimulation he needs to become fully erect. A woman who shows a man how to please her by guiding his hand or responding enthusiastically to his oral ministrations lets him off the erection hook. Male or female, review the hints for handling loss of erection during lovemaking.

COMMENTS: From a 50-year-old man: "The first time I made love to a new woman in 25 years, I said to her, 'Let me pleasure you.' I gave her orgasm after orgasm via cunnilingus. By the time she was sated, I was fully aroused and confident enough of my erection for intercourse. If you can give a woman several orgasms, you lose the fear of failing with your penis."

Fear of Rejection

How would it feel to be rejected by your first new lover in many years? Not good. That fear keeps some people from ever having a new lover. Others censor their words and feelings creating a false "me" to protect the true self from rejection. They rationalize that they are safe from emotional hurt if they take no chances. Withdrawal is not a good option.

HOW TO HANDLE: Go back to Chapter 2 and review the building blocks of passion. You have to overcome fear to have passion in your life. That isn't always easy to do, but it's worth the effort. Say to yourself: If I have sex with someone who never wants to see me again, there are other potential lovers who will want more of me.

COMMENTS: From a 49-year-old woman: "It's hell to be middle-aged and wondering, 'Is he going to call or not?' I found myself glancing through that asinine book, *The Rules*, in a bookstore after I met Rick and briefly wondering if I should wait until a certain time period had elapsed to have sex with him so he'd call me back. Ridiculous! I talked myself out of my rejection fears and plunged ahead. It's the only thing you can do."

Fear of Intimacy

Some people use exaggerated disease fears as a way of avoiding intimacy. Others look for excuses to reject a potential partner before they have sex or soon thereafter. Some avoid intimacy by pursuing fervently, then pulling back when the object of their affections returns their interest. That behavior pattern isn't limited only to the young.

HOW TO HANDLE: People who fear intimacy protect themselves emotionally. They don't become vulnerable. Good sex requires shared vulnerability. Review the material about overcoming intimacy fears. Talk to yourself about your fears. Say: I won't be overwhelmed by my partner's needs if I get close. I can handle closeness and retain my autonomy.

COMMENTS: From a 49-year-old man: "My ex-wife often accused me of avoiding intimacy, fearing intimacy, running from intimacy. I really got tired of hearing the word 'intimacy' in my marriage. I think she used it as a club. When I started sleeping with a woman I cared about after the divorce, I began to think a lot about the concept of intimacy. It's not such a bad idea if a woman isn't demanding it from you."

After a man and woman have had sex, they either move forward toward a deeper intimacy and have more sex, or they don't. Some couples don't develop a relationship for good reasons: They aren't right for each other. The timing is wrong. One or both have other priorities. But some couples don't develop a relationship for the wrong reasons: They let obstacles that could be overcome get in their way.

Overcoming the Five Obstacles to a New Sexual Relationship

"Matt and I became lovers on a holiday in Mexico," says Sandra, 46. "I hadn't been with a man in over a year. He hadn't been with a woman since his divorce almost a year to the day after we met. Our Mexican interlude was idyllic. The sex was wonderful. Then we went home, he to Chicago, me to St. Louis, not an impossible commute, but not convenient. Still, the relationship thrived.

"Our kids did us in. My teenagers and his adult children didn't want us to be together—with a vengeance. Not one of the four of them could deal with a parent having a sex life. We caved to the pressure and didn't see each other for three months. Now we are seeing each other when we can arrange it without the kids knowing. It's like an illicit affair. My friends say I need counseling, and they're probably right. But the sex is still wonderful. Maybe when my baby goes off to college next year, we'll work something out."

Once a new sexual relationship has been established in middle age, the participants may not get the same enthusiastic emotional support from family and friends that young lovers do. Unlike the twentysomething couple, they will find a dearth of media images celebrating their love. To be young in love at midlife is, in our culture's terms, an oxymoron. Don't expect rose petals to be tossed in your path.

Some of the obstacles you may encounter shortly after the first series of orgasms subsides:

1. *Teenaged or adult children.* Logically, adult children should have no effect on a single parent's sex life, but they can if you let them. Maybe they resent Dad for leaving Mom or vice versa. Maybe they're worried about their inheritance. Possibly they can't imagine their parents having sex, not even with each other, never mind with someone else. Teenagers are even less capable of imagining Mom or Dad having

sex with a suitable stranger. And their demands on a parent's time, energy, and emotions are more acceptable and understandable.

If the kids don't approve, can the adults have sex?

Tell your teenagers that you are old enough to understand and accept the responsibilities of a sexual relationship and can make your own partner choice. If you aren't comfortable with your choice, however, they'll know it. And will pounce.

How to Handle: Don't be provocative in front of the children. Avoid one-night stands that lead to a series of lovers staying over. You can counter your children's objections to your sexual behavior more authoritatively if your actions are consistent with your family's values. "Do as I say, not as I do," doesn't cut it with teens and young adults.

Don't get into a relationship with someone who makes you feel uncomfortable. That can lead you to become sexually active to prove your attractiveness or assuage neediness or allay fears of being left alone. Your kids won't miss those signals. They will hit you directly in the vulnerable zone. When your sexual choices aren't solid, you're more likely to have difficulty handling their reactions.

Finally, remember that your children's objections to a new lover may be rooted in their unspoken wish for a reconciliation between you and their other parent. Your sexual behavior is threatening because it indicates your intention of forming a new relationship. Discuss this with your children. You can't give them the power of choosing your sex partners.

2. *Past-relationship baggage.* His wife was critical and domineering, so he doesn't want to hear an opinion or suggestion from you. Your husband had an affair; and you don't trust men anymore. People bring issues from their families of origin into the first marriage. When they pack for the second, or later, marriage, they may still have the original bags, plus a new set. That's a heavy load to lug into the honeymoon suite.

How to Handle: Many people not only carry issues from a former partner into a new relationship, they also choose someone who is particularly suited to enact their unfinished business. The woman, for example, who has trust issues gets involved with a married man promising to leave his wife. Whether he keeps his promise or not, he's most likely trouble.

Be aware of the issues you bring into a new relationship and avoid the obvious reenactments. Stop blaming your ex for all your problems, and take a good look at yourself and your contribution to the failed relationship. When you do that, you'll be able to identify your own issues.

Finally, be open with a new partner. Discuss your issues. If you don't get a supportive response early in the relationship, you probably won't get it later.

3. *Health problems.* A 40-year-old woman married a healthy, vibrant 60-year-old man. Ten years later, she is nursing him through recovery from prostate-cancer surgery, a recovery complicated by his diabetes and heart condition. That dreaded scenario plays out in the minds of most middle-aged women involved with men their age or older. The chances of one or both partners facing health problems in the marriage is certainly higher than it was when she married for the first time in her twenties. There will likely be a bigger age gap between her and her second husband than there was between her and her first. On average, with each marriage, men marry younger than they did before. If she marries the man who is 5, 10, 15, 20 years older at this stage in her life, how likely is it that she will become his nurse?

How to Handle: Committing to someone considerably older does increase the likelihood that the partner will become ill and need care. Prevention is the best medicine here. In a loving relationship, each partner has a responsibility to be supportive of the other's health. Encourage your partner to eat well, exercise moderately, get regular medical checkups to spot problems early, and manage stress effectively.

If you have a partner in ill health, you can't devote yourself entirely to caring for him or her. The challenge for partners of seriously and/or chronically ill people is to refrain from becoming bitter and resentful. Make time for the activities and people that you enjoy because they recharge your emotional batteries. Get help with the caretaking from professionals and other family members and friends. Create a support system for both you and your partner. There are support groups for people with cancer and other diseases. Reach out for help. Doing that will enable you to be thankful for the good years you've had with your partner and make the most of your remaining time together.

4. *Unresolved personal issues.* If they haven't been resolved by midlife, how likely is it that they ever will be? Issues that can get in the way of establishing intimacy and maintaining a good sexual relationship

include unresolved anger and intimacy fears, behavioral problems such as heavy drinking or overspending, and sexual hang-ups. In middle age unresolved personal issues will very likely create relationship problems.

HOW TO HANDLE: Practice self-acceptance. Midlife is the perfect time to embrace ourselves, blemishes and all. At this point in our lives, we've addressed many of the concerns of youth: choosing a primary career path, starting a family, establishing a financial base. We have more time, and the inclination, for reflection. Sometimes that reflection leads to harsh self-analysis.

Most of us do our best. We have good intentions and decency in our hearts. Do we have to be Mother Teresa to feel good about ourselves? No. We'll take most of our imperfections to our graves. By being more self-accepting, we can be more open, less defensive, and stop living our lives in fear of being "found out." Problems such as intimacy fears, drinking, and anger decrease dramatically when we learn to accept ourselves.

If you jump over these obstacles in a rush to remarry, they may mysteriously reappear in your path someday.

"Rob and I got married last year on my fiftieth birthday after a six-month courtship," says Carla. "The sex was very good until we got married, and then there was a sudden drop-off in frequency. I was interested, and he wasn't. We started fighting about when and how often to have sex. Finally, one day he told me I was just like his first wife. A bell went off in my head.

"I literally dragged him to a marital-and-sex therapist. It took us six months, as long as the courtship, to work out the issues we'd carried over from our previous marriages. We are happy now, and the sex is good again. But I would advise other couples to do this before the wedding, not after."

THE LATE AFFAIR

"When a man has his first extramarital affair after his fortieth birthday, everyone assumes he's in the throes of a 'midlife crisis,'" says Martin, 46. "I resent being lumped into the category of 'typical middle aged man.'"

Having said this, Martin acknowledged that he's having an affair with his 25-year-old administrative assistant. To him, and presumably to his lover, they are a unique man and woman involved in a special relationship that has nothing in common with the cliché they undoubtedly resemble. There are, however, some commonalities in first-time midlife affairs. Often the participants invest them with more meaning and take them more seriously, or convince themselves they do, than either their counterparts who strayed earlier or younger first-time extramarital lovers. Often the older man does seek out the younger woman, typically a workplace subordinate. But statistics show that trend has leveled off somewhat with an increasing number of married men being attracted to their feminine equals in the workplace, women nearer their own age. Without small children at home to motivate them to stay in their marriages, older lovers in high emotional-involvement affairs may be more likely to divorce.

"My wife and I have been ships passing in the night for years now," he says. "Our marriage is a property partnership. Now that our son has left for college, the two of us have even less in common than we did and fewer shared activities to attend. The sexual part of our relationship has been dead for a long time."

Martin's lover, Tiffany, believes that he and his wife Georgia never have sex. He concedes they do, but, he says, "It's not very intimate lovemaking like I have with Tiffany, but it's better sex than we've been having. I think I bring more energy to the bedroom after being with Tiffany." Will Martin leave Georgia for Tiffany? "That would be complicated," he hedges.

The odds are still that Martin will break up with Tiffany, or she with him, and he will stay with his wife. Studies have shown that only about one in ten people leave their spouses for their lovers. He may or may not have another affair. Their marriage may or may not become close and intimate, but it probably has benefited sexually from his affair. Incidentally, his wife may be having, or have had, an affair of her own without Martin knowing.

Men and women become involved in affairs for the first time in middle age for many of the same reasons they might have earlier, but their age, and the length of time they've been married, may have supplied the impetus they needed to finally act on their erotic impulses. Those reasons include:

- *Emotional alienation from mate.* In the child-rearing years, a couple may be too busy to notice how alienated they are from each other. At middle age, when the household is quieter, they look across the breakfast or dinner table and realize they have nothing to say to each other. Their sex life is probably routine and boring because they have not deepened the intimate connection between them and moved to a higher plane of lovemaking. If the children were the raison d'être for the marriage, the marriage is in trouble now.

HOW IT MAY AFFECT THE MARRIAGE: Rather than working together to build a more intimate relationship, some couples choose to look elsewhere for the sexual excitement they crave. Unlike the frequent philanderer who spends a lifetime reliving the adolescent thrill of fresh attraction, the midlife first-timer is turning back sexual time in one big leap. The affair will probably be exhilarating for a while.

COMMENTS: From a 48-year-old woman: "I had an affair last year for the first time in a 21-year marriage and for all the classic reasons. I didn't feel close to my husband anymore. We made love infrequently. I needed to feel attractive and valued by someone else. The affair lasted three months and was a wake-up call for me. I got my husband into counseling. I really wanted to make my marriage better, not throw it away. He doesn't know about the affair; and I don't think he ever needs to know. We are closer now; and the sex is better."

• *Curiosity about what sex would be like with someone else.* A man or a woman who married young with not much of a sexual past may have some regrets about pleasures never tasted. He or she may have occasionally fantasized about missed opportunities over the years. Now the sense of erotic time running out creates a sense of urgency. An opportunity for sex with another person presents itself; and the formerly faithful spouse strays.

HOW IT MAY AFFECT THE MARRIAGE: An affair motivated by sheer curiosity will probably be a low emotional-involvement relationship and may not threaten the marriage. This may be the only taste of forbidden fruit the curious partner requires. He or she may return to the spouse, chastened, and determined to atone for the lapse by being more romantic, caring, and seductive. A cautionary note: Any affair can lead to a more intense involvement and can have lasting impact on the marriage.

COMMENTS: From a 50-year-old man: "I married my high-school sweetheart when I was 22. I'd had sex with one other girl, a total of four times. Over the years, I thought about other women. I have considered using a prostitute when I traveled on business just to see what it would be like, but fear of disease kept me from it. Last year I had a fling with a woman I know at work. She's happily married too. It was good for both of us. I felt like a real stud for the first time in my life. Lovemaking with my wife is better than it was with the other woman. She's a very good lover, and we bring a history of tenderness and passion to every encounter. But I needed to know that."

- *Unexpressed anger or hostility toward partner.* Some people have affairs to get back at a spouse. That may be their subconscious agenda, no matter how they rationalize the liaison to themselves. The man or woman may have personal-anger issues and be unable to express angry feelings within the marriage. Or the hostility may have developed over a long period of time between a couple who express anger often and loudly, without resolving any of the problems that are making them so mad. An affair in these circumstances can be a passive-aggressive act of revenge.

How It May Affect the Marriage: Anything can happen when a middle-aged person with a big emotional agenda has a first extramarital affair, including divorce and remarriage. It's possible the affair may remain undiscovered and will lessen some of the feelings of resentment toward the spouse. The marriage and the sex may improve. On the other hand, the affair may be exposed, leading the hostile couple into another battle and the repressed-anger couple into a confrontation. Neither couple is likely to resolve the issues and rebuild the marriage without some counseling, but the possibility for a stronger marriage is there if they do get help.

Comments: From a 48-year-old man: "My wife was the church secretary, PTA president, and all around loyal woman. A year ago she got involved with another man. Now we are in the process of getting a divorce so she can marry him. She tells me that she learned in therapy she'd been angry at me for 20 years because I was a workaholic and emotionally withdrawn from her. Interestingly, she wants her cut of the money I earned through my workaholic ways. The new guy doesn't make as much. Do I wish I'd paid attention to her unexpressed feelings and needs a long time ago? Yes. The truth is I always knew something was wrong. I just didn't ask what. I figured she'd tell me if it was important."

• *The desire for more sex or a different kind of sex from what a partner wants.* After 20 years of making love to a partner who won't or can't indulge an erotic desire, some people find a lover for that reason alone. The desire may be for more frequent sex or oral sex, or for sexual variations such as anal sex, bondage, or light S/M. In some cases, a man seeks a partner who will indulge a "kink" his wife finds distasteful, such as foot fetishism. Very often, a man or woman is simply looking for a partner who will be more creative and spontaneous in bed. At this stage in life, he or she is asking, 'Why can't I have what I want now?'

HOW IT MAY AFFECT THE MARRIAGE: The affair may become an ongoing sexual outlet with low emotional involvement and may coexist with the marriage. The relationship may remove some of the stress from the marriage, particularly if the partner who can't comply sexually has medical reasons for not doing so. Or, the sexual seeker may discover that he or she doesn't want or need this particular sexual activity once it's available.

COMMENTS: From a 48-year-old man: "My wife is not as highly sexed as I am. Nor is she as interested in exploring sexual variations. She will do things for me, like agreeing to tie me up, but she won't get into them. I accidentally discovered that a coworker was interested in some mildly kinky forms of sex when I overheard her talking to a friend on the phone. After thinking it over a long time, I made my move. I haven't regretted it, and I hope I can keep the affair going without my wife ever finding out. She thinks I've 'outgrown' some of my sexual 'ideas' and is happy with our life together."

• *The need for an ego boost.* The one-night stand, the out-of-town fling, the brief affair with an attractive subordinate—all may be nothing more than shots of testosterone to the ego. That doesn't mean every ego getting an illicit sexual boost is male. Women can have affairs rooted in the need for an ego boost, and their libidos are also fueled by testosterone. When a couple have been together a long time, they may have stopped giving each other the positive emotional feedback most people need. Compliments, romantic gestures, and lust-filled glances say, You are sexy and desirable.

HOW IT MAY AFFECT THE MARRIAGE: An ego-boost affair typically does not evolve into a long-lasting emotional relationship. The impact on the marriage will probably be minimal, and may be positive, if discovery is avoided. Sexual battery recharged, the errant lover may give the spouse an ego boost now.

COMMENTS: From a 49-year-old man: "I was tired of being taken for granted by my wife and by my kids away at college who had no interest in me beyond the answer to the question, 'Dad, did you send a check?' It had been a long time since a woman touched my hand or my arm and looked into my eyes while we were talking. This woman did. And she was a very classy and beautiful woman. I felt like a new man after our little fling."

• *Avoidance—of marital or personal problems.* Some people are beset by problems for the first time at midlife. Corporate downsizing, hitting the glass ceiling, dealing with aging parents, unexpected health problems, living with teenagers, and paying for college are some of the big problems that seem to accompany receding hairlines and waistlines. If a couple are experiencing sex problems too, one or both of them may not see that the solutions lie in adapting their lovemaking styles and deepening their intimate connection. They may have an affair instead.

HOW IT MAY AFFECT THE MARRIAGE: For some people, the temporary sexual diversion and respite from marital problems helps them gain a new perspective and tolerance. The affair may enable them to keep the marriage intact through the difficult period. If they become very emotionally involved with a lover, however, they may decide to leave the marriage, believing (likely falsely) that they'll be leaving all their problems behind too.

COMMENTS: From a 52-year-old woman: "Last year I had an affair that saved my marriage. We had my terminally ill mother-in-law staying with us when our daughter returned home pregnant and not married; and I had to take a pay cut to stay employed. My husband and I were at each other's throats all the time. I had an affair with a friend who'd also been downsized and was having marital difficulties. We called it our little vacation from reality. Both of us did go back to reality, because we helped each other be able to cope."

• *To dull the pain of loss, for example death of a loved one or a child going off to college.* Traumatic loss brings some couples closer together but it drives many apart, sometimes temporarily. The death of a loved one, an empty nest, even a devastating career blow can lead to an affair. A man or a woman who can't share painful feelings with a spouse may find it easier to open up to a stranger in bed or at least seek comfort there.

HOW IT MAY AFFECT THE MARRIAGE: Much depends again on how emotionally involved the lovers become. Most affairs are low emotional-involvement affairs. If the bond between the lovers becomes intense, a middle-aged man or woman coping with significant loss may seize upon the relationship as salvation.

COMMENTS: From a 52-year-old woman: "After our son was paralyzed in a diving accident three years ago, my husband had an affair with his secretary. After all these years and at a time like that, he had an affair. I was devastated. For a while he thought he was in love with her. He realized he wasn't and begged me to take him back. I want the marriage to stay together, but I don't really think I've forgiven him yet. When I first found out about the affair, I had the hottest sex with him I've had in years. But we've had problems off and on since then, with his erections, my low libido. Maybe time will heal."

In many cases, there is more than one reason motivating a man or woman to have an affair. While reliable statistics are hard to find, affairs are certainly more common than they were in the past. When a first-time affair happens at midlife, however, emotions can easily be magnified. If you or your partner are having an affair, or have recently ended one, talk to a therapist. You could probably use some help in putting things back together again on a more solid footing.

HOW TO AVOID THE RISKS OF STDS

More than 12 million Americans will contract a sexually transmitted disease (STD) this year, and almost 20 percent of them will be over 40. With the exception of AIDS, these diseases, transmitted through sexual contact, are curable, most of them easily treated by antibiotics. When left untreated, some of them can lead to serious complications such as pelvic inflammatory disease in women.

Five Keys for Avoiding Midlife STDs:

- Practice safe sex, using condoms and nonoxonyl 9 during intercourse, whether the woman can get pregnant or not, is on birth control or not.

- Ask your doctor to test you for STDs during regular checkups if you are not in a monogamous relationship.

- Don't assume you can tell if a partner is likely to carry the HIV virus (for AIDS) or another STD by the way he or she looks, his or her age, or how long he or she has been married. You can't. HIV infection among men and women over 50 is a growing problem.

- If you know you're going to have a one-night stand only, why risk intercourse, even with a condom?

- And if you are a man paying a prostitute to perform fellatio, use a condom. You can contract some STDs from oral sex.

SHOULD YOU HAVE AN AFFAIR?

No one can make that choice for you. As a therapist, I wouldn't advise an unhappy spouse to have an affair. I would suggest he or she deal with the relationship issues first. Then I would ask, "Why are you considering an affair?" It's hoped, in trying to answer that question, the man or woman would begin to examine his or her dissatisfaction and look for the root causes. An affair is more often another complication than an answer. But I wouldn't offer a blanket condemnation of a man or a woman who does have an affair either.

Are you dissatisfied with the marriage? Or with yourself?

If you are sorely tempted to stray but haven't acted upon your impulses yet, ask and answer the following questions:

1. *What do you want from an affair?*

Review the most common reasons for midlife affairs in this chapter. Are you looking for intimacy, a different kind of sex, more sex, an ego boost, escape from the pain of a midlife loss? Could you get what you need from your mate if you asked?

Sometimes we assume that our partners won't be willing to listen, change, compromise, when in fact they would be if only they had the chance. Before looking outside the marriage for what you need, talk to your mate about your dissatisfaction. Don't threaten to have an affair if your needs aren't met.

2. *Do you have a hidden agenda?*

Anger, resentment, emotional alienation, and other factors are often the subtext of an extramarital affair, particularly at midlife. The feelings have had years to ferment inside. Having an affair may be a way of letting the feelings out. But is it the best way? Is it fair to you, your spouse, your prospective lover?

An affair can be a means of avoidance. You avoid working on the marriage, on your own personal issues, on dealing with the fears and concerns common at midlife. Some people manufacture a dissatisfaction with the marriage as an excuse for having an affair that really masks a dissatisfaction with self—or with a fear of "growing old."

3. *Are your lover's expectations for the affair the same as yours?*

Having an affair with another unhappily married person with no plans to divorce, for example, is different from having an affair with a single person who hopes you will leave your spouse for her or him. Some people are content in emotionally limited marriages. They may from time to time seek out a lover, but they enjoy the safety and security of the marriage. Which kind of person are you? What kind is your lover?

4. *What are the risks inherent in this affair?*

Will you fall in love? Will your lover? Would your spouse leave you if the affair were discovered? What other repercussions might befall you? Trouble at work? Confrontations with teenaged or young-adult children? Financial consequences? Emotional wreckage?

In weighing the risks, don't forget to consider the emotional ones. When people get involved in highly emotionally charged affairs, they report conflict and pain upon discovery or separation. A casual affair may coexist with a marriage, but an intense amour competes with it. Are you prepared for the outcome should the extramarital relationship become intense?

5. *Are you prepared for the mistrust that will exist between you and your spouse if the affair is discovered and then ended?*

Even a casual affair can have a strong impact upon a marriage. The consequences can run the gamut from destructive to enhancing. After a brief undiscovered affair, you'll be more open, loving, and receptive to your spouse. Discovery will almost certainly complicate the situation.

One of the consequences of a discovered affair may well be mistrust. Once you have broken the bond of intimacy between you and your spouse, you may discover that the trust is gone. Even an undiscovered affair can result in mistrust. The straying spouse no longer trusts self or partner. "If I cheated, so can she/he," is a comment I've often heard from patients in the aftermath of an affair. And they may also say, "If I cheated once, I'm afraid I'll do it again. I don't trust myself anymore."

6. *Is your spouse physically unable to be a sexual partner?*

Your spouse may be suffering from a debilitating or terminal illness that precludes sexual activity. That makes answering the question, "Should I have an affair?" even more difficult. You are probably grieving for your partner's loss of sexuality as well as your own enforced celibacy. Review the suggestions for maintaining intimate contact during illness or disability. Then schedule an appointment with a therapist to talk about your needs and desires. I am not saying you shouldn't have an affair under any circumstances, but I want you to be very clear about what you're doing before you do it. You will need some help in dealing with the guilt that will accompany an affair under these circumstances, if nothing else.

Should you have an affair?

Affairs can contribute to the unraveling of the fabric of a marriage by sowing those seeds of mistrust. Only you can analyze your motives and weigh the risks. Only you can decide if you should have an affair or not.

SHOULD YOU LEAVE YOUR PARTNER FOR YOUR LOVER?

As mentioned earlier, according to several studies, only about one in ten people having an extramarital affair leave their partners to marry their lovers. The consequences of divorce are frequently as hard on the person who seeks it as they are on the other partner, particularly at midlife. Divorce can lead to financial hardship, personal emotional distress, and all the problems associated with angry teenaged or adult children and extended families. Embarrassment over divorce is more common among people over 50 than among those who are younger.

Even if your marriage is unsatisfactory, you can expect a great deal of sadness and upheaval upon deciding to end it. Discomfort accompanies any loss. The end of a longstanding marriage is a major loss.

Divorce is sometimes the best choice for a couple, but not one that should ever be made in anger or haste, especially after they've been together for many years. See a counselor before leaving your spouse. And take all the time you need in making a decision. Don't be hurried by an impatient lover.

Finally, the difficulties of starting over with a new partner may be greater than you are imagining now, particularly if the partner is much younger than you.

If you think leaving is the right thing to do, keep this checklist handy.

1. *I have considered the financial consequences of divorce at midlife; and I am dealing with them.* Talk to your lawyer, tax accountant, financial planner. Unless you are wealthy, a midlife divorce will almost surely mean a reduction is lifestyle for both partners.

2. *I have anticipated the emotional impact of divorce, and I am getting help to deal with it.* Too many people assume they will be happy once they get the divorce they want. Before experiencing happiness, they will almost inevitably go through periods of grief, guilt, anxiety, and doubt.

3. *I have done everything I can to be fair to my spouse.* Some people get angry at the partner they're leaving because they need the anger as an impetus to action. Assigning full blame for the failure of the marriage to your partner is unfair and unrealistic. You will be able to move on with your new life faster if you accept responsibility for your own part in the dissolution of your marriage—and if you treat your spouse fairly, both emotionally and financially.

4. *I have communicated my feelings to my children, but I haven't tried to put them in the middle of their parents' divorce.* If your children are teenagers or older, they need and deserve some kind of explanation form you. Without going into the details of your sex life, you should be honest with them. Don't attack their other parent. And don't force them into a position where they feel they have to take the side of one parent against another. If they're angry at you, understand and leave the emotional doors open for them.

5. *I have been fair to my lover too.* It isn't fair to let your lover be blamed for the breakup of your marriage. If you were committed to the marriage, you wouldn't be getting a divorce. The third party makes a convenient target for the ex-spouse, children, other family members, and friends. In their view, the marriage was "perfect" until the "homewrecker" came along. You play into that myth if you say, "I'm doing this for you, honey."

If you're getting a divorce, you're doing it for you. Otherwise, you shouldn't be getting one.

SHOULD YOU LEAVE YOUR PARTNER OVER AN AFFAIR?

Assuming your spouse doesn't want a divorce, you have to decide if you want to rebuild the marriage, leave, or perhaps accept a non-monogamous relationship. You need to make the decision based on what you want, not on what friends or family tell you to do. Don't make a choice based on immediate hurt and anger. You may choose divorce as an act of revenge, but once the act is over, you'll be alone with the hurt and anger that didn't go away when the final decree was stamped.

Before making a decision:

1. *Don't say anything you don't really mean.* Threatening to get a divorce puts you in a corner. Issuing an ultimatum weakens your position. If you say, "I'll leave if you don't stop seeing him/her," then you have to leave or lose bargaining power when your spouse doesn't end the affair.

2. *See a therapist.* If your mate won't go with you, go alone. You need to work through a process of grieving that will probably include blame and self-pity. And you will need to learn how to reestablish communication with your partner. A communication breakdown typically accompanies the discovery of an affair.

3. *Expect the healing process to take some time.* If the marriage is to be healed, the betrayed spouse has to work through feelings of resentment and animosity before she/he can examine the problems that have led to the affair. This will likely take months rather than weeks. The situation didn't develop overnight, and it won't be resolved that quickly either.

4. *Consider a temporary separation.* For some couples, a temporary separation provides an important "time-out" period. The difficulty in separation lies in how it is used. Often, rather than employing a brief separation constructively, the betrayed spouse withdraws, and the straying spouse continues to play. Set up some ground rules. And continue talking, preferably with the help of a counselor.

5. *Define your terms.* What do you want from your spouse? What are you willing to give in return? What accommodations must each of you make now to put the marriage back on solid ground?
The obvious first issue is: Will she/he give up the other person?
If not, are you willing to live with a nonmonogamous spouse?
If your partner wants to end the relationship and heal the marriage, she/he will have to be willing to work at reestablishing trust.

An extramarital affair typically does not end a marriage. In some cases, it can be, in retrospect, good for the relationship. Before deciding to leave a marriage because of an affair, yours or your partner's, give yourself at least six months of consideration time. At midlife, the stakes are higher. You have more invested—and more to lose.

Sizzler # **14**

NEW BEGINNINGS

Anne was widowed in her early forties when her beloved husband died of cancer. For five years following his death she didn't have a date. Then she had "a flurry" of arranged first dates with men who either didn't call back if she wished they had—or did call back when she wished they hadn't. Finally she met Ted, also a widower. He was everything she wanted in a man, including age appropriate. She desired him, and the feeling came as a shock.

"I feel like Sleeping Beauty's grandmother," she joked to friends. "To experience lust stirring in my loins again is a strange experience." She didn't add, *and very scary.*

Underneath her bravado, Anne was as frightened of making love to Ted as she was desirous of doing so. His hands on her body when he caressed her during good-bye kisses at her door promised something she wanted him to deliver. But what if seeing that body fully unclothed turned him off? After they'd had several dates, she knew the inevitable "big moment" was coming. She planned the big seduction dinner, complete with candles, flowers, his favorite meal, soft music, and she in her new and flattering long hostess gown.

Anne knew she was drinking too much wine, but couldn't seem to stop herself from gulping it down. He picked up on her nervousness, and that steadied his own nerves. Her fearfulness gave him more courage than he'd had. He, too, wanted to make love, but feared disappointing her. Would she measure him against her late husband, the man she remembered in his erotic prime? Had there been other men in between—and had they perhaps been younger, more virile than he?

After dinner, they sat side by side on the sofa, her hand in his, listening to soft jazz playing in the background. He let go of her hand, put his arm around her shoulder, and pulled her closer to him. First he kissed her hairline, then her cheeks, nose, chin, and finally her lips. His hand caressed her breast. Emboldened by the heat of her body beneath her dress, he pressed harder. She pulled away.

"Did I hurt you?" he asked, surprised and confused by her response.

"No!" she exclaimed, grabbing his hand and clasping it to her chest. Her heart was pounding; and her face was flushed. "I was just . . ."

She couldn't finish the thought, so he added his own interpretation: She, she was just shy. He kissed her, thrusting his tongue into her mouth. Her girlish behavior made him feel like a young buck. He felt his penis stirring hopefully. For her part, she was imagining the look of disgust on his face as she removed her clothes, exposing less than perfect flesh. She wasn't the woman she'd been all those years ago when she'd experienced a first time with a man she wanted. Again, she pulled out of his embrace.

"What's wrong?" he asked.

"I can't," she said, and she began to cry.

Her tears doused the flames of his passion. After trying his best, however briefly, to comfort her, he made a hasty retreat. Alone in her misery, she drank the coffee she'd intended to share with him. What was wrong with her? Surely other women were able to start over again in bodies that had known their share of wear and tear.

Anne made up her mind to invite him over to consummate their relationship on the spot the moment he called. But he didn't call. Days, then weeks passed. She didn't hear from him. Mutual friends hinted that he, considering himself rejected by her, was never going to call her again.

Now she couldn't get Ted out of her mind. She lay in bed some nights, with her hand clamped between her legs in that space so abnormally hot, fantasizing about him. More than once, her hand reached for the phone. Once or twice, she dialed his number and hung up on the first ring. "You're a coward," she told herself.

Fortifying herself with a small brandy, she punched in his phone number, held her breath, and willed herself to let it ring. When he answered, she didn't hang up. He was happy to hear her voice.

"I'm lying alone in my bed, naked, thinking carnal thoughts about you," she said.

"Share them by all means," he replied, and she did.

She told the story of Sleeping Beauty's grandmother who'd allowed her vanity regarding her physical imperfections to keep her imprisoned within her celibate state. Then she described her longing, allowing her fingers to play with her clitoris as she spoke. Her voice grew huskier, her breath more jagged.

"I want you to come," he said, and she did.

Later that night she came again and again after he'd joined her in bed.

15

KEEPING THE ROMANCE ALIVE FOREVER

"Can you keep the romance alive?" Janet asked wistfully.

At 52, she and her husband have just reconciled after a separation. The romance is very much alive again, and they would like to keep it that way.

"We took each other for granted and drifted apart," she says, "like too many couples do. He had an affair, and I found out. We had been separated for six months when we started dating again. We've been through marital counseling, and we're taking a second honeymoon. This time I want it to last for the rest of forever."

When romance is missing from people's lives, they may not feel loved and desired by their partners. They might be open to an affair or closed to sexual activity. Romance keeps the connecting doors between a man and a woman open. Some evidence suggests that mature couples may actually be more romantic than younger ones. At midlife, men and women are more well matched sexually and emotionally and in this state of simpatico are more likely to speak the tender words and make the thoughtful gestures of romance. Not surprisingly, romance is more important to men at this age than to younger men.

Friendship: the Hidden Component of Romance

Few of us are surprised when friendship turns into love, yet we may not realize that friendship remains an important component of a love relationship, particularly a long-term one. Like romantic love, friendship has an arc. The young couple before children are close friends who explore each other's likes and dislikes, feelings and beliefs through long discussions. As their lives become more complex, the friendship may be less close. The birth of children, the acquisition of a home, career development, and the pull of other emotional ties work together to diminish the amount of time the couple can spend having long intimate conversations about the meaning of life. If the friendship matters to them, however, they will make the time to be intimate with each other, verbally as well as physically.

When a husband and wife speak to each other only about their schedules, duties, and chores, they are putting their friendship as well as their passion at risk. These are the couples who at midlife discover they have nothing to say to each other now that they have the time to talk. How likely is it that they'll have romance in their relationship if they don't have even conversation?

A lasting relationship is, among other things, a friendship agreement. Even with sexual feelings, a successful division of family responsibilities, and mutual respect, a couple who do not have companionship at midlife will probably have a less satisfying sexual and romantic life than they would like. If the romance has gone out of your relationship, try to put the friendship back in first.

The Six Steps to Reviving Friendship

1. *Don't say, "You never talk to me,"* when faced with an uncommunicative partner. Assigning blame will only put him or her in the defensive position. If the lack of real conversation disturbs you, initiate dialogue by snuggling up and musing, "Honey, do you remember when we used to talk into the wee hours of the morning?"

2. *Ask questions.* The "talk to me" demand is typically followed by, "What do you want me to say?" Be sure your questions show both your knowledge of and interest in your partner's life apart from you. Pretend you've just met someone shy and use your wiles to draw him/her out.

3. *Ask questions that can't be answered in monosyllables.* "Yes, dear," and "No, dear," aren't going to take you anywhere you want to go.

4. *Don't assume you know the other "like the back of your hand."* People change and forget to tell each other. But good friends don't let that happen. They say, "Hey, I don't think the same way about politics as I once did."

5. *Talk and you will be talked to.* Share information. In the beginning, you told your partner everything. Maybe you called each other at work several times a day. Now one or the other is often chagrined at being the last to know that a neighborhood couple is splitting, the daughter is scheduled for a sonogram, or the pastor is leaving the parish.

6. *Show your friend you care.* Do a favor without being asked. Go out of your way to get tickets to a game or play that he/she wants to see. Share companionable silent activities. Remember when you read magazines on the sofa beside him while he watched football—just because you enjoyed being near him?

Once you've reconnected as friends, add a little romance to the mix.

What Romance Is—And Isn't

There is a difference between "romance" and the romantic love stage of sexual attraction, between "romance" and sexual passion, between employing romantic gestures to seduce a partner and genuinely being romantic.

- The *romantic love stage* is a period of euphoria lasting from three to six months at the beginning of a love relationship, a time in which the lovers idealize each other. This euphoria plays an important role in the early development of an intimate and lasting relationship. To reinforce the bond, the body produces a chemical cocktail creating a natural high, the "lovesick" feeling. The primary ingredient in the love cocktail is phenylethylamine (PEA). In the euphoric days, the lovers crave each other's company because their PEA levels shoot back up when they're together. "Love sickness" is nothing more than the pangs of PEA deprivation. Eventually the body's PEA production slows down to normal, and the romantic love stage cannot be sustained.

- *Romance does help keep sexual passion alive*, but passion ebbs and flows in any healthy ongoing relationship while romance can remain constant.

- *Romance is an ongoing expression of love between two people.* Through words and actions, they demonstrate their love, affection, and respect for each other. *It can last forever.*

The Five Midlife Romantic Misconceptions

Five misconceptions shared by many middle-aged couples keep romance from lasting forever for them. They are:

1. Believing romance can't endure because they equate "romance" with the image of youth and beauty—or the feeling of euphoria in the romantic love stage.

2. Giving up on romance when the partner is less than a romantic ideal.

3. Assuming that it isn't possible to sustain romance over decades of togetherness.

4. Thinking that full knowledge, disclosure, and understanding of each other kill romance, because the "mystery" is gone.

5. Refusing to ask for the kind of romantic words and gestures they crave, because they believe true romantics intuit the desires of the other and fulfill them.

If these misconceptions have been keeping the romance out of your life, banish them and get romantic.

The Romance Quiz

How much romance do you have in your life? Take a few minutes to assess the romantic aspect of your relationship. Whatever you want that you're not getting now may be more easily achieved if you try a little romance. More sex? More closeness? Better communication? A stronger intimacy bond? Heartfelt romantic words and gestures may smooth the path to your relationship goals.

1. When was the last time you said, "I love you," and under what circumstances?

2. Can you remember the most recent *unrequested* favor you did for your mate? What was it?

3. How often do you offer to give a neck or back rub?

4. How long has it been since you looked deeply into your partner's eyes and held the gaze as she/he spoke?

5. When was the last time he brought home flowers for no special reason?

6. How often do you dine by candlelight using the good china for the two of you alone?

7. When did you last buy the other a no-occasion little gift?

8. How long has it been since you rushed home to freshen up before the other arrived?

9. How long has it been since you listened to music alone together and danced by firelight in the living room? Or rented a movie and cuddled up together to watch it?

10. When was the last time you took a shower or bath together?

11. When did she last buy new lingerie?

12. And when did you last write your partner a love note or letter, a poem, or an endearment scrawled at the bottom of a greeting card?

If most of your answers to these twelve questions are "I can't remember," it's time to recapture the romance.

THE TEN STEPS TO REDISCOVERING ROMANCE

"I equated romance with the jittery feeling you have when you first fall in love," says Joan. "I thought it was gone, long gone, after 22 years of marriage. My husband said we needed 'a little romance' in our lives; and I thought he meant more sex. I'm an avid consumer of pop psychology, but nothing had quite prepared me for the changes that have come over him in the past few years. He wants to talk. He wants to cuddle. Now, he wants romance.

"As a joke, I sent him flowers to his office. He was thrilled. The sex was better that night than it had been in months. He worshiped my clitoris. I am learning how to be a romantic woman, which was never my style. But I'm enjoying this new phase of our lives. It's sexy."

Rediscover your lost romantic side and you may recapture some of the sexual passion you thought had subsided too. The ten steps are:

1. *See each other as lovers again.* After a couple have settled well into marriage, they view each other as "husband" and "wife," "father" and "mother." Some married couples even call each other "Mom" and "Dad." Try this simple exercise: Look at your partner with fresh eyes and *see* your lover.

2. *Use each other's names or occasional terms of endearment, like "darling."* Stop calling each other Mom and Dad. Go back to the days when you were Harry and Sally and all that implied.

3. *Tell your partner how special she/he is.* Choose your words carefully. While you appreciate your mate for all the stalwart qualities that enable him or her to share the load of family responsibilities, don't mention them now. What are the qualities that first attracted you, that made this person more special to you than others you'd known? They may include warmth, charm, wit, intelligence, and a beautiful smile, among others.

4. *Be affectionate, not as a prelude to lovemaking.* If a hug, a kiss, or a caress are immediately interpreted as sexual invitations, the romance has seeped out of your relationship. Get physical. Holding hands, both publicly and privately, is a very romantic thing to do. Small gestures of affection in public say, "I'm proud to be with this wonderful person."

5. *Take time to do things for each other.* Some couples have daily power struggles over the small chores, like who will pick up the cleaning, stop at the supermarket, or mail the bills. Stop confronting your partner as if the two of your were opposing sides in a labor negotiation. Do something thoughtful and unexpected, such as stop at an out-of-the-way market to buy the raspberries she craves in the early days of the season.

6. *Buy love gifts.* Love gifts are little tokens of romantic esteem given when no occasion demands them. A few ideas: the single red rose wrapped in tissue and tied with a ribbon, a miniature box of fine chocolates or a bag of gourmet jelly beans, a paperback book or stack of magazines, a snowglobe paperweight of a sentimental scene, an ornament for the Christmas tree, a silly souvenir from the ballpark. A 52-year-old woman who has been married 30 years still remembers the big bottle of hand lotion her husband brought her from a grocery-shopping trip their first year of marriage. He was in the Army, and they were "broker than broke." The hand lotion represented his spending money for two days.

7. *Date each other.* Call your partner and ask him/her out on a date. You take charge of reservations, getting directions, or whatever planning needs to be done. Put the same effort into your appearance that you did when you were first dating. Suggest that your partner make the next date. After a few dates, ask your lover to go away for the weekend.

8. *Don't neglect the accoutrements of romance.* Light candles at the dinner table when the two of you are dining alone. Buy fresh flowers as often as you can afford. Use fragrance again, if you've stopped. And, buy some new lingerie for her and silk robes for both of you.

9. *Accompany your partner somewhere you really don't want to go.* At midlife, many couples go their separate ways to sporting events, concerts, movies, plays, and other events if they don't share each other's tastes. Independence is a good thing. No one is suggesting you face life like conjoined twins, but occasionally accompanying your partner to an event that doesn't interest you because it's special to him or her is a very romantic gesture.

10. *Say "I love you" often.* Those three little words are the most romantic words you can say.

The ten steps will almost surely rekindle your romance. Having regained the feelings of excitement and discovery, you don't want to lose them again.

HOW TO KEEP THE ROMANCE ALIVE

"Whenever people talk about 'working on a relationship,' I want to yawn," says Chuck, 48. "I know I'm in for a boring conversation about their earnest approach to relating. Why not try playing at a relationship for a change? In our Puritan society, everything is work. Marriage is work. Sex is work. Work is work. I think there's a lot of room for play in life. You can get your job done well and enjoy doing it. You can have a good relationship without approaching it like the plans for a nuclear reactor. And you can certainly have better sex if you learn to lighten up. Adults have forgotten how to play.

"My wife gave me the greatest compliment recently. She told me I'm the most romantic guy she's ever known because I can always make her giggle. She said, 'Chuck, sometimes you make me feel like I have champagne bubbling up inside.' What a sexy thing to say to a man."

Romance is not all soft lighting and candles any more than sex is always a deeply emotional and intimate experience. A take-out pizza eaten in bed can be the most romantic dinner a couple have shared in months if it leads to exciting sex. The ability to make a lover laugh can be the most romantic quality anyone possesses. How can one measure the value of a partner who can lighten each day with smiles?

To keep the romance alive in a long-term relationship, you need the right attitudes. Without them, you'll always be consulting a romantic calendar for the suggestion of the day. Romantic spontaneity is a product of attitudes.

THE SEVEN INDISPENSABLE ROMANTIC ATTITUDES

1. *Empathetic.* True romantics are able to put themselves in their partner's place. They can see and feel the world as he or she does. Empathy makes it possible for them to personalize the words

and gestures of love, to give what the partner desires, not what the giver would like to give.

2. *Adventuresome.* Excitement, adventure, and risk cause the body to produce PEA, the same potent hormone that gives the romantic love stage its power. If you want to duplicate the feeling of falling in love, take a hot-air balloon ride or go hang gliding together, travel to foreign countries where you've never been and can't speak the language, explore New York City by subway. Be sexually adventurous too.

3. *Affectionate.* Affectionate gestures and words are the basic communication components of romance. As a relationship deepens, the gestures of romance will likely be more varied and creative than the gift of a single red rose. A romantic man or woman says words and makes gestures that reflect intimate knowledge of the beloved. These small daily doses of affection reinforce the bond of intimacy.

4. *Flirtatious.* Flirting is both playful and sexy, a way of making your partner feel desired as he or she was in the beginning of love. Contrary to what many think, flirting is not the province of the young in love. A romantic couple continue to flirt throughout their lives.

5. *Humorous.* Lighthearted lovers have the gift of romance. Most people take sex, relationships, *life* far too seriously. Sex is supposed to be fun, and sometimes it's funny too. Romantics who have the humorous touch can be irresistible to their partners. They put the spontaneity and joy into being together.

6. *Sensual.* Romantic people revel in all the senses: taste, smell, sight, touch, and sound. They are good lovers because they know that lovemaking is more than technique and genital connection, more than orgasm. When both partners are focused on sensual pleasure, they experience everything from a shared sunset to sex more fully, too.

7. *Generous.* In romance as in sex, those who are able to give and share enhance their own and their partner's experience. The soul of romance is generosity. Empathy cannot exist without it. It is difficult for a miser and a romantic exist in the same person?

HOW SOME COUPLES NEVER LOSE THE MAGIC

Mike and Barb are an attractive and sexy couple in their early fifties. They fell in love in high school, married when she was 20 and he was 21, evolved separately into secure, exciting, interesting individuals and together as a warm and charismatic couple. People like to be around them because they have never lost the aura of magic surrounding the young in love.

"We've had our problems over the years like every couple who's been married a long time and raised a family together," Barb says, "but we never stopped loving each other or being romantic with each other. In our second year of marriage, Mike's father, a volunteer sheriff, was shot to death trying to resolve a domestic dispute, and a few months later, I miscarried our first child. I remember waking up in the hospital after the miscarriage. Mike was gently applying chapstick to my lips. He'd run out to buy a tube while I was sleeping because he'd noticed my lips were dry and wanted to make me comfortable in any way he could. I knew then everything would eventually be all right.

"For my fiftieth birthday, Mike took me to a resort for the weekend. We had a beautiful suite. He'd arranged for a lovely bouquet of flowers and chilled champagne. And he gave me diamond earrings, an extravagance I didn't know I wanted so much until I held them in my hand. It was like our wedding night all over again."

A friend who has known them since they were engaged says, "They always have and still do radiate sexual energy. And they have a good time together. I've watched them go through hard times and good times, and I've never known them to lose their ability to laugh easily or fail to comfort each other. I like to be with them. It cheers me up to be around them."

Mike and Barb embody the seven indispensable romantic attitudes. After 30 years of marriage, the magic lingers. Another couple, Ellen and Dick, in their seventies, recently celebrated their fiftieth anniversary, and they, too, embody the attitudes and have the magic. Like Mike and Barb, they have a wide circle of family and friends who find joy and comfort in being around them.

"We have a good time, even in the bad times," Ellen says. "My heart still beats a little faster when he comes into the room if we've been apart for the day. I can't imagine what my life would have been like without him." Dick retired before Ellen did, and in her last year of working, he had dinner waiting when she came home. "One of the nicest things he did for me last year was plant hundreds of bulbs, irises and tulips. He knew they would be blooming around the time of my retirement, and he wanted me to have something to look forward to in those first days of missing my job. We had lunch on the porch on warm days and admired the flowers."

Dick adds, "Life with Ellen has never been dull, not one moment since I met her over 50 years ago at a ball park. I was playing amateur ball. She came with a girlfriend to the game. I was attracted to her hair; she had beautiful long, wavy hair that shone with burnished highlights in the sun. After the game I got someone to introduce us, and I asked her out. We were married six weeks after we met. We just knew right away that we wanted to be together for the rest of our lives."

These two couples and others like them have a special relationship that attracts others to them. Most of us like to be around lovers. We want to believe in the magic, and we can, because this magic is real.

If your partner is not as romantic as you would like, don't despair. Here are some ways you can encourage the development of romantic attitudes:

- *Start with yourself.* Change your own attitudes and behaviors to more positive and romantic ones. You have to give romance to get it. Without realizing that you are, you might be sabotaging the romance in your relationship by not appearing to be open to it.

- *Give positive reinforcement.* Show appreciation for any romantic gesture, no matter how small or how generic. A handful of flowers that aren't your favorite. A brief good-bye kiss. A heartfelt "thank you" for a favor done. Don't wait for your partner to behave like a romantic ideal before you melt.

- *Withhold criticism.* Criticizing someone for not being romantic won't make the loving words and gestures flow. People do not respond romantically to being criticized or nagged.

- *Give your partner what he or she needs to feel loved.* The best way to inspire romance is to show your partner that you really understand his/her desires. Personalize your own displays of affection.

THE LAST WORDS

The following points encapsulate the advice found in this book.

1. *Live a life outside the bedroom that is vital and adventurous.* Stay out of ruts. Avoid stale routines. Expand your experiences. Live a counterphobic lifestyle and take chances. Then bring this bold attitude to the bedroom.

2. *Yes, living with the same person for decades really is boring.* So don't stay the same person you were when you met and married. Change. Evolve. Grow. You have a responsibility to your partner to do that. Expand your personal boundaries. Keep learning. An active, curious mind is a sexual turn-on.

3. *Keep your relationship emotionally open.* Don't become one of those couples who have nothing substantial to say to each other because they've eliminated so many issues of discussion over the years. Retain the sexy openness that new lovers share. It's a form of verbal foreplay.

4. *Remember that good sex involves friction and fiction.* Stay sexually stimulated by watching erotic films, reading sexy books, indulging your fantasies. Don't be afraid of a good fight.

5. *Accept that you and your partner's sexuality evolves and changes over the years.* Adapt your lovemaking style to the changes. Be flexible and adaptive. Rigidity is deadly, especially in the bedroom. Find the good in the changes, and make the most of each new phase of life.

6. *Stay active, fit, and healthy.* You probably can't maintain a good sex life unless you do.

7. *Last, remember that attitude is everything.* When you approach life with hope and enthusiasm, you make the best of the bad days and enjoy the good ones to the fullest. A good attitude creates sexual energy. By midlife, negative people are too tired and defeated to enjoy sex.

If you think you can, you can.

Sizzler # **15**

THE "LIKE" CONNECTION

For their thirty-fifth wedding anniversary, Matt presented Carol with an elegant diamond necklace. She gave him a new set of golf clubs. Carol doesn't care much for diamonds, and Matt hasn't played enough golf to wear out his "old" set of clubs. Family and friends teased them about their gift choices at the surprise party their sons threw for them.

"Do you two even know each other?" Carol's sister asked.

Sudden tears welled in Carol's eyes. Another question had sprung to mind: Do we even like each other? She, the aging girl next door, and he, the poor boy who made good with his veneer of carefully cultivated sophistication grown as thick a a plank, seemed a world apart. From across the room, he saw the look on her face, and his own face fell in response.

After the party, they had a serious discussion about their marriage. Neither wanted a divorce, but, on the other hand, neither felt "happy" anymore.

"Maybe we expect too much?" he mused. "What does 'happy' mean at our age anyway?"

So they agreed to "work harder" on their "relationship" and "try to put some romance" back in their life together. Toward that end, each made the stereotypical gestures. He brought roses and fine chocolates home. She lit candles and served his favorite meals.

"Matt's probably right," she confided to her sister. "We expect too much. Romantic gestures aren't very meaningful when you already live as well as we do."

"The accoutrements of romance aren't as meaningful as the thought behind them," her sister replied, but Carol looked at her doubtfully.

That night Matt told her she'd be receiving several large boxes soon, but she wasn't to open them until he gave her permission. Her interest piqued, she tried to get him to tell her what the secret cartons would contain. He wouldn't. When they arrived later in the week, she was baffled.

"Can we open them now?" she demanded as soon as he came home.

"No. They sit here untouched for two weeks from this Friday. Block four days off the calendar then, by the way."

"It's going to take us four days to open these boxes?" she asked incredulously.

"In a manner of speaking," he said.

She hadn't seen him have so much fun with a surprise since the Christmas the children were small. He'd earned his first major bonus and had literally covered the floor of the small living room in their old house with gifts for her and them. Seeing him like this reminded her of how much Matt genuinely enjoyed giving. She thought guiltily of the unworn diamond necklace in its blue velvet-lined box and put her hand instinctively to her throat. He met her eyes, and she could swear he knew what she was thinking. How long had it been since she'd felt he could read her mind?

He didn't go into the office on the day scheduled for the opening of the boxes. Eagerly, she tore open the first one and pulled out—a backpack. Mystified, she looked at him with raised eyebrows. A backpack?

"There should be another one of those," he said offhandedly.

There was. And a tent and all the accompanying gear, including fishing rods and waterproof disposable cameras. They were going camping for four days. She'd long ago stopped asking him if they could take off in the car, drive to a nearby national-park camping ground, and pitch a tent. Now they were doing it.

"Oh, Matt," she cried, throwing her arms around him and hugging hard. "I don't know what to say."

They were ebullient on the drive to the campgrounds. He proved so much more adept at pitching a tent than she'd expected that she was suspicious.

"Where'd you learn how to do this?" she asked.

"I took a seminar at the sporting-goods store," he said sheepishly.

Again she threw her arms around him. In the middle of the forest, with the sound of a trout stream running nearby and birds chirping, the years fell away. She was young again. So was he.

After eating the dinner they'd prepared on the campfire, they retired to the tent. They were awkward at first, fumbling with zippers and buttons, fingers trembling. She pulled the turtleneck cotton sweater over her head. The diamond necklace gleamed in the soft light inside the tent.

"I've never loved you more," he said; and everything else was said with their bodies.

CONCLUSION:
YOU'RE STILL SEXY

Many of the sex "taboos" that existed when we were younger no longer do. Oral sex, masturbation, anal sex, even many forms of kinky sex such as spanking and bondage have come out of the closet. Women can have partners younger than themselves—as men always could have; and they are not penalized for being sexually active before marriage. The "virgin clause" isn't part of the marital contract anymore. Enlightened people no longer regard homosexuality or bisexuality as evil or perverse.

One "taboo" that has outlasted the others: elder sex. Everyone's definition of "elder" seems to depend, of course, upon his or her own age. Twenty year olds probably think we are very old; and it wouldn't surprise me to hear they don't think sex is possible after the age of 40, if not 35. On the other hand, a 70-year-old man who is still sexually active with his wife of 48 years told me he considers "old" 15 years older than whatever age he is. With laughter in his eyes, he said, "Obviously I will never get old." He added, "and as long as Paul Newman is still sexy, so am I." It's a good thing to think of yourself as "sexy," not "old."

As I noted in the introduction, the Baby Boom generation, with another one of its members turning 50 every seven or eight seconds, will change the way our society views aging and sexuality. Eventually the age "taboo" will seem silly as believing brides must be virgins or that oral sex is perverse does to us now. Meanwhile, subscribing to that belief is the one major obstacle standing between you and great sex at this point in your life. Don't let yourself fall into a sex-negative mind-set or your body will follow you into the shutdown mode.

Sex does change as we age. And aren't we fortunate that it does? Like fine wine and art masterpieces, great lovers appreciate in value and are more appreciated by their partners as time goes by. In your twenties, passion was everything, but passion didn't always, for either gender, lead to pleasure. Young men long for the kind of ejaculatory control that mature men take for granted, and young women strain to reach orgasm when that response comes easily to a mature woman.

Older is not only beautiful. It's better. Men are more tender, women more physically responsive. Each has the wisdom and experience to celebrate the other.

I hope you will refer to this book whenever you need help over a rough patch or need a new approach to lovemaking—or a reminder that you're still sexy after all. Some other books that you may find useful or inspirational in maintaining a sex-positive frame of mind include:

- *My Summer with George*, a novel by Marilyn French about passionate love between an older couple

- *Little Birds* and other erotica by Anaïs Nin

- *Sex: An Oral History*, interviews with real people of all ages about their sex lives, by Harry Maurer

- *The Autobiography of My Body*, a novel by David Guy

- *Inventing Memory*, a novel by Erica Jong

- *An Erotic Beyond Sade*, by Octavia Paz.

- *Boomer Babes* by Linda Stasi and Rosemary Rogers.

- *His Secret Life*, a study of male fantasies by Bob Berkowitz

- *Aphrodite*, a memoir of the senses by Isabelle Allende

- *Vox*, a novel about phone sex by Nicholson Baker

- *Kama Sutra*, the illustrated edition; buy it for the art

- *Herotica*, volumes I, II, III, and IV, and *Best American Erotica*, collections of erotic short fiction.

And don't forget previous books by the authors:

- *Secrets of Better Sex* and *The Romance of Sex* by Joel Block, Ph.D.

- *Sexational Secrets; Kink: The Hidden Sex Lives of Americans; What Men Really Want* and *Sexual Pleasures* by Susan Crain Bakos.

Good sources for buying erotic books and videos are:

- Adam & Eve Catalogue
  800-765-ADAM. Web site: www.adameve.com

The photos are more explicit than in other catalogues. Their best sellers include Dr. Ruth's Eroscillator, a smaller, streamlined, and quiet vibrator with detachable heads for different kinds of stimulation. The company also coproduces and markets high-quality erotic films and instructional videos. If you see their name of the box, you can be sure it's a good product.

- Good Vibrations
  800-BUY-VIBE. Web site: www.goodvibes.com.

Catalogue illustrations tend more toward the soft and pretty, with a lot of drawings mixed among the photos. An ordering plus: The company guarantees they will not give, sell, or trade your name to other mail-order businesses. The sell books, videos, and sex toys and probably have a greater range of G-spot vibrators and informational material than other catalogues.

They also have a retail store in San Francisco, and Cleis Press (also in San Francisco) publishes *The New Good Vibrations Guide to Sex: Tips and Techniques from America's Favorite Sex Store*, by Cathy Winks and Anne Semans.

- The Xandria Catalogue
  800-242-2823. Web site: www.xandria.com.

This company also guarantees not to give, sell, or trade your name to other mail-order businesses. Their mail catalogue is an interesting combination of the tasteful and the slightly raunchy, but exuberantly raunchy. In addition to the standard mix of books, videos, and sex toys, they also market excellent publications on such topics as sexuality and cancer and sexuality and disability. These booklets contain information on where to buy specialized products to aid sexual expression, other resource information, and fine illustrations on adapting sexual positions and skills to the situations.

There are many good erotic and instructional videos available today. In addition to the Adam and Eve label, look for Candida Royalle's Femme Productions erotic videos and instructional videos in both The Better Sex Video Series by the Townsend Institute and The Sinclair Institute Series.

Increasingly, novels and some films feature older characters involved in romantic relationships. Look for them. Teenagers aren't the only ones who can benefit from spending time with good role models.

It's also important to keep up with the latest and most accurate information available in the areas of medicine, general health, diet, and exercise. As you now know, everything you take into your body can have a potential effect on sexuality. Every week it seems that some study appears contradicting the results of a previous study. You have to evaluate carefully what you read. Often a study quoted in an explosive headline article is merely a small sampling, its conclusions distorted in the press release, the distortions magnified by the resulting coverage.

Again, I caution you to stay abreast of current developments and read everything with an open and analytical mind. As the population ages, more antiaging products and "miracle aging cures" will compete for our dollars and our hopes. You'll have to be a careful consumer of both information and products.

It's unlikely that the "cure" for aging will be discovered in our lifetime, but the secrets of enduring sexuality are already available to you in this book. I'll leave you with a quote from the actor Jack

Nicholson, a comment made several years ago on his fifty-fifth birthday: "I feel exactly the same as I've always felt: a lightly reined-in voracious beast." If that doesn't make you feel good about your age, has anyone told you that rock icon Tina Turner of the glorious legs is pushing 60?

INDEX

A

Adam & Eve Catalogue, 289
Adult children, as obstacle to new sex-
    ual relationship, 251–52
Adventure, sense of, and romance, 279
AFE zone, 77
Affairs, 261–63
    hidden agendas, 262
    lover's expectations, 262
    mistrust, 262–63
    reasons for having, 261–62
    risks, 262
    sexually inactive spouse, 263
Affection, and romance, 279
Age issues, 126
Aggressor role, in erotic role playing,
    108
Alcoholism, and impotence, 208
Anal sex, 146–47

Anger:
    and impotence, 208
    as sexual energy drainer, 18
Anti-sex myths, 127–28
Aphrodisiacs, and impotence, 210–11
Arthritis, effect on sexuality, 232
Attitudes:
    checking, 130
    testing validity of, 8

B

Big draw technique, 169–70
Body image anxiety, and new partner,
    248–49
Bondage, 147–48
Boredom:
    as obstacle to great sex, 6

293